Be Hopeful

Warren W. Wiersbe

This book is designed for your personal reading pleasure and profit. It is also designed for group study. A leader's guide with helps and hints for teachers and visual aids (Victor Multiuse Transparency Masters) is available from your local bookstore or from the publisher.

VICTOR BOOKS a division of SP Publications, Inc.

WHEATON, ILLINOIS 60187

Offices also in
Whitby, Ontario, Canada
Amersham-on-the-Hill, Bucks, England

Second printing, 1983

Most of the Scripture quotations in this book are from the *King James Version*. Other quotations are from the *New International Version* (NIV), © 1978 by New York International Bible Society; the *New American Standard Bible* (NASB), © 1960, 1962, 1963, 1968, 1971, 1973 by the Lockman Foundation, La Habra, California.

Recommended Dewey Decimal Classification: 227.87
   Suggested Subject Heading: BIBLE, N.T. 1 PETER

Library of Congress Catalog Card Number: 82-60581
ISBN: 0-88207-382-6

Contents

Dedicated to our daughter-in-law
SUSAN WIERSBE

and our sons-in-law
DAVID JACOBSEN
and
DAVID JOHNSON

It's great to have you
in the family!

Preface

If you know something about suffering and persecution, then 1 Peter has a message for you: "Be hopeful!"

Peter wrote this letter to Christians who were going through various trials. The apostle knew that a severe "fiery trial" was just around the corner, and he wanted to prepare believers for it. After all, what life does to us depends on what life finds in us.

For the most part, Christians in the western world have enjoyed comfortable lives. Our brothers and sisters behind iron and bamboo curtains have suffered for their faith. Now there is every indication that the time is approaching when it will cost us to take a stand for Christ. The only "comfortable" Christian will be a "compromising" Christian, and his comfort will be costly.

But God's message to us is, "Be hopeful! Suffering leads to glory! I can give you all the grace you need to honor Me when the going gets tough!"

The future is still as bright as the promises of God, so—BE HOPEFUL!

WARREN W. WIERSBE

1
Where There's Christ, There's Hope

1 Peter 1:1; 5:12-14

"While there's life, there's hope!"

That ancient Roman saying is still quoted today and, like most adages, it has an element of truth but no guarantee of certainty. It is not the *fact* of life that determines hope, but the *faith* of life. A Christian believer has a "living hope" (1 Peter 1:3, NASB) because his faith and hope are in God (1:21). This "living hope" is the major theme of Peter's first letter. He is saying to all believers, "Be hopeful!"

Before we study the details of this fascinating letter, let's get acquainted with the man who wrote it, the people to whom he sent it, and the particular situation that prompted him to write.

1. The writer

He identified himself as "Peter, an apostle of Jesus Christ" (1:1). Some liberals have questioned whether a common fisherman could have penned this letter, especially since Peter and John were both called "unlearned and ignorant men" (Acts 4:13). However, this phrase only means "laymen without for-

7

mal schooling"; that is, they were not professional religious leaders. We must never underestimate the training Peter had for three years with the Lord Jesus, nor should we minimize the work of the Holy Spirit in his life. Peter is a perfect illustration of the truth expressed in 1 Corinthians 1:26-31.

His given name was Simon, but Jesus changed it to Peter, which means "a stone" (John 1:35-42). The Aramaic equivalent of "Peter" is "Cephas," so Peter was a man with three names. Nearly fifty times in the New Testament, he is called "Simon"; and often he is called "Simon Peter." Perhaps the two names suggest a Christian's two natures: an old nature (Simon) that is prone to fail, and a new nature (Peter) that can give victory. As Simon, he was only another human piece of clay; but Jesus Christ made a rock out of him!

Peter and Paul were the two leading apostles in the early church. Paul was assigned especially to minister to the Gentiles, and Peter to the Jews (Gal. 2:1-10). The Lord had commanded Peter to strengthen his brethren (Luke 22:32) and to tend the flock (John 21:15-17; also see 1 Peter 5:1-4), and the writing of this letter was a part of that ministry. Peter told his readers that this was a letter of encouragement and personal witness (1 Peter 5:12). Some writings are manufactured out of books, the way freshmen students write term papers; but this letter grew out of a life lived to the glory of God. A number of events in Peter's life are woven into the fabric of this epistle.

This letter is also associated with Silas (Silvanus, 5:12). He was one of the "chief men" in the early church (Acts 15:22) and a prophet (15:32). This means that he communicated God's messages to the congregations as he was directed by the Holy Spirit (see 1 Cor. 14). The apostles and prophets worked together to lay the foundation of the church (Eph. 2:20); and, once that foundation was laid, they passed off the scene. There are no apostles and prophets *in the New Testament sense* in the church today.

It is interesting that Silas was associated with Peter's ministry, because originally he went with Paul as a replacement for Barnabas (Acts 15:36-41). Peter also mentioned John Mark (1 Peter 5:13) whose failure on the mission field helped to cause the rupture between Paul and Barnabas. Peter had led Mark to faith in Christ ("Mark, my son") and certainly would maintain a concern for him. No doubt one of the early assemblies met in John Mark's home in Jerusalem (Acts 12:12). In the end, Paul forgave and accepted Mark as a valued helper in the work (2 Tim. 4:11).

Peter indicated that he wrote this letter "at Babylon" (1 Peter 5:13) where there was an assembly of believers. There is no evidence either from church history or tradition that Peter ministered in ancient Babylon which, at that time, did have a large community of Jews. There was another town called "Babylon" in Egypt, but we have no proof that Peter ever visited it. "Babylon" is probably another name for the city of Rome, and we do have reason to believe that Peter ministered in Rome and was probably martyred there. Rome is called "Babylon" in Revelation 17:5 and 18:10. It was not unusual for persecuted believers during those days to write or speak in "code."

In saying this, however, we must not assign more to Peter than is due him. He did *not* found the church in Rome nor serve as its first bishop. It was Paul's policy not to minister where any other apostle had gone (Rom. 15:20); so Paul would not have ministered in Rome had Peter arrived there first. Peter probably arrived in Rome after Paul was released from his first imprisonment, about the year A.D. 62. First Peter was written about the year 63. Paul was martyred about 64, and perhaps that same year, or shortly after, Peter laid down his life for Christ.

2. The recipients

Peter called them "strangers" (1 Peter 1:1), which means "resident aliens, sojourners." They are called "strangers and pilgrims" in 1 Peter 2:11. These people were citizens of heaven through faith in Christ (Phil. 3:20), and therefore were not permanent residents on earth. Like Abraham, they had their eyes of faith centered on the future city of God (Heb. 11:8-16). They were in the world, but not of the world (John 17:16).

Because Christians are "strangers" in the world, they are considered to be "strange" in the eyes of the world (1 Peter 4:4). Christians have standards and values different from those of the world, and this gives opportunity both for witness and for warfare. We will discover in this epistle that some of the readers were experiencing suffering because of their different lifestyle.

These believers were a "scattered" people as well as a "strange" people. The word translated "scattered" *(diaspora)* was a technical term for the Jews who lived outside of Palestine. It is used this way in John 7:35 and James 1:1. However, Peter's use of this word does not imply that he was writing only to Jewish Christians; because some statements in his letter suggest that some of his readers were converted out of Gentile paganism (1:14, 18; 2:9-10;

4:1-4). There was undoubtedly a mixture of both Jews and Gentiles in the churches that received this letter. We will notice a number of Old Testament references and allusions in these chapters.

These Christians were scattered in five different parts of the Roman Empire, all of them in northern Asia Minor (modern Turkey). The Holy Spirit did not permit Paul to minister in Bithynia (Acts 16:7), so he did begin this work. There were Jews at Pentecost from Pontus and Cappadocia (2:9), and perhaps they carried the Gospel to their neighboring province. Possibly Jewish believers who had been under Peter's ministry in other places had migrated to towns in these provinces. People were "on the move" in those days, and dedicated believers shared the Word wherever they went (8:4).

The important thing for us to know about these "scattered strangers" is that they were going through a time of suffering and persecution. At least fifteen times in this letter, Peter referred to suffering; and he used eight different Greek words to do so. Some of these Christians were suffering because they were living godly lives and doing what was good and right (1 Peter 2:19-23; 3:14-18; 4:1-4, 15-19). Others were suffering reproach for the name of Christ (4:14) and being railed at by unsaved people (3:9-10). Peter wrote to encourage them to be good witnesses to their persecutors, and to remember that their suffering would lead to glory (1:6-7; 4:13-14; 5:10).

But Peter had another purpose in mind. He knew that a "fiery trial" was about to begin, official persecution from the Roman Empire (4:12). When the church began in Jerusalem, it was looked upon as a "sect" of the traditional Jewish faith. The first Christians were Jews, and they met in the temple precincts. The Roman government took no official action against the Christians since the Jewish religion was accepted and approved. But when it became clear that Christianity was not a "sect" of Judaism, Rome had to take official steps.

Several events occurred that helped to precipitate this "fiery trial." To begin with, Paul had defended the Christian faith before the official court in Rome (Phil. 1:12-24). He had been released but then was arrested again. This second defense failed, and he was martyred (2 Tim. 4:16-18). Second, the deranged emperor, Nero, blamed the fire of Rome (July, A.D. 64) on the Christians, using them as a scapegoat. Peter was probably in Rome about that time and was slain by Nero, who had also killed Paul. Nero's persecution of Christians was local at first, but it probably spread. At any rate, Peter wanted to prepare the churches.

We must not get the idea that all Christians in every part of the Empire were going through the same trials to the same degree at the same time. It varied from place to place, though suffering and opposition were pretty general (1 Peter 5:9). Nero introduced official persecution of the church and other emperors followed his example in later years. Peter's letter must have been a tremendous help to Christians who suffered during the reigns of Trajan (98-117), Hadrian (117-138), and Diocletian (284-305). Christians in the world today may yet learn the value of Peter's letter when their own "fiery trials" of persecution begin. While I personally believe that the church will not go through *the* tribulation, I do believe that these latter days will bring much suffering and persecution to the people of God.

It is possible that Silas was the bearer of this letter to the believers in the provinces, and also the secretary who wrote the epistle.

3. The message

First Peter is a letter of encouragement (5:12). We have noted that the theme of *suffering* runs throughout the letter, but so also does the theme of *glory* (see 1:7-8, 11, 21; 2:12; 4:11-16; 5:1, 4, 10-11). One of the encouragements that Peter gives suffering saints is the assurance that their suffering will one day be transformed into glory (1:6-7; 4:13-14; 5:10). This is possible only because the Saviour suffered for us and then entered into His glory (1:11; 5:1). The sufferings of Christ are mentioned often in this letter (1:11; 3:18; 4:1, 13; 5:1).

Peter is preeminently the apostle of *hope,* as Paul is the apostle of *faith* and John of *love.* As believers, we have a "living hope" because we trust a living Christ (1:3). This hope enables us to keep our minds under control and "hope to the end" (1:13) when Jesus Christ shall return. We must not be ashamed of our hope but ready to explain it and defend it (3:15). Like Sarah, the Christian wives can hope in God (3:5, where "trusted" should be translated "hoped"). Since suffering brings glory, and because Jesus is coming again, we can indeed be hopeful!

But suffering does not *automatically* bring glory to God and blessing to God's people. Some believers have fainted and fallen in times of trial and have brought shame to the name of Christ. It is only when we depend on the grace of God that we can glorify God in times of suffering. Peter also emphasized God's grace in this letter. "I have written to you briefly, encouraging you and testifying that this is the true grace of God. Stand fast in it" (5:12, NIV).

The word "grace" is used in every chapter of 1 Peter: 1:2, 10, 13; 2:19 ("thankworthy") and 2:20 ("acceptable"); 3:7; 4:10; 5:5, 10, 12. Grace is God's generous favor to undeserving sinners and needy saints. When we depend on God's grace, we can endure suffering and turn trials into triumphs. It is grace alone that saves us (Eph. 2:8-10). God's grace can give us strength in times of trial (2 Cor. 12:1-10). Grace enables us to serve God in spite of difficulties (1 Cor. 15:9-10). Whatever begins with God's grace will always lead to glory (Ps. 84:11; 1 Peter 5:10).

As we study 1 Peter, we will see how the three themes of suffering, grace, and glory unite to form an encouraging message for believers experiencing times of trial and persecution. These themes are summarized in 1 Peter 5:10, a verse we would do well to memorize.

The cynical editor and writer H. L. Mencken once defined hope as "a pathological belief in the occurrence of the impossible." But that definition does not agree with the New Testament meaning of the word. True Christian hope is more than "hope so." It is confident assurance of future glory and blessing.

An Old Testament believer called God "the Hope of Israel" (Jer. 14:8). A New Testament believer affirms that Jesus Christ is his hope (1 Tim. 1:1; and see Col. 1:27). The unsaved sinner is "without hope" (Eph. 2:12); and if he dies without Christ, he will be hopeless forever. The Italian poet, Dante, in his *Divine Comedy*, put this inscription over the world of the dead: "Abandon all hope, you who enter here!"

This confident hope gives us the encouragement and enablement we need for daily living. It does not put us in a rocking chair where we complacently await the return of Jesus Christ. Instead, it puts us in the marketplace, on the battlefield, where we keep on going when the burdens are heavy and the battles are hard. Hope is not a sedative; it is a shot of adrenaline, a blood transfusion. Like an anchor, our hope in Christ stabilizes us in the storms of life (Heb. 6:18-19); but unlike an anchor, our hope moves us forward, it does not hold us back.

It is not difficult to follow Peter's train of thought. Everything begins with salvation, our personal relationship to God through Jesus Christ. If we know Christ as Saviour, then we have hope! If we have hope, then we can walk in holiness and in harmony. There should be no problem submitting to those around us in society, the home, and the church family. Salvation and submission are preparation for suffering; but if we focus on Christ, we can overcome and God will transform suffering into glory.

Here is one way to outline 1 Peter

   I. GOD'S GRACE AND SALVATION—
      1:1—2:10
      A. Live in hope—1:1-12
      B. Live in holiness—1:13-21
      C. Live in harmony—1:22—2:10

  II. GOD'S GRACE AND SUBMISSION—
      2:11—3:12
      A. Submit to authorities—2:11-17
      B. Submit to masters—2:18-25
      C. Submit in the home—3:1-7
      D. Submit in the church—3:8-12

 III. GOD'S GRACE AND SUFFERING—
      3:13—5:11
      A. Make Jesus Christ Lord—3:13-22
      B. Have Christ's attitude—4:1-11
      C. Glorify Christ's name—4:12-19
      D. Look for Christ's return—5:1-6
      E. Depend on Christ's grace—5:7-11

Additional Notes: 1 Peter and Ephesians
Many Bible scholars have noted the numerous
parallels between Ephesians and 1 Peter. These
parallels refute the notion that Paul and Peter
preached different messages. In fact, Peter himself
refuted this notion! (2 Peter 3:15-16) While Paul and
Peter agreed to work in different spheres of ministry
(Gal. 2:1-10), they preached the same Gospel and
exalted the same Lord. You may want to examine
some of these parallel passages for yourself.

Ephesians	1 Peter
1:3	1:3
3:5, 10	1:12
3:6, 21	4:11
3:8	1:8
4:2	3:9
4:7, 11	4:10
4:13, 15	2:2

God's Word is without flaw. Whatever the Holy
Spirit has written is true, and there can be no con-
tradictions. While studying 1 Peter, you may want to
refer to the cross references in your Bible and see
what other passages have to say about a topic.

1 Peter and the Gospels
We would expect Peter to make reference to the
words of Christ and to events and conversations
recorded in the Gospel record. Here are some references for you to study.

1 Peter	Gospels
1:16	Matthew 5:48
1:17	Matthew 22:16
1:18	Mark 10:45

1:22	John 15:12
2:19	Matthew 5:39; Luke 6:32
3:9	Matthew 5:38ff
3:14	Matthew 5:10
4:11	Matthew 5:16
4:13	Matthew 5:10ff
4:18	Matthew 24:22
5:3	Matthew 20:25ff
5:5	John 13:1ff
5:7	Matthew 6:25ff
5:8	Luke 22:31ff

2
It's Glory
All the Way!

1 Peter 1:2-12

On a balmy summer day, my wife and I visited one of the world's most famous cemeteries located at Stoke Poges, a little village not far from Windsor Castle in England. On this site Thomas Gray penned his famous "Elegy Written in a Country Church-yard," a poem most of us had to read at one time or another in school.

As we stood quietly in the midst of ancient graves, one stanza of that poem came to mind:

> The boast of heraldry, the pomp of power,
> And all that beauty, all that wealth e'er gave,
> Awaits alike the inevitable hour,
> The paths of glory lead but to the grave.

Man's glory simply does not last, but God's glory is eternal; and He has deigned to share that glory with us! In this first section of his letter, Peter shared four wonderful discoveries that he had made about the glory of God.

1. Christians are born for glory (1:2-4)

Because of the death and resurrection of Jesus Christ, believers have been "begotten again" to a living hope, and that hope includes the glory of God. But, what do we mean by "the glory of God"?

The glory of God means the sum total of all that God is and does. "Glory" is not a separate attribute or characteristic of God, such as His holiness, wisdom, or mercy. Everything that God is and does is characterized by glory. He is glorious in wisdom and power, so that everything He thinks and does is marked by glory. He reveals His glory in creation (Ps. 19), in His dealings with the people of Israel, and especially in His plan of salvation for lost sinners.

When we were born the first time, we were not born for glory. "For all flesh is like grass, and all the glory of man like the flower of grass" (1 Peter 1:24, quoted from Isa. 40:6). Whatever feeble glory man has will eventually fade and disappear; but the glory of the Lord is eternal. The works of man done for the glory of God will last and be rewarded (1 John 2:17). But the selfish human achievements of sinners will one day vanish to be seen no more. One reason that we have encyclopedias is so that we can learn about the famous people who are now forgotten!

Peter gave two descriptions to help us better understand this wonderful truth about glory.

A. A CHRISTIAN'S BIRTH DESCRIBED (1:2-3).
This miracle all began with God: we were chosen by the Father (Eph. 1:3-4). This took place in the deep counsels of eternity, and we knew nothing about it until it was revealed to us in the Word of God. This election was not based on anything we had done, because we were not even on the scene. Nor was it based on anything God saw that we would be or do.

God's election was based wholly on His grace and love. We cannot explain it (Rom. 11:33-36), but we can rejoice in it.

"Foreknowledge" does not suggest that God merely knew ahead of time that we would believe, and therefore He chose us. This would raise the question, "Who or what made us decide for Christ?" and would take our salvation completely out of God's hands. In the Bible, "to foreknow" means "to set one's love upon a person or persons in a personal way." It is used this way in Amos 3:2: "You only have I known of all the families of the earth." God set His electing love on the nation of Israel. Other verses that use "know" in this special sense are 1 Corinthians 8:3; John 10:14, 27; Matthew 7:23; and Psalm 1:6.

But the plan of salvation includes more than the Father's electing love; it also includes the work of the Spirit in convicting the sinner and bringing him to faith in Christ. The best commentary on this is 2 Thessalonians 2:13-14. Also, the Son of God had to die on the cross for our sins, or there could be no salvation. We have been chosen by the Father, purchased by the Son, and set apart by the Spirit. It takes all three if there is to be a true experience of salvation.

As far as God the Father is concerned, I was saved when He chose me in Christ before the foundation of the world. As far as the Son is concerned, I was saved when He died for me on the cross. But as far as the Spirit is concerned, I was saved one night in May, 1945 when I heard the Gospel and received Christ. Then it all came together, but it took all three Persons of the Godhead to bring me to salvation. If we separate these ministries, we will either deny divine sovereignty or human responsibility;

and that would lead to heresy.

Peter does not deny man's part in God's plan to save sinners. In 1 Peter 1:23 he emphasizes the fact that the Gospel was preached to these people, and that they heard it and believed (see also 1:12). Peter's own example at Pentecost is proof that we do not "leave it all with God" and never urge lost sinners to come to Christ (Acts 2:37-40). The same God who ordains the end—our salvation—also ordains *the means to the end*—the preaching of the Gospel of the grace of God.

B. A CHRISTIAN'S HOPE DESCRIBED (1:3-4). To begin with, it is *a living hope* because it is grounded on the living Word of God (1:23), and was made possible by the living Son of God who arose from the dead. A "living hope" is one that has life in it and therefore can give life to us. Because it has life, it grows and becomes greater and more beautiful as time goes on. Time destroys most hopes; they fade and then die. But the passing of time only makes a Christian's hope that much more glorious.

Peter called this hope *an inheritance* (1:4). As the children of the King, we share His inheritance in glory (Rom. 8:17-18; Eph. 1:9-12). We are included in Christ's last will and testament, and we share the glory with Him (John 17:22-24).

Note the description of this inheritance, for it is totally unlike any earthly inheritance. For one thing, it is *incorruptible,* which means that nothing can ruin it. Because it is *undefiled,* it cannot be stained or cheapened in any way. It will never grow old because it is eternal; it cannot wear out, nor can it disappoint us in any way.

In verses 5 and 9, this inheritance is called "salvation." The believer is already saved through faith in Christ (Eph. 2:8-9), but the completion of that salvation awaits the return of the Saviour. Then we shall have new bodies and enter into a new environment, the heavenly city. In verse 7, Peter called this hope "the appearing of Jesus Christ." Paul called this "the blessed hope" (Titus 2:13).

What a thrilling thing it is to know that we were born for glory! When we were born again, we exchanged the passing glory of man for the eternal glory of God!

2. Christians are kept for glory (1:5)

Not only is the glory being "reserved" for us, but we are being kept for the glory! In my travels, I have sometimes gone to a hotel or motel, only to discover that the reservations have been confused or cancelled. This will not happen to us when we arrive in heaven, for our future home and inheritance are guaranteed and reserved.

"But suppose *we* don't make it?" a timid saint might ask. But, we will; for all believers are being "kept by the power of God." The word translated "kept" is a military word that means "guarded, shielded." The tense of the verb reveals that we are *constantly* being guarded by God, assuring us that we shall safely arrive in heaven. This same word is used to describe the soldiers guarding Damascus when Paul made his escape (2 Cor. 11:32). See also Jude 24-25 and Romans 8:28-39.

Believers are not kept by their own power, but by the power of God. Our faith in Christ has so united us to Him that His power now guards us and guides us. We are not kept by our strength, but by His faithfulness. How long will He guard us? Until Jesus Christ returns and we will share in the full revelation of His great salvation. This same truth is repeated in verse 9.

It is encouraging to know that we are "guarded for glory." According to Romans 8:30, we have *already* been glorified. All that awaits is the public revelation of this glory (Rom. 8:18-23). If any believer were lost, it would rob God of His glory. God is so certain that we will be in heaven that He has already given us His glory as the assurance (John 17:24; Eph. 1:13-14).

The assurance of heaven is a great help to us today. As Dr. James M. Gray expressed it in one of his songs, "Who can mind the journey, when the road leads home?" If suffering today means glory tomorrow, then suffering becomes a blessing to us. The unsaved have their "glory" now, but it will be followed by eternal suffering *away from the glory of God* (2 Thes. 1:3-10). In the light of this, ponder 2 Corinthians 4:7-18—and rejoice!

3. Christians are being prepared for glory (1:6-7)

We must keep in mind that all God plans and performs here is preparation for what He has in store for us in heaven. He is preparing us for the life and service yet to come. Nobody yet knows all that is in store for us in heaven; but this we do know: life today is a school in which God trains us for our future ministry in eternity. This explains the presence of trials in our lives: they are some of God's tools and textbooks in the school of Christian experience.

Peter used the word "trials" rather than "tribulations" or "persecutions," because he was dealing with the *general* problems that Christians face as they are surrounded by unbelievers. He shared several facts about trials.

A. Trials meet needs. The phrase "if need be"

indicates that there are special times when God
knows that we need to go through trials. Sometimes
trials discipline us when we have disobeyed God's
will (Ps. 119:67). At other times, trials prepare us for
spiritual growth, or even help to prevent us from
sinning (2 Cor. 12:1-9). We do not always know the
need being met, but we can trust God to know and
to do what is best.

B. TRIALS ARE VARIED. Peter used the word "manifold," which literally means "variegated, many-col-
ored." He used the same word to describe God's
grace in 4:10. No matter what "color" our day may
be—a "blue" Monday or a "gray" Tuesday—God
has grace sufficient to meet the need. We must not
think that because we have overcome one kind of
trial that we will automatically "win them all." Trials
are varied, and God matches the trial to our
strengths and needs.

C. TRIALS ARE NOT EASY. Peter did not suggest that
we take a careless attitude toward trials, because this
would be deceitful. Trials produce what he called
"heaviness." The word means "to experience grief
or pain." It is used to describe our Lord in Gethsemane (Matt. 26:37), and the sorrow of saints at the
death of loved ones (1 Thes. 4:13). To deny that our
trials are painful is to make them even worse. Christians must accept the fact that there are difficult
experiences in life and not put on a brave front just
to appear "more spiritual."

D. TRIALS ARE CONTROLLED BY GOD. They do not last
forever; they are "for a season." When God permits
His children to go through the furnace, He keeps His
eye on the clock and His hand on the thermostat. If
we rebel, He may have to reset the clock; but if we
submit, He will not permit us to suffer one minute
too long. The important thing is that we learn the

lesson He wants to teach us and that we bring glory to Him alone.

Peter illustrated this truth by referring to the goldsmith. No goldsmith would deliberately waste the precious ore. He would put it into the smelting furnace long enough to remove the cheap impurities; then he would pour it out and make from it a beautiful article of value. It has been said that the eastern goldsmith kept the metal in the furnace until he could see his face reflected in it. So our Lord keeps us in the furnace of suffering until we reflect the glory and beauty of Jesus Christ.

The important point is that this glory is not fully revealed until Jesus returns for His church. Our trying experiences today are preparing us for glory tomorrow. When we see Jesus Christ, we will bring "praise and honor and glory" to Him if we have been faithful in the sufferings of this life. (See Rom. 8:17-18.) This explains why Peter associated *rejoicing* with *suffering*. While we may not be able to rejoice as we look *around* in our trials, we can rejoice as we look *ahead*. The word "this" in verse 6 (NASB) refers back to the "salvation" (the return of Christ) mentioned in verse 5.

Just as the assayer tests the gold to see if it is pure gold or counterfeit, so the trials of life test our faith to prove its sincerity. A faith that cannot be tested cannot be trusted! Too many professing Christians have a "false faith" and this will be revealed in the trials of life. The seed that fell on shallow soil produced rootless plants, and the plants died when the sun came up (see Matt. 13:1-9, 18-23). The sun in the parable represents "tribulation or persecution." The person who abandons "his faith" when the going gets tough is only proving that he really had no faith at all.

The patriarch Job went through many painful trials, all of them with God's approval; and yet he understood somewhat of this truth about the refiner's fire. "But He knoweth the way that I take; when He hath tried me, I shall come forth as gold" (Job 23:10). And he did!

It is encouraging to know that we are born for glory, kept for glory, and being prepared for glory. But the fourth discovery Peter shared with his readers is perhaps the most exciting of all.

4. Christians can enjoy the glory now (1:8-12)

The Christian philosophy of life is not "pie in the sky by and by." It carries with it a *present* dynamic that can turn suffering into glory *today*. Peter gave four directions for enjoying the glory now, even in the midst of trials.

A. Love Christ (1:8). Our love for Christ is not based on physical sight, because we have not seen Him. It is based on our spiritual relationship with Him and what the Word has taught us about Him. The Holy Spirit has poured out God's love into our hearts (Rom. 5:5), and we return that love to Him. When you find yourself in some trial, and you hurt, immediately lift your heart to Christ in true love and worship. Why? Because this will take the poison out of the experience and replace it with healing medicine.

Satan wants to use life's trials to bring out the worst in us, but God wants to bring out the best in us. If we love ourselves more than we love Christ, then we will not experience any of the glory *now*. The fire will *burn* us, not *purify* us.

B. Trust Christ (1:8). We must live by faith and not by sight. An elderly lady fell and broke her leg while attending a summer Bible conference. She said to the pastor who visited her, "I know the Lord led me to the conference. But I don't see why this had to happen! And I don't see any good coming from it." Wisely, the pastor replied, "Romans 8:28 doesn't say that we *see* all things working together for good. It says that we *know* it."

Faith means surrendering all to God and obeying His Word in spite of circumstances and consequences. Love and faith go together: when you love someone, you trust him. And faith and love together help to strengthen hope; for where you find faith and love, you will find confidence for the future.

How can we grow in faith during times of testing and suffering? The same way we grow in faith when things seem to be going well: by feeding on the Word of God (Rom. 10:17). Our fellowship with Christ through His Word not only strengthens our faith, but it also deepens our love. It is a basic principle of Christian living that we spend much time in the Word when God is testing us and Satan is tempting us.

C. REJOICE IN CHRIST (1:8). You may not be able to rejoice *over* the circumstances, but you can rejoice *in* them by centering your heart and mind on Jesus Christ. Each experience of trial helps us learn something new and wonderful about our Saviour. Abraham discovered new truths about the Lord on the mount where he offered his son (Gen. 22). The three Hebrew children discovered His nearness when they went through the fiery furnace (Dan. 3). Paul learned the sufficiency of His grace when he suffered with a thorn in the flesh (2 Cor. 12).

Note that the joy He produces is "unspeakable and full of glory." This joy is so deep and so wonderful that we cannot even express it. Words fail us! Peter had seen some of the glory on the Mount of

Transfiguration where Jesus discussed with Moses and Elijah His own impending suffering and death (Luke 9:28-36).

D. RECEIVE FROM CHRIST (1:9). "Believing . . . receiving . . ." is God's way of meeting our needs. If we love Him, trust Him, and rejoice in Him, then we can receive from Him all that we need to turn trials into triumphs. Verse 9 can be translated, "For you are receiving the consummation of your faith, that is, the final salvation of your souls." In other words, we can experience *today* some of that future glory. Charles Spurgeon used to say, "Little faith will take your soul to heaven, but great faith will bring heaven to your soul." It is not enough that we long for heaven during times of suffering, for anybody can do that. What Peter urged his readers to do was exercise love, faith, and rejoicing, so that they might experience some of the glory of heaven in the midst of suffering *now*.

The amazing thing is that this "salvation" we are awaiting—the return of Christ—was a part of God's great plan for us from eternity. The Old Testament prophets wrote about this salvation and studied closely what God revealed to them. They saw the sufferings of the Messiah, and also the glory that would follow; but they could not fully understand the connection between the two. In fact, in some of the prophecies, the Messiah's sufferings and glory are blended in one verse or paragraph.

When Jesus came to earth, the Jewish teachers were awaiting a conquering Messiah who would defeat Israel's enemies and establish the glorious kingdom promised to David. Even His own disciples were not clear about the need for His death on the cross (Matt. 16:13-28). They were still inquiring about the Jewish kingdom even after His resurrection (Acts 1:1-8). If the *disciples* were not clear about God's program, certainly the Old Testament *prophets* could be excused!

God told the prophets that they were ministering for a *future* generation. Between the suffering of Messiah and His return in glory comes what we call "the age of the church." The truth about the church was a hidden "mystery" in the Old Testament period (Eph. 3:1-13). The Old Testament believers looked ahead by faith and saw, as it were, two mountain peaks: Mount Calvary, where Messiah suffered and died (Isa. 53), and Mount Olivet, where He will return in glory (Zech. 14:4). They could not see the "valley" in between, the present age of the church.

Even the angels are interested in what God is doing in and through His church! Read 1 Corinthians 4:9 and Ephesians 3:10 for further information on how God is "educating" the angels through the church.

If the Old Testament prophets searched so diligently into the truths of salvation, and yet had so little to go on, how much more ought we to search into this subject, now that we have a complete Word from God! The same Holy Spirit who taught the prophets and, through them, wrote the Word of God, can teach us the truths in it (John 16:12-15).

Furthermore, we can learn these truths from the Old Testament as well as from the New Testament. You can find Christ in every part of the Old Testament Scriptures (Luke 24:25-27). What a delight it is to meet Christ in the Old Testament Law, the types, the Psalms, and the writings of the prophets. In times of trial, you can turn to the Bible, both the Old and New Testaments, and find all that you need for encouragement and enlightenment.

Yes, for Christians, it is glory all the way! When

we trusted Christ, we were born for glory. We are being kept for glory. As we obey Him and experience trials, we are being prepared for glory. When we love Him, trust Him, and rejoice in Him, we experience the glory here and now.

Joy unspeakable and full of glory!

3
Staying Clean in a Polluted World

1 Peter 1:13-21

In the first section of this chapter, Peter emphasized *walking in hope;* but now his emphasis is *walking in holiness.* The two go together, for "every man that hath this hope in him purifieth himself, even as He is pure" (1 John 3:3).

The root meaning of the word translated *holy* is "different." A holy person is not an odd person, but a different person. His life has a quality about it that is different. His present "lifestyle" is not only different from his past way of life, but it is different from the "lifestyles" of the unbelievers around him. A Christian's life of holiness appears strange to the lost (1 Peter 4:4), but it is not strange to other believers.

However, it is not easy to live in this world and maintain a holy walk. The anti-God atmosphere around us that the Bible calls "the world" is always pressing against us, trying to force us to conform. In this paragraph, Peter presented to his readers five spiritual incentives to encourage them (and us) to maintain a different lifestyle, a holy walk in a polluted world.

1. The glory of God (1:13)

"The revelation of Jesus Christ" is another expression for the "living hope" and "the appearing of Jesus Christ." Christians live in the future tense; their present actions and decisions are governed by this future hope. Just as an engaged couple makes all their plans in the light of that future wedding, so Christians today live with the expectation of seeing Jesus Christ.

"Gird up the loins of your mind" simply means, "Pull your thoughts together! Have a disciplined mind!" The image is that of a robed man, tucking his skirts under the belt, so he can be free to run. When you center your thoughts on the return of Christ, and live accordingly, you escape the many worldly things that would encumber your mind and hinder your spiritual progress. Peter may have borrowed the idea from the Passover supper, because later in this section he identifies Christ as the Lamb (v. 19). The Jews at Passover were supposed to eat the meal in haste, ready to move (Ex. 12:11).

Outlook determines outcome; attitude determines action. A Christian who is looking for the glory of God has a greater motivation for present obedience than a Christian who ignores the Lord's return. The contrast is illustrated in the lives of Abraham and Lot (Gen. 12—13; Heb. 11:8-16). Abraham had his eyes of faith on that heavenly city, so he had no interest in the world's real estate. But Lot, who had tasted the pleasures of the world in Egypt, gradually moved toward Sodom. Abraham brought blessing to his home, but Lot brought judgment. Outlook determined outcome.

Not only should we have a disciplined mind, but we should also have a *sober* mind. The word means "to be calm, steady, controlled; to weigh matters."

Unfortunately some people get "carried away" with prophetic studies and lose their spiritual balance. The fact that Christ is coming should encourage us to be calm and collected (1 Peter 4:7). The fact that Satan is on the prowl is another reason to be sober-minded (5:8). Anyone whose mind becomes undisciplined, and whose life "falls apart," because of prophetic studies, is giving evidence that he does not really understand Bible prophecy.

We should also have an *optimistic* mind. "Hope to the end" means "set your hope fully." Have a hopeful outlook! A friend of mine sent me a note one day that read: "When the *out*look is gloomy, try the *up*look!" Good advice, indeed! It has to be dark for the stars to appear.

The result of this spiritual mind-set is that a believer experiences the grace of God in his life. To be sure, we will experience grace when we see Jesus Christ; but we can also experience grace today as we look for Him to return. We have been saved by grace and we depend moment by moment on God's grace (1:10). Looking for Christ to return strengthens our faith and hope in difficult days, and this imparts to us more of the grace of God. Titus 2:10-13 is another passage that shows the relationship between grace and the coming of Jesus Christ.

2. The holiness of God (1:14-15)

The argument here is logical and simple. Children inherit the nature of their parents. God is holy; therefore, as His children, we should live holy lives. We are "partakers of the divine nature" (2 Peter 1:4) and ought to reveal that nature in godly living.

Peter reminded his readers of what they were before they trusted Christ. They had been *children of disobedience* (Eph. 2:1-3), but now they were to be obedient children. True salvation always results in obedience (Rom. 1:5; 1 Peter 1:2). They had also been *imitators of the world,* "fashioning themselves" after the standards and pleasures of the world. Romans 12:2 translates this same word as "conformed to this world." Unsaved people tell us that they want to be "free and different"; yet they all imitate one another!

The cause of all this is *ignorance* that leads to *indulgence.* Unsaved people lack spiritual intelligence, and this causes them to give themselves to all kinds of fleshly and worldly indulgences. (See Acts 17:30; Eph. 4:17ff.) Since we were born with a fallen nature, it was natural for us to live sinful lives. Nature determines appetites and actions. A dog and a cat behave differently because they have different natures.

We would still be in that sad sinful plight were it not for the grace of God. He called us! One day, Jesus called to Peter and his friends and said, "Come, follow Me, . . . and I will make you fishers of men" (Mark 1:17, NIV). They responded by faith to His call, and this completely changed their lives.

Perhaps this explains why Peter used the word "called" so often in this letter. We are called to be holy (1:15). We are called "out of darkness into His marvelous light" (2:9). We are called to suffer and follow Christ's example of meekness (2:21). In the midst of persecution, we are called "to inherit a blessing" (3:9). Best of all, we are called to "His eternal glory" (5:10). God called us before we called on Him for salvation. It is all wholly of grace.

But God's gracious election of sinners to become saints always involves responsibility, and not just privilege. He has chosen us in Christ "that we should be holy and without blame before Him" (Eph. 1:4).

God has called us to Himself, and He is holy; therefore, we should be holy. Peter quoted from the Old Testament Law to back up his admonition (Lev. 11:44-45; 19:2; 20:7, 26).

God's holiness is an essential part of His nature. "God is light, and in Him is no darkness at all" (1 John 1:5). Any holiness that we have in character and conduct must be derived from Him. Basically, to be "sanctified" means to be "set apart for God's exclusive use and pleasure." It involves separation from that which is unclean and complete devotion to God (2 Cor. 6:14—7:1). We are to be holy "in all manner of conversation [behavior]," so that everything we do reflects the holiness of God.

To a dedicated believer, there is no such thing as "secular" and "sacred." All of life is holy as we live to glorify God. Even such ordinary activities as eating and drinking can be done to the glory of God (1 Cor. 10:31). If something cannot be done to the glory of God, then we can be sure it must be out of the will of God.

3. The Word of God (1:16)

"It is written!" is a statement that carries great authority for the believer. Our Lord used the Word of God to defeat Satan, and so may we (Matt. 4:1-11, and see Eph. 6:17). But the Word of God is not only a sword for battle; it is also a light to guide us in this dark world (2 Peter 1:19; Ps. 119:105), food that strengthens us (Matt. 4:4; 1 Peter 2:2), and water that washes us (Eph. 5:25-27).

The Word of God has a sanctifying ministry in the lives of dedicated believers (John 17:17). Those who delight in God's Word, meditate on it, and seek to obey it will experience God's direction and blessing in their lives (Ps. 1:1-3). The Word reveals God's mind, so we should *learn* it; God's heart, so we should *love* it; God's will, so we should *live* it. Our whole being—mind, will, and heart—should be controlled by the Word of God.

Peter quoted from the Book of Leviticus, "Ye shall be holy; for I am holy" (11:44). Does this mean that the Old Testament Law is authoritative today for New Testament Christians? Keep in mind that the early Christians did not even have the New Testament. The only Word of God they possessed was the Old Testament, and God used that Word to direct and nurture them. Believers today are not under the ceremonial laws given to Israel; however, even in these laws we see moral and spiritual principles revealed. Nine of the Ten Commandments are repeated in the epistles, so we must obey them. (The Sabbath commandment was given especially to Israel and does not apply to us today. See Rom. 14:1-9.) As we read and study the Old Testament, we will learn much about God's character and working, and we will see truths pictured in types and symbols.

The first step toward keeping clean in a filthy world is to ask, "What does the Bible say?" In the Scriptures, we will find precepts, principles, promises, and persons to guide us in today's decisions. If we are really willing to obey God, He will show us His truth (John 7:17). While God's methods of working may change from age to age, His character remains the same and His spiritual principles never vary. We do not study the Bible just to get to know the Bible. We study the Bible that we might get to know God better. Too many earnest Bible students are content with outlines and explanations, and do not really get to know God. It is good to know the Word of God, but this should help us better know the God of the Word.

4. The judgment of God (1:17)

As God's children, we need to be serious about sin and about holy living. Our heavenly Father is a holy (John 17:11) and righteous Father (17:25). He will not compromise with sin. He is merciful and forgiving, but He is also a loving disciplinarian who cannot permit His children to enjoy sin. After all, it was sin that sent His Son to the cross. If we call God "Father," then we should reflect His nature.

What is this judgment that Peter wrote about? It is the judgment of a believer's works. It has nothing to do with salvation, except that salvation ought to produce good works (Titus 1:16; 2:7, 12). When we trusted Christ, God forgave our sins and declared us righteous in His Son (Rom. 5:1-10; 8:1-4; Col. 2:13). Our sins have already been judged on the cross (1 Peter 2:24), and therefore they cannot be held against us (Heb. 10:10-18).

But when the Lord returns, there will be a time of judgment called "the Judgment Seat of Christ" (Rom. 14:10-12; 2 Cor. 5:9-10). Each of us will give an account of his works, and each will receive the appropriate reward. This is a "family judgment," the Father dealing with His beloved children. The Greek word translated *judgeth* carries the meaning "to judge in order to find something good." God will search into the motives for our ministry; He will examine our hearts. But He assures us that His purpose is to glorify Himself in our lives and ministries, "and then shall every man have praise of God" (1 Cor. 4:5). What an encouragement!

God will give us many gifts and privileges, as we grow in the Christian life; but He will never give us the privilege to disobey and sin. He never pampers His children or indulges them. He is no respecter of persons. He "shows no partiality and accepts no bribes" (Deut. 10:17, NIV). "For God does not show favoritism" (Rom. 2:11, NIV). Years of obedience cannot purchase an hour of disobedience. If one of His children disobeys, God must chasten (Heb. 12:1-13). But when His child obeys and serves Him in love, He notes that and prepares the proper reward.

Peter reminded his readers that they were only "sojourners" on earth. Life was too short to waste in disobedience and sin (see 1 Peter 4:1-6). It was when Lot stopped being a sojourner, and became a resident in Sodom, that he lost his consecration and his testimony. Everything he lived for went up in smoke! Keep reminding yourself that you are a "stranger and pilgrim" in this world (1:1; 2:11).

In view of the fact that the Father lovingly disciplines His children today, and will judge their works in the future, we ought to cultivate an attitude of godly fear. This is not the cringing fear of a slave before a master, but the loving reverence of a child before his father. It is not fear of judgment (1 John 4:18), but a fear of disappointing Him or sinning against His love. It is "godly fear" (2 Cor. 7:1), a sober reverence for the Father.

I sometimes feel that there is today an increase in carelessness, even flippancy, in the way we talk about God or talk to God. Nearly a century ago, Bishop B. F. Westcott said, "Every year makes me tremble at the daring with which people speak of spiritual things." The godly bishop should hear what is said today! A worldly actress calls God "the Man upstairs." A baseball player calls Him "the great Yankee in the sky." An Old Testament Jew so feared God that he would not even pronounce His holy name, yet we today speak of God with carelessness and irreverence. In our public praying, we sometimes get so familiar that other people wonder whether we are trying to express our requests or impress the listeners with our nearness to God!

5. The love of God (1:18-21)

This is the highest motive for holy living. In this paragraph, Peter reminded his readers of their salvation experience, a reminder that all of us regularly need. This is one reason our Lord established the Lord's Supper, so that regularly His people would remember that He died for them. Note the reminders that Peter gave.

He reminded them of *what they were*. To begin with, they were slaves who needed to be set free. The word *redeemed* is, to us, a theological term; but it carried a special meaning to people in the first-century Roman Empire. There were probably 50 million slaves in the Empire! Many slaves became Christians and fellowshiped in the local assemblies. A slave could purchase his own freedom, if he could collect sufficient funds; or his master could sell him to someone who would pay the price and set him free. Redemption was a precious thing in that day.

We must never forget the slavery of sin (Titus 3:3). Moses urged Israel to remember that they had been slaves in Egypt (Deut. 5:15; 16:12; 24:18, 22). The generation that died in the wilderness forgot the bondage of Egypt and always wanted to go back!

Not only did we have a life of slavery, but it was also a life of *emptiness*. Peter called it "the empty way of life handed down to you from your forefathers" (1:18, NIV), and he described it more specifically in 4:1-4. At the time, these people thought their lives were "full" and "happy," when they were really empty and miserable. Unsaved people today are blindly living on substitutes.

While ministering in Canada, I met a woman who told me she had been converted early in life but had drifted into a "society life" that was exciting and satisfied her ego. One day, she was driving to a card party and happened to tune in a Christian radio broadcast. At that very moment, the speaker said, "Some of you women know more about cards than you do your Bible!" Those words arrested her. God spoke to her heart, she went back home, and from that hour her life was dedicated fully to God. She saw the futility and vanity of a life spent out of the will of God.

Peter not only reminded them of what they were, but he also reminded them of *what Christ did*. He shed His precious blood to purchase us out of the slavery of sin and set us free forever. "To redeem" means "to set free by paying a price." A slave could be freed with the payment of money, but no amount of money can set a lost sinner free. Only the blood of Jesus Christ can redeem us.

Peter was a witness of Christ's sufferings (5:1) and mentioned His sacrificial death often in this letter (2:21ff; 3:18; 4:1, 13; 5:1). In calling Christ "a Lamb," Peter was reminding his readers of an Old Testament teaching that was important in the early church, and that ought to be important to us today. It is the doctrine of substitution: an innocent victim giving his life for the guilty.

The doctrine of sacrifice begins in Genesis 3, when God killed animals that He might clothe Adam and Eve. A ram died for Isaac (Gen. 22:13) and the Passover lamb was slain for each Jewish household (Ex. 12). Messiah was presented as an innocent Lamb in Isaiah 53. Isaac asked the question, "Where is the lamb?" (Gen. 22:7), and John the Baptist answered it when he pointed to Jesus and said,

"Behold the Lamb of God, which taketh away the sin of the world" (John 1:29). In heaven, the redeemed and the angels sing, "Worthy is the Lamb!" (Rev. 5:11-14)

Peter made it clear that Christ's death was an appointment, not an accident; for it was ordained by God before the foundation of the world (Acts 2:23). From the human perspective, our Lord was cruelly murdered; but from the divine perspective, He laid down His life for sinners (John 10:17-18). But He was raised from the dead! Now, anyone who trusts Him will be saved for eternity.

When you and I meditate on the sacrifice of Christ for us, certainly we should want to obey God and live holy lives for His glory. When only a young lady, Frances Ridley Havergal saw a picture of the crucified Christ with this caption under it: "I did this for thee? What hast thou done for Me?" Quickly, she wrote a poem, but was dissatisfied with it and threw it into the fireplace. The paper came out unharmed! Later, at her father's suggestion, she published the poem, and today we sing it.

> I gave My life for thee,
>   My precious blood I shed;
> That thou might ransomed be,
>   And quickened from the dead.
> I gave, I gave, My life for thee,
> What hast thou given for Me?

A good question, indeed! I trust we can give a good answer to the Lord.

Additional note: "corruptible" and "precious"
Note that Peter used the words "corruptible" or "incorruptible" several times: 1 Peter 1:4, 18, 23;

3:4. Also the word "precious": 1:19; 2:4, 6, 7; 2 Peter 1:1, 4.

4
Christian Togetherness

1 Peter 1:22—2:10

One of the painful facts of life is that the people of God do not always get along with each other. You would think that those who walk in *hope* and *holiness* would be able to walk in *harmony,* but this is not always true. From God's divine point of view, there is only one body (see Eph. 4:4-6); but what we see with human eyes is a church divided and sometimes at war. There is today a desperate need for spiritual unity.

In this section of his letter, Peter emphasized spiritual unity by presenting four vivid pictures of the church.

1. We are children in the same family
(1:22—2:3)
When you consider the implications of this fact, you will be encouraged to build and maintain unity among God's people.

A. WE HAVE EXPERIENCED THE SAME BIRTH (23-25). The only way to enter God's spiritual family is by a spiritual birth, through faith in Jesus Christ (John 3:1-16). Just as there are two parents in physical

birth, so there are two parents in spiritual birth: the
Spirit of God (3:5-6) and the Word of God (1 Peter
1:23). The new birth gives to us a new nature
(2 Peter 1:4) as well as a new and living hope
(1 Peter 1:3).

Our first birth was a birth of "flesh," and the flesh
is corruptible. Whatever is born of flesh is destined
to die and decay. This explains why mankind cannot
hold civilization together: it is all based on human
flesh and is destined to fall apart. Like the beautiful
flowers of spring, man's works look successful for a
time, but then they start to decay and die. All the
way from the Tower of Babel in Genesis 11, to
"Babylon the Great" in Revelation 17 and 18, man's
great attempts at unity are destined to fail.

If we try to build unity in the church on the basis
of our first birth, we will fail; but if we build unity on
the basis of the new birth, it will succeed. Each
believer has the same Holy Spirit dwelling within
(Rom. 8:9). We call upon the same Father (1 Peter
1:17) and share His divine nature. We trust the same
Word, and that Word will never decay or disappear.
We have trusted the same Gospel and have been
born of the same Spirit. The *externals* of the flesh
that could divide us mean nothing when compared
with the *eternals* of the Spirit that unite us.

B. WE EXPRESS THE SAME LOVE (22). Peter used two
different words for love: *philadelphia,* which is
"brotherly love," and *agape,* which is Godlike sacrificial love. It is important that we share both kinds of
love. We share brotherly love because we are brothers and sisters in Christ and have likenesses. We
share *agape* love because we belong to God and
therefore can overlook differences.

By nature, all of us are selfish; so it took a miracle
of God to give us this love. Because we "obeyed the

truth through the Spirit," God purified our souls and poured His love into our hearts (Rom. 5:5). Love for the brethren is an evidence that we truly have been born of God (1 John 4:7-21). Now we are "obedient children" (1 Peter 1:14) who no longer want to live in the selfish desires of the old life.

It is tragic when people try to "manufacture" love, because the product is obviously cheap and artificial. "The words of his mouth were smoother than butter, but war was in his heart: his words were softer than oil, yet were they drawn swords" (Ps. 55:21). The love that we share with each other, and with a lost world, must be generated by the Spirit of God. It is a *constant* power in our lives, and not something that we turn on and off like a radio.

Not only is this love a spiritual love, but it is a *sincere* love ("unfeigned"). We love "with a pure heart." Our motive is not to get but to give. There is a kind of "success psychology" popular today that enables a person to subtly manipulate others in order to get what he wants. If our love is sincere and from a pure heart, we could never "use people" for our own advantage.

This love is also a *fervent* love, and this is an athletic term that means "striving with all of one's energy." Love is something we have to work at, just as an Olympic contestant has to work at his particular skills. Christian love is not a feeling; it is a matter of the will. We show love to others when we treat them the same way God treats us. God forgives us, so we forgive others. God is kind to us, so we are kind to others. It is not a matter of *feeling* but of *willing,* and this is something we must constantly work at if we are to succeed.

We have two wonderful "assistants" to help us: the Word of God and the Spirit of God. The same truth that we trusted and obeyed to become God's children also nurtures and empowers us. *It is impossible to love the truth and hate the brethren.* The Spirit of God produces the "fruit of the Spirit" in our lives, and the first of these is love (Gal. 5:22-23). If we are filled with the Word of God (Col. 3:16ff) and the Spirit of God (Eph. 5:18ff), we will manifest the love of God in our daily experiences.

C. We enjoy the same nourishment (2:1-3). God's Word *has* life, *gives* life, and *nourishes* life. We should have appetites for the Word just like hungry newborn babes! We should want the *pure* Word, unadulterated, because this alone can help us grow. When I was a child, I did not like to drink milk (and my father worked for the Borden Dairy!), so my mother used to add various syrups and powders to make my milk tastier. None of them really ever worked. It is sad when Christians have no appetite for God's Word, but must be "fed" religious entertainment instead. As we grow, we discover that the Word is milk for babes, but also strong meat for the mature (Heb. 5:11-14; 1 Cor. 3:1-4). It is also bread (Matt. 4:4) and honey (Ps. 119:103).

Sometimes children have no appetite because they have been eating the wrong things. Peter warned his readers to "lay aside" certain wrong attitudes of heart that would hinder their appetite and spiritual growth. "Malice" means wickedness in general. "Guile" is craftiness, using devious words and actions to get what we want. Of course, if we are guilty of malice and guile, we will try to hide it; and this produces "hypocrisies." Often the cause of ill will is *envy,* and one result of envy is *evil speaking,* conversation that tears the other person down. If these attitudes and actions are in our lives, we will lose our appetite for the pure word of God. If we stop feeding on the Word, we stop growing, and we stop enjoying ("tasting") the grace that we find in the Lord. When Christians are growing in the Word, they are peacemakers, not troublemakers, and they promote the unity of the church.

2. We are stones in the same building (2:4-8)

There is only one Saviour, Jesus Christ, and only one spiritual building, the church. Jesus Christ is the chief cornerstone of the church (Eph. 2:20), binding the building together. Whether we agree with each other or not, all true Christians belong to each other as stones in God's building.

Peter gave a full description of Jesus Christ, the stone. He is a *living* stone because He was raised from the dead in victory. He is the *chosen* stone of the Father, and He is *precious*. Peter quoted Isaiah 28:16 and Psalm 118:22 in his description and pointed out that Jesus Christ, though chosen by God, was rejected by men. He was not the kind of Messiah they were expecting, so they stumbled over Him. Jesus referred to this same Scripture when He debated with the Jewish leaders (Matt. 21:42ff, and see Ps. 118:22). Though rejected by men, Jesus Christ was exalted by God!

The real cause of this Jewish stumbling was their refusal to submit to the Word (1 Peter 2:8). Had they believed and obeyed the Word, they would have received their Messiah and been saved. Of course, people today still stumble over Christ and His cross (1 Cor. 1:18ff). Those who believe on Christ "shall not be confounded [ashamed]."

In His first mention of the church, Jesus compared it to a building: "I will build My church" (Matt. 16:18). Believers are living stones in His building. Each time someone trusts Christ, another stone is quarried out of the pit of sin and cemented by grace into the building. It may look to us that the church on earth is a pile of rubble and ruins, but God sees the total structure as it grows (Eph. 2:19-22). What a privilege we have to be a part of His church, "an habitation of God through the Spirit."

Peter wrote this letter to believers living in five different provinces, yet he said that they all belonged to *one* "spiritual house." There is a unity of God's people that transcends all local and individual assemblies and fellowships. We belong to each other because we belong to Christ. This does not mean that doctrinal and denominational distinctives are wrong, because each local church must be fully persuaded by the Spirit. But it does mean that we must not permit our differences to destroy the spiritual unity we have in Christ. We ought to be mature enough to disagree without in any sense becoming disagreeable.

A contractor in Michigan was building a house and the construction of the first floor went smoothly. But when they started on the second floor, they had nothing but trouble. None of the materials from the lumber yard would fit properly. Then they discovered the reason: they were working with two different sets of blueprints! Once they got rid of the old set, everything went well and they built a lovely house.

Too often, Christians hinder the building of the church because they are following the wrong plans. When Solomon built his temple, his workmen followed the plans so carefully that everything fit together on the construction site (1 Kings 6:7). If all of us would follow God's blueprints, given in His Word, we would be able to work together without discord and build His church for His glory.

3. We are priests in the same temple (2:5, 9)

We are a "holy priesthood" and a "royal priest-hood." This corresponds to the heavenly priesthood of our Lord, for He is both King and Priest (see Heb. 7). In the Old Testament, no king in Israel served as a priest; and the one king who tried was judged by God (2 Chron. 26:16-21). Our Lord's heavenly throne is a throne of grace from which we may obtain by faith all that we need to live for Him and serve Him (Heb. 4:14-16).

In the Old Testament period, God's people *had* a priesthood; but today, God's people *are* a priest-hood. Each individual believer has the privilege of coming into the presence of God (Heb. 10:19-25). We do not come to God through any person on earth, but only through the one Mediator, Jesus Christ (1 Tim. 2:1-8). Because He is alive in glory, interceding for us, we can minister as holy priests.

This means that our lives should be lived as though we were priests in a temple. It is indeed a privilege to serve as a priest. No man in Israel could serve at the altar, or enter the tabernacle or temple holy places, except those born into the tribe of Levi and consecrated to God for service. Each priest and Levite had different ministries to perform, yet they were together under the high priest, serving to glorify God. As God's priests today, we must work together at the direction of our great High Priest. Each ministry that we perform for His glory is a service to God.

Peter mentioned especially the privilege of offer-ing "spiritual sacrifices." Christians today do not bring animal sacrifices as did the Old Testament worshipers; but we do have our own sacrifices to present to God. We ought to give *our bodies* to Him as living sacrifices (Rom. 12:1-2), as well as the *praise* of our lips (Heb. 13:15) and the *good works* we do for others (13:16). The *money* and other material things we share with others in God's service is also a spiritual sacrifice (Phil. 4:10-20). Even the *people* we win to Christ are sacrifices for His glory (Rom. 15:16). We offer these sacrifices through Jesus Christ, for only then are they acceptable with God. If we do any of this for our own pleasure or glory, then it will not be accepted as a spiritual sacrifice.

God wanted His people Israel to become "a kingdom of priests" (Ex. 19:6), a spiritual influence for godliness; but Israel failed Him. Instead of being a positive influence on the godless nations around them, Israel imitated those nations and adopted their practices. God had to discipline His people many times for their idolatry, but they still persisted in sin. Today, Israel has no temple or priesthood.

It is important that we, as God's priests, maintain our separated position in this world. We must not be isolated, because the world needs our influence and witness; but we must not permit the world to infect us or change us. Separation is not isolation; it is contact without contamination.

The fact that each individual believer can go to God personally and offer spiritual sacrifices should not encourage selfishness or "individualism" on our part. We are priests *together,* serving the same High Priest, ministering in the same spiritual temple. The fact that there is but *one* High Priest and heavenly Mediator indicates unity among the people of God. While we must maintain our personal walk with God, we must not do it at the expense of other Christians by ignoring or neglecting them.

Several social scientists have written books dealing with what they call the "me complex" in modern society. The emphasis today is on taking care of yourself and forgetting about others. This same attitude has crept into the church, as I see it. Too much modern church music centers on the individual and ignores the fellowship of the church. Many books and sermons focus on *personal* experience to the neglect of ministry to the whole body. I realize that the individual must care for himself if he is to help others, but there must be balance.

4. We are citizens of the same nation (2:9-10)

The description of the church in these verses parallels God's description of Israel, in Exodus 19:5-6 and Deuteronomy 7:6. In contrast to the disobedient and rebellious nation of Israel, God's people today are His chosen and holy nation. This does not suggest that God is through with Israel, for I believe He will fulfill His promises and His covenants and establish the promised kingdom. But it does mean that the church today is to God and the world what Israel was meant to be.

We are a *chosen generation*, which immediately speaks of the grace of God. God did not choose Israel because they were a great people, but because He loved them (Deut. 7:7-8). God has chosen us purely because of His love and grace. "You did not choose Me, but I chose you" (John 15:16, NIV).

We are a *holy nation*. We have been set apart to belong exclusively to God. Our citizenship is in heaven (Phil. 3:20), so we obey heaven's laws and seek to please heaven's Lord. Israel forgot that she was a holy nation and began to break down the walls of separation that made her special and distinct. God commanded them to put a "difference between holy and unholy, and between unclean and clean" (Lev.

10:10); but they ignored the differences and disobeyed God.

We are the *people of God*. In our unsaved condition, we were not God's people; because we belonged to Satan and the world (Eph. 2:1-3, 11-19). Now that we have trusted Christ, we are a part of God's people. We are a "people of His own special possession," because He purchased us with the blood of His own Son (Acts 20:28).

All of these privileges carry with them one big responsibility: revealing the praises of God to a lost world. The verb translated "show forth" means "to tell out, to advertise." Because the world is "in the dark," people do not know the "excellencies" of God; but they should see them in our lives. Each citizen of heaven is a living "advertisement" for the virtues of God and the blessings of the Christian life. Our lives should radiate the "marvelous light" into which God has graciously called us.

After all, we have obtained mercy from God! Were it not for His mercy, we would be lost and on the way to eternal judgment! God reminded Israel many times that He had delivered them from the bondage of Egypt that they might glorify and serve Him, but the nation soon forgot and the people drifted back into their sinful ways. We are God's chosen people only because of His mercy, and it behooves us to be faithful to Him.

We are living in enemy territory, and the enemy is constantly watching us, looking for opportunities to move in and take over. As citizens of heaven, we must be united. We must present to the world a united demonstration of what the grace and mercy of God can do. As I write these words, the newspapers are reporting "dissentions" among the men who serve with the President of the United States. These men are not presenting a united front, and the nation is a bit uneasy. I wonder what the unsaved people think when they see the citizens of heaven and servants of God fighting among themselves.

Each of these four pictures emphasizes the importance of unity and harmony. We belong to one family of God and share the same divine nature. We are living stones in one building and priests serving in one temple. We are citizens of the same heavenly homeland. It is Jesus Christ who is the source and center of this unity. If we center our attention and affection on Him, we will walk and work together; if we focus on ourselves, we will only cause division.

Unity does not eliminate diversity. Not all children in a family are alike, nor are all the stones in a building identical. In fact, it is diversity that gives beauty and richness to a family or building. The absence of diversity is not *unity;* it is *uniformity,* and uniformity is dull. It is fine when the choir sings in unison, but I prefer that they sing in harmony.

Christians can differ and still get along. All who cherish the "one faith" and who seek to honor the "one Lord" can love each other and walk together (Eph. 4:1-6). God may call us into different ministries, or to use different methods, but we can still love each other and seek to present a united witness to the world.

After all, one day all of us will be together in heaven (John 17:24); so it might be a good idea if we learned to love each other down here!

St. Augustine said it perfectly: "In essentials, unity. In nonessentials, liberty. In all things, charity."

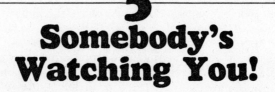

5
Somebody's Watching You!

1 Peter 2:11-25

The central section of Peter's letter (2:11—3:12) emphasizes *submission* in the life of a believer. This is certainly not a popular topic in this day of lawlessness and the quest for "personal fulfillment," but it is an important one. Peter applied the theme of submission to the life of a believer as a citizen (2:11-17), a worker (2:18-25), a marriage partner (3:1-7), and a member of the Christian assembly (3:8-12).

Submission does not mean slavery or subjugation but simply the recognition of God's authority in our lives. God has established the home, human government, and the church, and He has the right to tell us how these institutions should be run. God wants each of us to exercise authority; but before we can *exercise* authority, we must be *under* authority. Satan's offer to our first parents was freedom without authority, but they ended up losing both freedom and authority. The Prodigal Son found his freedom when he yielded to his father's will.

Peter shared with his readers three excellent motives for submitting to authority and thus living dedicated, obedient Christian lives.

1. For the sake of the lost (2:11-12)

As Christians, we must constantly remind ourselves *who we are;* and Peter did this in verse 11. To begin with, we are *God's dearly beloved children.* Eight times in his two epistles, Peter reminded his readers of God's love for them (1 Peter 2:11; 4:12; 2 Peter 1:7; 3:1, 8, 14-15, 17). In ourselves, there is nothing that God can love; but He loves us because of Jesus Christ. "This is My beloved Son, in whom I am well pleased" (2 Peter 1:17). Because of our faith in Jesus Christ, we are "accepted in the beloved" (Eph. 1:6).

Our "love relationship" to Jesus Christ ought to be motivation enough for us to live godly lives in this godless world. "If ye love Me, keep My commandments" (John 14:15). There is something deeper than obedience because of duty, and that is obedience because of devotion. "If a man love Me, he will keep My words" (John 14:23).

Not only are we God's beloved children, but we are also "strangers [sojourners] and pilgrims" in this world. We are "resident aliens" who have our citizenship in another country—heaven. Like the patriarchs of old, we are temporary in this life, traveling toward the heavenly city (Heb. 11:8-16). If you have ever lived in a foreign land, you know that the citizens watch you and are prone to find things to criticize. (In all fairness, we must confess that sometimes we are critical of foreigners in our own country.) Some years ago, a best-selling novel called *The Ugly American* depicted the struggles of an American as he tried to meet the needs of a foreign people, and still maintain his credibility with his fellow Americans, who, unfortunately, completely misunderstood the situation.

We are also *soldiers involved in a spiritual battle*.
There are sinful desires that war against us and want
to defeat us. (See Gal. 5:16-26.) Our real battle is
not with people around us, but with passions within
us. D. L. Moody said, "I have more trouble with D.
L. Moody than with any man I know." If we yield to
these sinful appetites, then we will start living like
the unsaved around us, and will become ineffective
witnesses. The word translated "war" carries the
idea of "a military campaign." We do not win one
battle, and the war is over! It is a constant warfare,
and we must be on our guard.

Most of all, we are *witnesses to the lost around us*.
The word "Gentiles" here has nothing to do with
race, since it is a synonym for "unsaved people"
(1 Cor. 5:1; 12:2; 3 John 7). Unsaved people are
watching us, speaking against us (1 Peter 3:16; 4:4),
and looking for excuses to reject the Gospel.

If we are going to witness to the lost people
around us, we must live "honest" lives. This word
implies much more than telling the truth and doing
what is right. It carries with it the idea of beauty,
comeliness, that which is admirable and honorable.
To use a cliché of the '60s, we must be "beautiful
people" in the best sense of the word.

We do not witness only with our lips; we must
back up our "talk" with our "walk." There should
be nothing in our conduct that will give the unsaved
ammunition to attack Christ and the Gospel. Our
good works must back up our good words. Jesus said
this in Matthew 5:16, and the entire Bible echoes
this truth.

In more than thirty years of ministry, I have seen
the powerful impact Christians can make on the lost
when they combine a godly life with a loving witness.
I remember many instances of some wonderful con-

versions simply because dedicated Christians let their lights shine. On the other hand, I recall with grief some lost persons who rejected the Word because of the inconsistent lives of professed believers.

Peter encouraged his readers to bear witness to the lost, by word and deed, so that one day God might visit them and save them. "The day of visitation" could mean that day when Christ returns and every tongue will confess that He is Lord. But I think the "visitation" Peter mentioned here is the time when God visits lost sinners and saves them by His grace. The word is used in this sense in Luke 19:44. When these people do trust Christ, they will glorify God and give thanks because we were faithful to witness to them even when they made life difficult for us.

In the summer of 1805, a number of Indian chiefs and warriors met in council at Buffalo Creek, New York, to hear a presentation of the Christian message by a Mr. Cram from the Boston Missionary Society. After the sermon, a response was given by Red Jacket, one of the leading chiefs. Among other things, the chief said:

"Brother, you say that there is but one way to worship and serve the Great Spirit. If there is but one religion, why do you white people differ so much about it? Why not all agree, as you can all read the Book?

"Brother, we are told that you have been preaching to the white people in this place. These people are our neighbors. We are acquainted with them. We will wait a little while and see what effect your preaching has upon them. If we find it does them good, makes them honest and less disposed to cheat Indians, we will then consider again of what you have said."

2. For the Lord's sake (2:13-17)

Of course, *everything* we do should be for the glory of the Lord and the good of His kingdom! But Peter was careful to point out that Christians in society are representatives of Jesus Christ. It is our responsibility to "advertise God's virtues" (1 Peter 2:9, author's translation). This is especially true when it comes to our relationship to government and people in authority.

As Christian citizens, we should submit to the authority vested in human government. The word translated "ordinance" in our Authorized Version simply means "creation or institution." It does not refer to each individual law, but to the institutions that make and enforce the laws. It is possible to submit to the institutions and still disobey the laws.

For example, when Daniel and his three friends refused to obey the king's dietary regulations, they disobeyed the law; but the *way* that they did it proved that they honored the king and respected the authorities (Dan. 1). They were not rebels; they were careful not to embarrass the official in charge or get him into trouble; and yet they stood their ground. They glorified God and, at the same time, honored the authority of the king.

Peter and the other apostles faced a similar challenge shortly after Pentecost (Acts 4—5). The Jewish council commanded them to stop preaching in the name of Jesus, but Peter and his associates refused to obey. (See Acts 4:19; 5:29.) They did not cause a rebellion or in any way question or deny the authority of the council. They submitted to the institution but they refused to stop preaching. They showed respect to their leaders even though these men were opposed to the Gospel.

It is important that we respect the office even

though we cannot respect the man or woman in the office. As much as possible, we should seek to cooperate with the government and obey the law; but we must never allow the law to make us violate our conscience or disobey God's Word. Unfortunately, some zealous but ignorant Christians use these differences as opportunities for conflict and loud sermons about "freedom" and "separation of church and state."

When a local church constructs and furnishes a building, there is a local code that must be obeyed. (I have been through several building programs and I know!) The government has no right to control the pulpit or the business meeting, but it has every right to control matters that relate to safety and operation. If the law requires a certain number of exits, or fire extinguishers, or emergency lights, the church must comply. The state is not persecuting when it sets up the code, nor is the church compromising when it obeys the code. But I know some overly-zealous saints who have disgraced the name of the Lord by their attitudes and actions relating to these matters.

Peter named the offices we are to respect. "The king" meant "the emperor." In democratic nations, we have a president or premier. Peter did not criticize the Roman government or suggest that it be overthrown. God's church has been able to live and grow in all kinds of political systems. The "governors" are those under the supreme authority who administer the laws and execute justice. Ideally, they should punish those who do evil and praise those who do good. This ideal was not always reached in Peter's day (see Acts 24:24-27), nor is it reached in our own. Again, we must remind ourselves to respect the office even if we cannot respect the officer.

Two phrases are important: "the will of God" (1 Peter 2:15) and "the servants of God" (v. 16). When we do something in the will of God and as the servants of God, then we are doing it "for the Lord's sake." God has willed that we silence the critics by doing good, not by opposing the authority. The word "silence" in verse 15 is literally "muzzle," as though the pagan critics were like a pack of yelping, snapping dogs!

Someone may argue, "But, as Christians, are we not free?" Yes, we are free in Christ; but we must never use our freedom for ourselves. We must always use it for others. Sad to say, there are "religious racketeers" who prey upon ignorant people and use "religion" to veil their evil actions. A true Christian submits himself to authority because he is first of all submitted to Christ. He uses his freedom as a tool to build with and not as a weapon to fight with. A good example of this attitude is Nehemiah, who willingly gave up his own rights that he might help his people and restore the walls of Jerusalem.

If we are sincerely submitted to authority "for the Lord's sake," then we will show honor to all who deserve it. We may not agree with their politics or their practices, but we must respect their position. (See Rom. 13.) We will also "love the brotherhood," meaning, of course, the people of God in the church. This is a recurring theme in this letter (1:22; 3:8; 4:8; 5:14). One way we show love to the brethren is by submitting to the authority of the "powers that be," for we are bound together with one another in our Christian witness.

"Fear God" and "honor the king" go together, since "the powers that be are ordained of God" (Rom. 13:1). Solomon had the same counsel: "My son, fear thou the Lord and the king" (Prov. 24:21).

We honor the king because we do fear the Lord. It is worth noting that the tenses of these verbs indicate that we should *constantly* maintain these attitudes. "Keep loving the brotherhood! Keep fearing God! Keep honoring the king!"

As Christians, we must exercise discernment in our relationship to human government. There are times when the right thing is to set aside our own privileges, and there are other times when *using* our citizenship is the right thing. Paul was willing to suffer personally in Philippi (Acts 16:16-24), but he was unwilling to "sneak out of town" like a criminal (16:35-40). When he was arrested on false charges, Paul used his citizenship to protect himself (22:22-29) and to insist on a fair trial before Caesar (25:1-12).

3. For our own sake (2:18-25)

In this paragraph Peter addressed the Christian slaves in the congregations, and again he stressed the importance of submission. Some newly converted slaves thought that their spiritual freedom also guaranteed personal and political freedom, and they created problems for themselves and the churches. Paul dealt with this problem in 1 Corinthians 7:20-24, and also touched on it in his letter to his friend Philemon. The Gospel eventually overthrew the Roman Empire and the terrible institution of slavery, even though the early church did not preach against either one.

There are no Christian slaves today, at least in the New Testament sense; but what Peter wrote does have application to employees. We are to be submissive to those who are over us, whether they are kind or unkind to us. Christian employees must never take advantage of Christian employers. Each

worker should do a good day's work and honestly
earn his pay.

Sometimes a Christian employee may be wronged
by an unbelieving co-worker or supervisor. For
conscience' sake, he must "take it" even though he
is not in the wrong. A Christian's relationship to
God is far more important than his relationship to
men. "For this is grace [thankworthy]" to bear reproach when you are innocent (see Matt. 5:10-12).
Anybody, including an unbeliever, can "take it pa-
tiently" when he is in the wrong! It takes a dedicated
Christian to "take it" when he is in the right. "This is
grace [acceptable] with God." God can give us the
grace to submit and "take it" and in this way glorify
God.

Of course, the human tendency is to fight back
and to demand our rights. But that is the natural
response of the unsaved person, and we must do
much more than they do (Luke 6:32-34). Anybody
can fight back; it takes a Spirit-filled Christian to
submit and let God fight his battles (Rom. 12:16-21).

In the Bible, duty is always connected with doctrine. When Paul wrote to the slaves, he related his
admonitions to the doctrine of the grace of God
(Titus 2:9-15). Peter connected his counsels to the
example of Jesus Christ, God's "Suffering Servant"
(2:21-25; and see Isa. 52:13—53:12). Peter had
learned in his own experience that God's people
serve through suffering. At first, Peter had opposed
Christ's suffering on the cross (Matt. 16:21ff); but
then he learned the important lesson that we lead by
serving and serve by suffering. He also learned that
this kind of suffering always leads to glory!

Peter encouraged these suffering slaves by presenting three "pictures" of Jesus Christ.

A. HE IS OUR EXAMPLE IN HIS LIFE (2:21-23). All that

Jesus did on earth, as recorded in the four Gospels, is a perfect example for us to follow. But He is especially our example in the way He responded to suffering. In spite of the fact that He was sinless in both word and deed, He suffered at the hands of the authorities. This connects, of course, to Peter's words in verses 19 and 20. We wonder how he would have responded in the same circumstances! The fact that Peter used his sword in the garden suggests that he would have fought rather than submitted to the will of God.

Jesus proved that a person could be in the will of God, be greatly loved by God, and still suffer unjustly. There is a shallow brand of popular theology today that claims that Christians will *not* suffer if they are in the will of God. Those who promote such ideas have not meditated much on the cross.

Our Lord's humility and submission were not an evidence of weakness, but of power. Jesus could have summoned the armies of heaven to rescue Him! His words to Pilate in John 18:33-38 are proof that He was in complete command of the situation. It was Pilate who was on trial, not Jesus! Jesus had committed Himself to the Father, and the Father always judges righteously.

We are not saved by following Christ's example, because each of us would stumble over verse 22: "who did no sin." Sinners need a Saviour, not an Example. But after a person is saved, he will want to "follow closely upon His steps" (literal translation) and imitate the example of Christ.

B. HE IS OUR SUBSTITUTE IN HIS DEATH (2:24). He died as the sinner's Substitute. This entire section reflects that great "Servant Chapter," Isaiah 53, especially verses 5-7, but also verses 9 and 12. Jesus did not die as a martyr; He died as a Saviour, a sinless Substitute. The word translated "bare" means "to carry as a sacrifice." The Jewish people did not crucify criminals; they stoned them to death. But if the victim was especially evil, his dead body was hung on a tree until evening, as a mark of shame (Deut. 21:23). Jesus died on a tree—a cross—and bore the curse of the Law against our sins (Gal. 3:13).

The paradoxes of the cross never cease to amaze us. Christ was wounded that we might be healed. He died that we might live. We died with Him, and thus we are "dead to sin" (Rom. 6) so that we might "live unto righteousness." The healing Peter mentioned in verse 24 is not physical healing, but rather the spiritual healing of the soul (Ps. 103:3). One day, when we have glorified bodies, all sicknesses will be gone; but meanwhile, even some of God's choicest servants may have physical afflictions (see Phil. 2:25-30; 2 Cor. 12:1ff).

It is not Jesus the Example or the Teacher who saves us, but Jesus the spotless Lamb of God who takes away the sins of the world (John 1:29).

C. He is our Watchful Shepherd in heaven (2:25). In the Old Testament, the sheep died for the shepherd; but at Calvary, the Shepherd died for the sheep (John 10). Every lost sinner is like a sheep gone astray: ignorant, lost, wandering, in danger, away from the place of safety, and unable to help himself. The Shepherd went out to search for the lost sheep (Luke 15:1-7). He died for the sheep!

Now that we have been returned to the fold and are safely in His care, He watches over us lest we stray and get into sin. The word "bishop" simply means "one who watches over, who oversees." Just as the elder-bishop oversees the flock of God, the local church (1 Peter 5:2), so the Saviour in glory watches over His sheep to protect them and perfect them (Heb. 13:20-21).

Here, then, is the wonderful truth Peter wanted to share: as we live godly lives, and submit in times of suffering, we are following Christ's example *and becoming more like Him.* We submit and obey, not only for the sake of lost souls and for the Lord's sake, but also for our own sake, that we might grow spiritually and become more like Christ.

The unsaved world is watching us, but the Shepherd in heaven is also watching over us; so we have nothing to fear. We can submit to Him and know that He will work everything together for our good and His glory.

6
Wedlock or Deadlock?

1 Peter 3:1-7

A strange situation exists in society today. We have more readily available information about sex and marriage than ever before; yet we have more marital problems and divorces. Obviously something is wrong. It is not sufficient to say that God is needed in these homes, because even many *Christian* marriages are falling apart.

The fact that a man and a woman are both saved is no guarantee that their marriage will succeed. Marriage is something that we have to work at; success is not automatic. And when one marriage partner is not a Christian, that can make matters even more difficult. Peter addressed this section of his letter to Christian wives who had unsaved husbands, telling them how to win their mates to Christ. Then he added some important admonitions for Christian husbands.

No matter what your marital status may be, you can learn from Peter the essentials for a happy and successful marriage.

1. The example of Christ (3:1a, 7a)

The phrases "in the same manner" and "in like manner" refer us back to Peter's discussion of the example of Jesus Christ (2:21-25). Just as Jesus was submissive and obedient to God's will, so a Christian husband and wife should follow His example.

Much of our learning in life comes by way of imitation. Grandparents have a delightful time watching their grandchildren "pick up" new skills and words as they grow up. If we imitate the best models, we will become better people and better achievers; but if we imitate the wrong models, it will cripple our lives and possibly ruin our characters. The "role models" that we follow influence us in every area of life.

While standing in the checkout line in a supermarket, I overheard two women discussing the latest Hollywood scandal that was featured on the front page of a newspaper displayed on the counter. As I listened (and I could not *help* but hear them!), I thought: "How foolish to worry about the sinful lives of matinee idols. Why clutter up your mind with such trash? Why not get acquainted with decent people and learn from their lives?" A few days later, I overheard a conversation about the marital problems on a certain television "soap serial," and the same thoughts came to me.

When Christian couples try to imitate the world and get their standards from Hollywood instead of from heaven, there will be trouble in the home. But if both partners will imitate Jesus Christ in His submission and obedience, and His desire to serve others, then there will be triumph and joy in the home. A psychiatrist friend of mine states that the best thing a Christian husband can do is pattern himself after Jesus Christ. In Christ we see a beautiful blending of strength and tenderness, and that is what it takes to be a successful husband.

Peter also pointed to Sarah as a model for Christian wives to follow. To be sure, Sarah was not perfect; but she proved to be a good helpmeet to Abraham, and she is one of the few women named in Hebrews 11. I once made a pastoral visit on a woman who said she had marital problems, and I noticed a number of "movie fan club magazines" in the magazine rack. After listening to the woman's problems, I concluded that she needed to follow some Bible examples and models and get her mind off of the worldly examples.

We cannot follow Christ's example unless we first know Him as our Saviour, and then submit to Him as our Lord. We must spend time with Him each day, meditating on the Word and praying; and a Christian husband and wife must pray together and seek to encourage each other in the faith.

2. Submission (3:1-6)

Twice in this paragraph Peter reminded Christian wives that they were to be submissive to their husbands (1, 5). The word translated "subjection" is a military term that means "to place under rank." God has a place for everything; He has ordained various levels of authority (see 1 Peter 2:13-14). He has ordained that the husband be the head of the home (Eph. 5:21ff) and that, as he submits to Christ, his wife should submit to him. Headship is not dictatorship, but the loving exercise of divine authority under the Lordship of Jesus Christ.

Peter gave three reasons why a Christian wife should submit to her husband, even if the husband (as in this case) is not saved.

A. SUBMISSION IS AN OBLIGATION (3:1). God has commanded it because, in His wisdom, He knows that this is the best arrangement for a happy, fulfilling marriage. Subjection does not mean that the wife is inferior to the husband. In fact, in verse 7, Peter made it clear that the husband and wife are "heirs together." The man and woman are made by the same Creator out of the same basic material, and both are made in God's image. God gave dominion to both Adam and Eve (Gen. 1:28), and in Jesus Christ they are one (Gal. 3:28).

Submission has to do with order and authority, not evaluation. For example, the slaves in the average Roman household were superior in many ways to their masters, but they still had to be under authority. The buck private in the army may be a better person than the five-star general, but he is still a buck private. Even Christ Himself became a servant and submitted to God's will. There is nothing degrading about submitting to authority or accepting God's order. If anything, it is the first step toward fulfillment. And Ephesians 5:21 makes it clear that *both* husband and wife must first be submitted to Jesus Christ.

Husbands and wives must be partners, not competitors. After a wedding ceremony, I often privately say to the bride and groom, "Now, remember, from now on it's no longer *mine* or *yours*, but *ours*." This explains why Christians must always marry other Christians, for a believer cannot enter into any kind of deep "oneness" with an unbeliever (2 Cor. 6:14-18).

B. Submission is an opportunity (3:1b-2). An opportunity for what? To win an unsaved husband to Christ. God not only *commands* submission, but He *uses it* as a powerful spiritual influence in a home. This does not mean that a Christian wife "gives in" to her unsaved husband in order to subtly manipulate him and get him to do what she desires. This kind of selfish psychological persuasion ought never to be found in a Christian's heart or home.

An unsaved husband will not be converted by preaching or nagging in the home. The phrase "without the word" does not mean "without the Word of God," because salvation comes through the Word (John 5:24). It means "without talk, without a lot of speaking." Christian wives who preach at their husbands only drive them farther from the Lord. I know one zealous wife who used to keep religious radio programs on all evening, usually very loud, so that her unsaved husband would "hear the truth." She only made it easier for him to leave home and spend his evenings with his friends.

It is the character and conduct of the wife that will win the lost husband—not arguments, but such attitudes as submission, understanding, love, kindness, patience. These qualities are not manufactured; they are the fruit of the Spirit that comes when we are submitted to Christ and to one another. A Christian wife with "purity and reverence" will reveal in her life "the praises" of God (1 Peter 2:9) and influence her husband to trust Christ.

One of the greatest examples of a godly wife and mother in church history is Monica, the mother of the famous St. Augustine. God used Monica's witness and prayers to win both her son and her husband to Christ, though her husband was not converted until shortly before his death. Augustine wrote in his *Confessions,* "She served him as her lord; and did her diligence to win him unto Thee . . . preaching Thee unto him by her conversation [behavior]; by which Thou ornamentest her, making her reverently amiable unto her husband."

In a Christian home, we must minister to each other. A Christian husband must minister to his wife and help to "beautify her" in the Lord (Eph. 5:25-30). A Christian wife must encourage her husband and help him grow strong in the Lord. Parents and children must share burdens and blessings and seek to maintain an atmosphere of spiritual excitement and growth in the home. If there are unsaved people in the home, they will be won to Christ more by what they see in our lives and relationships than by what they hear in our witness.

C. Submission is an ornament (3:3-6). The word translated "adorning" is *kosmos* in the Greek, and gives us our English words "cosmos" (the ordered universe) and "cosmetic." It is the opposite of *chaos*. Peter warned the Christian wife not to major on external decorations but on internal character. Roman women were captivated by the latest fashions of the day, and competed with each other in dress and hairdos. It was not unusual for the women to have elaborate *coiffures,* studded with gold and silver combs and even jewels. They wore elaborate and expensive garments, all for the purpose of impressing each other.

A Christian wife with an unsaved husband might think that she must imitate the world if she is going to win her mate; but just the opposite is true. Glamor is artificial and external; true beauty is real and internal. Glamor is something a person can put on and take off, but true beauty is always present. Glamor is corruptible; it decays and fades. True beauty from the heart grows more wonderful as the years pass. A Christian woman who cultivates the beauty of the inner person will not have to depend on cheap externals. God is concerned about values, not prices.

Of course, this does not mean that a wife should neglect herself and not try to be up-to-date in her apparel. It simply means that she is not *majoring* on being a "fashion plate" just to "keep up with the crowd." Any husband is proud of a wife who is attractive, but that beauty must come from the heart, not the store. We are not *of* this world, but we must not look as though we came from *out of* this world!

Peter did not forbid the wearing of jewelry any more than the wearing of apparel. The word "wearing" in verse 3 means "the putting around," and refers to a gaudy display of jewelry. It is possible to wear jewelry and still honor God, and we must not judge one another in this matter.

Peter closed this section by pointing to Sarah as an example of a godly, submissive wife. Read Genesis 18 for the background. Christian wives today would probably embarrass their husbands if they called them "lord," but their attitudes ought to be such that they could call them "lord" and people would believe it. The believing wife who submits to Christ and to her husband, and who cultivates a "meek and quiet spirit" will never have to be afraid. (The "fear" in this verse means "terror," while in verse 2 it means "reverence.") God will watch over her even when her unsaved mate creates problems and difficulties for her.

3. Consideration (3:7)

Why did Peter devote more space to instructing the wives than the husbands? Because the Christian wives were experiencing a whole new situation and needed guidance. In general, women were kept down in the Roman Empire, and their new freedom in Christ created new problems and challenges. Furthermore, many of them had unsaved husbands and needed extra encouragement and enlightenment.

As Peter wrote to the Christian husbands, he reminded them of four areas of responsibility in their relationship with their mates.

A. PHYSICAL—"DWELL WITH THEM." This implies much more than sharing the same address. Marriage is fundamentally a physical relationship: "They two shall be one flesh" (Eph. 5:31). Of course, Christian mates enjoy a deeper spiritual relationship, but the two go together (1 Cor. 7:1-5). A truly spiritual husband will fulfill his marital duties and love his wife.

The husband must make time to be home with his wife. Christian workers and church officers who get too busy running around solving other people's problems, may end up creating problems of their own at home. One survey revealed that the average husband and wife had thirty-seven minutes a week together in actual communication! Is it any wonder that marriages fall apart after the children grow up and leave home? The husband and wife are left alone—to live with strangers!

"Dwell with them" also suggests that the husband provide for the physical and material needs of the home. While it is not wrong for a wife to have a job or career, her first responsibility is to care for the home (Titus 2:4-5). It is the husband who should provide (1 Tim. 5:8).

B. INTELLECTUAL—"ACCORDING TO KNOWLEDGE." Somebody asked Mrs. Albert Einstein if she understood Dr. Einstein's theory of relativity, and she replied, "No, but I understand the Doctor." In my premarital counseling as a pastor, I often gave the couple pads of paper and asked them to write down the three things each one thinks the other enjoys doing the most. Usually, the prospective bride made her list immediately; the man would sit and ponder. And usually the girl was right but the man wrong! What a beginning for a marriage!

It is amazing that two married people can live together and not really know each other! Ignorance is dangerous in any area of life, but it is especially dangerous in marriage. A Christian husband needs to know his wife's moods, feelings, needs, fears, and hopes. He needs to "listen with his heart" and share meaningful communication with her. There must be in the home such a protective atmosphere of love and submission that the husband and wife can disagree and still be happy together.

"Speaking the truth in love" is the solution to the communications problem (Eph. 4:15). It has well been said that love without truth is hypocrisy, and truth without love is brutality. We need both truth and love if we are to grow in our understanding of one another. How can a husband show consideration for his wife if he does not understand her needs or problems? To say "I never knew you felt that way!" is to confess that, at some point, one mate excommunicated the other. When either mate is afraid to be open and honest about a matter, then you are building walls and not bridges.

C. EMOTIONAL—"GIVING HONOR UNTO THE WIFE." Chivalry may be dead, but every husband must be a "knight in shining armor" who treats his wife like a princess. (By the way, the name Sarah means "princess.") Peter did not suggest that a wife is "the weaker vessel" mentally, morally, or spiritually, but rather physically. There are exceptions, of course, but generally speaking, the man is the stronger of the two when it comes to physical accomplishments. The husband should treat his wife like an expensive, beautiful, fragile vase, in which is a precious treasure.

When a young couple starts dating, the boy is courteous and thoughtful. After they get engaged, he shows even more courtesy and always acts like a gentleman. Sad to say, soon after they get married, many a husband forgets to be kind and gentlemanly and starts taking his wife for granted. He forgets that happiness in a home is made up of many *little* things, including the small courtesies of life.

Big resentments often grow out of small hurts. Husbands and wives need to be honest with each other, admit hurts, and seek for forgiveness and healing. "Giving honor unto the wife" does not mean "giving in to the wife." A husband can disagree with his wife and still respect and honor her. As the spiritual leader in the home, the husband must sometimes make decisions that are not popular; but he can still act with courtesy and respect.

"Giving honor" means that the husband respects his wife's feelings, thinking, and desires. He may not agree with her ideas, but he respects them. Often God balances a marriage so that the husband needs what the wife has in her personality, and she likewise needs his good qualities. An impulsive husband often has a patient wife, and this helps to keep him out of trouble!

The husband must be the "thermostat" in the home, setting the emotional and spiritual temperature. The wife often is the "thermometer," letting him know what that temperature is! Both are necessary. The husband who is sensitive to his wife's feelings will not only make her happy, but will also grow himself and help his children live in a home that honors God.

D. SPIRITUAL—"THAT YOUR PRAYERS BE NOT HINDERED."

Peter assumed that husbands and wives would pray together. Often, they do not; and this is the reason for much failure and unhappiness. If unconverted people can have happy homes *without prayer* (and they do), how much happier Christian homes would be *with prayer!* In fact, it is the prayer life of a couple that indicates how things are going in the home. If something is wrong, their prayers will be hindered.

A husband and wife need to have their own private, individual prayer time each day. They also need to pray together and to have a time of "family devotion." How this is organized will change from home to home, and even from time to time as the children grow up and schedules change. The Word of God and prayer are basic to a happy, holy home (Acts 6:4).

A husband and wife are "heirs together." If the wife shows submission and the husband consideration, and if both submit to Christ and follow His example, then they will have an enriching experience in their marriage. If not, they will miss God's best and rob each other of blessing and growth. "The grace of life" may refer to children, who certainly are a heritage from God (Ps. 127:3); but even childless couples can enjoy spiritual riches if they will obey Peter's admonitions.

It might be good if husbands and wives occasionally took inventory of their marriages. Here are some questions, based on what Peter wrote.

1. Are we partners or competitors?
2. Are we helping each other become more spiritual?
3. Are we depending on the externals or the eternals? The artificial or the real?
4. Do we understand each other better?
5. Are we sensitive to each other's feelings and

ideas, or taking each other for granted?

6. Are we seeing God answer our prayers?

7. Are we enriched because of our marriage, or robbing each other of God's blessing?

Honest answers to these questions might make a difference!

7
Preparing
for the Best!

1 Peter 3:8-17

A devoted pastor was facing serious surgery, and a friend visited him in the hospital to pray with him. "An interesting thing happened today," the pastor told him. "One of the nurses looked at my chart and said, 'Well, I guess you're preparing for the worst!' I smiled at her and said, 'No, I'm preparing for the best. I'm a Christian, and God has promised to work all things together for good.' Boy, did she drop that chart and leave this room in a hurry!"

Peter wrote this letter to prepare Christians for a "fiery trial" of persecution, yet his approach was optimistic and positive. "Prepare for the best!" was his message. In this section, he gave them three instructions to follow if they would experience the best blessings in the worst times.

1. Cultivate Christian love (3:8-12)
We have noted that love is a recurring theme in Peter's letters, not only God's love for us, but also our love for others. Peter had to learn this important lesson himself, and he had a hard time learning it! How patient Jesus had to be with him!

78

We should begin with *love for God's people* (3:8). The word "finally" means "to sum it all up." Just as the whole of the Law is summed up in love (Rom. 13:8-10), so the whole of human relationships is fulfilled in love. This applies to every Christian and to every area of life.

This love is evidenced by a *unity of mind* (see Phil. 2:1-11). Unity does not mean uniformity; it means cooperation in the midst of diversity. The members of the body work together in unity, even though they are all different. Christians may differ on *how* things are to be done, but they must agree on *what* is to be done and *why.* A man criticized D. L. Moody's methods of evangelism, and Moody said, "Well, I'm always ready for improvement. What are *your* methods?" The man confessed that he had none! "Then I'll stick to my own," said Moody. Whatever methods we may use, we must seek to honor Christ, win the lost, and build the church. Some methods are definitely not scriptural, but there is plenty of room for variety in the church.

Another evidence of love is *compassion,* a sincere "feeling for and with" the needs of others. Our English word "sympathy" comes from this word. We dare not get hardhearted toward each other. We must share both joys and trials (Rom. 12:15). The basis for this is the fact that we are brethren in the same family (see 1 Peter 1:22; 2:17; 4:8; 5:14). We are "taught of God to love one another" (1 Thes. 4:9).

Love reveals itself in *pity,* a tenderness of heart toward others. In the Roman Empire, this was not a quality that was admired; but the Christian message changed all of that. Today, we are deluged with so much bad news that it is easy for us to get insulated and unfeeling. We need to cultivate compassion, and actively show others that we are concerned.

"Be courteous" involves much more than acting like a lady or gentleman. "Be humble-minded" is a good translation; and, after all, humility is the foundation for courtesy, for the humble person puts others ahead of himself.

Not only should we love God's people, but we should also *love our enemies* (1 Peter 3:9). The recipients of this letter were experiencing a certain amount of personal persecution because they were doing the will of God. Peter warned them that *official* persecution was just around the corner, so they had better prepare. The church today had better prepare, because difficult times are ahead.

As Christians, we can live on one of three levels. We can return evil for good, which is the Satanic level. We can return good for good and evil for evil, which is the human level. Or, we can return good for evil, which is the divine level. Jesus is the perfect example of this latter approach (2:21-23). As God's loving children, we must not give "an eye for an eye, and a tooth for a tooth" (Matt. 5:38-48), which is the basis for *justice*. We must operate on the basis of *mercy*, for that is the way God deals with us.

This admonition must have meant much to Peter himself, because he once tried to fight Christ's enemies with a sword (Luke 22:47-53). When he was an unconverted rabbi, Paul used every means possible to oppose the church; but when he became a Christian, Paul never used human weapons to fight God's battles (Rom. 12:17-21; 2 Cor. 10:1-6). When Peter and the apostles were persecuted, they depended on prayer and God's power, not on their own wisdom or strength. (See Acts 4:23ff.)

We must always be reminded of our *calling* as Christians, for this will help us love our enemies and do them good when they treat us badly. We are called to "inherit a blessing." The persecutions we experience on earth today only add to our blessed inheritance of glory in heaven someday (Matt. 5:10-12). But we also inherit a blessing *today* when we treat our enemies with love and mercy. By sharing a blessing with them, we receive a blessing ourselves! Persecution can be a time of spiritual enrichment for a believer. The saints and martyrs in church history all bear witness to this fact.

We should love one another, love our enemies, and *love life* (1 Peter 3:10-12). The news of impending persecution should not cause a believer to give up on life. What may appear to be "bad days" to the world can be "good days" for a Christian, if he will only meet certain conditions.

First, *we must deliberately decide to love life.* This is an act of the will: "He who wills to love life." It is an attitude of faith that sees the best in every situation. It is the opposite of the pessimistic attitude expressed in Ecclesiastes 2:17: "Therefore I hated life . . . for all is vanity and vexation of spirit." We can decide to *endure* life and make it a burden, *escape* life as though we were running from a battle, or *enjoy* life because we know God is in control. Peter was not suggesting some kind of unrealistic psychological gymnastics that refused to face facts. Rather, he was urging his readers to take a positive approach to life and *by faith* make the most of every situation.

Second, *we must control our tongues.* Many of the problems of life are caused by the wrong words, spoken in the wrong spirit. Every Christian should read James 3 regularly and pray Psalm 141:3 daily. How well Peter knew the sad consequences of hasty speech! There is no place for lies in the life of a saint.

Third, *we must do good and hate evil*. We need both the positive and the negative. The Old English word "eschew" means more than just "avoid." It means "to avoid something because you despise and loathe it." It is not enough for us to avoid sin because sin is wrong; we ought to shun it because we hate it.

Finally, *we must seek and pursue peace.* "Blessed are the peacemakers: for they shall be called the children of God" (Matt. 5:9). If we go out and seek trouble, we will find it; but if we seek peace, we can find it as well. This does not mean "peace at any price," because righteousness must always be the basis for peace (James 3:13-18). It simply means that a Christian exercises moderation as he relates to people and does not create problems because he wants to have his own way. "If it be possible, as much as lieth in you, live peaceably with all men" (Rom. 12:18). Sometimes it is not possible! See Romans 14:19 where we are also admonished to *work hard* to achieve peace. It does not come automatically.

"But what if our enemies take advantage of us?" a persecuted Christian might ask. "We may be seeking peace, but they are seeking war!" Peter gave them the assurance that God's eyes are upon His people and His ears open to their prayers. (Peter learned that lesson when he tried to walk on the water without looking to Jesus—Matt. 14:22-33.) We must trust God to protect and provide, for he alone can defeat our enemies (Rom. 12:17-21).

Peter quoted these statements from Psalm 34:12-15, so it would be profitable for you to read the entire psalm. It describes what God means by "good days." They are not necessarily days free from problems, for the psalmist wrote about fears (v. 4), troubles (vv. 6, 17), afflictions (v. 19), and even a broken heart (v. 18). A "good day" for the believer who "loves life" is not one in which he is pampered and sheltered, but one in which he experiences God's help and blessing *because of* life's problems and trials. It is a day in which he magnifies the Lord (vv. 1-3), experiences answers to prayer (vv. 4-7), tastes the goodness of God (v. 8), and senses the nearness of God (v. 18).

The next time you think you are having a "bad day," and you hate life, read Psalm 34 and you may discover you are really having a "good day" to the glory of God!

2. Practice the lordship of Christ (3:13-15)

These verses introduce the third main section of 1 Peter—God's grace in suffering. They introduce the important spiritual principle that the fear of the Lord conquers every other fear. Peter quoted Isaiah 8:13-14 to back up his admonition: "But in your hearts set apart Christ as Lord" (3:15, NIV).

The setting of the Isaiah quotation is significant. Ahaz, King of Judah, faced a crisis because of an impending invasion by the Assyrian army. The kings of Israel and Syria wanted Ahaz to join them in an alliance, but Ahaz refused; so Israel and Syria threatened to invade Judah! Behind the scenes, Ahaz confederated himself with Assyria! The Prophet Isaiah warned him against ungodly alliances and urged him to trust God for deliverance. "Sanctify the Lord of hosts [armies] Himself; and let Him be your fear, and let Him be your dread" (Isa. 8:13).

As Christians, we are faced with crises, and we are tempted to give in to our fears and make the wrong decisions. But if we "sanctify Christ as Lord" in our hearts, we need never fear men or circumstances.

Our enemies might *hurt* us, but they cannot *harm* us. Only we can harm ourselves if we fail to trust God. Generally speaking, people do not oppose us if we do good; but even if they do, it is better to suffer for righteousness' sake than to compromise our testimony. Peter discussed this theme in detail in 4:12-19.

Instead of experiencing fear as we face the enemy, we can experience blessing, if Jesus Christ is Lord in our hearts. The word "happy" in verse 14 is the same as "blessed" in Matthew 5:10ff. This is a part of the "joy unspeakable and full of glory" (1 Peter 1:8).

When Jesus Christ is Lord of our lives, each crisis becomes an opportunity for witness. We are "ready always to give an answer." Our English word *apology* comes from the Greek word translated "answer," but it does not mean "to say I am sorry." Rather, it means "a defense presented in court." "Apologetics" is the branch of theology that deals with the defense of the faith. Every Christian should be able to give a reasoned defense of his hope in Christ, *especially in hopeless situations*. A crisis creates the opportunity for witness when a believer behaves with faith and hope, because the unbelievers will then sit up and take notice.

This witness must be given "with meekness and fear [respect]" and not with arrogance and a know-it-all attitude. We are witnesses, not prosecuting attorneys! We must also be sure that our lives back up our defense. Peter did not suggest that Christians argue with lost people, but rather that we present to the unsaved an account of what we believe and why we believe it, in a loving manner. The purpose is not to win an argument but to win lost souls to Christ.

What does it mean to "sanctify Christ as Lord" in

our hearts? It means to turn everything over to Him, and to live only to please Him and glorify Him. It means to fear displeasing Him rather than fear what men might do to us. How wonderfully this approach simplifies our lives! It is Matthew 6:33 and Romans 12:1-2 combined into a daily attitude of faith that obeys God's Word in spite of consequences. It means being satisfied with nothing less than the will of God in our lives (John 4:31-34). One evidence that Jesus Christ is Lord in our lives is the readiness with which we witness to others about Him and seek to win them to Christ.

3. Maintain a good conscience (3:16-17)

Our word "conscience" comes from two Latin words: *con,* meaning "with," and *scio,* meaning "to know." The conscience is that internal judge that witnesses to us, that enables us to "know with," either approving our actions or accusing. (See Rom. 2:14-15.) Conscience may be compared to a window that lets in the light of God's truth. If we persist in disobeying, the window gets dirtier and dirtier, until the light cannot enter. This leads to a "defiled conscience" (Titus 1:15). A "seared conscience" is one that has been so sinned against that it no longer is sensitive to what is right and wrong (1 Tim. 4:2). It is even possible for the conscience to be so poisoned that it approves things that are bad and accuses when the person does good! This the Bible calls "an evil conscience" (Heb. 10:22). A criminal feels guilty if he "squeals" on his friends, but happy if he succeeds in his crime!

Conscience depends on knowledge, the "light" coming through the window. As a believer studies the Word, he better understands the will of God, and his conscience becomes more sensitive to right

and wrong. A "good conscience" is one that accuses
when we think to do wrong and approves when we
do right. It takes "exercise" to keep the conscience
strong and pure (Acts 24:16). If we do not grow in
spiritual knowledge and obedience, we have a
"weak conscience" that is upset very easily by trifles
(1 Cor. 8).

How does a good conscience help a believer in
times of trial and opposition? For one thing, it for-
tifies him with courage because he knows he is right
with God and men, so that he need not be afraid.
Inscribed on Martin Luther's monument at Worms,
Germany are his courageous words spoken before
the church council on April 18, 1521: "Here I stand;
I can do no other. God help me. Amen." His conscience, bound to God's Word, gave him the courage to defy the whole established church!

A good conscience also gives us peace in our
hearts; and when we have peace within, we can face
battles without. The restlessness of an uneasy conscience divides the heart and drains the strength of a
person, so that he is unable to function at his best.
How can we boldly witness for Christ if conscience is
witnessing against us?

A good conscience removes from us the fear of
what other people may know about us, say against
us, or do to us. When Christ is Lord and we fear only
God, we need not fear the threats, opinions, or
actions of our enemies. "The Lord is on my side; I
will not fear: what can man do unto me?" (Ps. 118:6)
It was in this matter that Peter failed when he feared
the enemy and denied the Lord.

Peter made it clear that conscience *alone* is not the
test of what is right or wrong. A person can be
involved in either "welldoing" or "evil-doing." For a
person to disobey God's Word and claim it is right

simply because his conscience does not convict him, is to admit that something is radically wrong with his conscience. Conscience is a safe guide only when the Word of God is the teacher.

More and more, Christians in today's society are going to be accused and lied about. Our personal standards are not those of the unsaved world. As a rule, Christians do not *create* problems; they *reveal* them. Let a born-again person start to work in an office, or move into a college dormitory, and in a short time there will be problems. Christians are lights in this dark world (Phil. 2:15), and they reveal "the unfruitful works of darkness" (Eph. 5:11).

When Joseph began to serve as steward in Potiphar's house, and refused to sin, he was falsely accused and thrown into prison. The government officials in Babylon schemed to get Daniel in trouble because his life and work were a witness against them. Our Lord Jesus Christ by His very life on earth revealed the sinful hearts and deeds of people, and this is why they crucified Him (see John 15:18-25). "Yea, and all that will live godly in Christ Jesus shall suffer persecution" (2 Tim. 3:12).

If we are to maintain a good conscience, we must deal with sin in our lives and confess it immediately (1 John 1:9). We must "keep the window clean." We must also spend time in the Word of God and "let in the light." A strong conscience is the result of obedience based on knowledge, and a strong conscience makes for a strong Christian witness to the lost. It also gives us strength in times of persecution and difficulty.

No Christian should ever suffer because of evildoing, and no Christian should be surprised if he suffers for welldoing. Our world is so mixed up that people "call evil good, and good evil" and "put darkness for light, and light for darkness . . ." (Isa. 5:20). The religious leaders of Jesus' day called Him "a malefactor," which means "a person who does evil things" (John 18:29-30). How wrong people can be!

As times of difficulty come to the church, we must cultivate Christian love; for we will need one another's help and encouragement as never before. We must also maintain a good conscience, because a good conscience makes for a strong backbone and a courageous witness. The secret is to practice the lordship of Jesus Christ. If we fear God, we need not fear men. "Shame arises from the fear of men," said Samuel Johnson. "Conscience, from the fear of God."

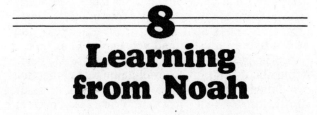

8
Learning from Noah

1 Peter 3:18-22

A pastor was teaching a Bible study on Matthew 16, explaining the many interpretations of our Lord's words to Peter, "Thou art Peter, and upon this rock I will build My church" (v. 18). Afterward, a woman said to him, "Pastor, I'll bet if Jesus had known all the trouble those words would cause, He would never have said them!"

When Peter wrote this section of his letter, he had no idea that it would be classified as one of the most difficult portions of the New Testament. Good and godly interpreters have wrestled with these verses, debated and disagreed, and have not always left behind a great deal of spiritual help. We may not be able to solve all the problems found in this section, but we do want to get the practical help that Peter gave to encourage Christians in difficult days.

The section presents three different ministries. If we understand these ministries, we will be better able to suffer in the will of God and glorify Christ.

1. The ministry of Christ

Everything else in this paragraph is incidental to
what Peter had to say about Jesus Christ. This material is parallel to what Peter wrote in 2:21ff. Peter
presented Jesus Christ as the perfect example of one
who suffered unjustly, and yet obeyed God.

A. THE DEATH OF CHRIST (3:18). In verse 17, Peter
wrote about suffering for well-doing rather than for
evil-doing; and then he gave the example of Jesus
Christ. Jesus was the "just One" (Acts 3:14), and yet
He was treated unjustly. Why? That He might die
for the unjust ones and bring them to God! He died
as a substitute (1 Peter 2:24), and He died only once
(Heb. 9:24-28). In other words, Jesus suffered for
well-doing; He did not die because of His own sins,
for He had none (1 Peter 2:22).

The phrase "bring us to God" is a technical term
that means "gain audience at court." Because of the
work of Christ on the cross, we now have an open
access to God (Eph. 2:18; 3:12). We may come
boldly to His throne (Heb. 10:19ff)! We also have
access to His marvelous grace to meet our daily
needs (Rom. 5:2). When the veil of the temple was
torn, it symbolized the new and open way to God
through Jesus Christ.

B. THE PROCLAMATION OF CHRIST (3:19-20). The
phrase "made alive by the Spirit" (KJV, SCO) creates a
problem for us. In the Greek manuscripts, there
were no capital letters; so we have no authority to
write "Spirit" rather than "spirit." Greek scholars
tell us that the end of verse 18 should read: "Being
put to death with reference to the flesh, but made
alive with reference to the spirit." The contrast is
between flesh and spirit, as in Matthew 26:41 and
Romans 1:3-4, and not between Christ's flesh and
the Holy Spirit.

Our Lord had a real body (Matt. 26:26), soul (John 12:27), and spirit (Luke 23:46). He was not God inhabiting a man; He was the true God-Man. When He died, He yielded His spirit to the Father (Luke 23:46, and see James 2:26). However, it seems evident that, if He was "made alive in the spirit," at some point His spirit must have died. It was probably when He was made sin for us and was forsaken by the Father (Mark 15:34; 2 Cor. 5:21). The phrase "quickened in [with reference to] the spirit" cannot mean resurrection, because resurrection has to do with *the body.*

So, on the cross, our Lord suffered and died. His body was put to death, and His spirit died when He was made sin. But His spirit was made alive and He yielded it to the Father. Then according to Peter, sometime between His death and His resurrection Jesus made a special proclamation to "the spirits in prison." This raises two questions: Who were these "spirits" that He visited? What did He proclaim to them?

Those who say that these "spirits in prison" were the spirits of lost sinners in hell, to whom Jesus brought the good news of salvation, have some real problems to solve. To begin with, Peter referred to *people* as "souls" and not "spirits" (3:20). In the New Testament, the word "spirits" is used to describe angels or demons, not human beings; and verse 22 seems to argue for this meaning. Furthermore, nowhere in the Bible are we told that Jesus visited hell. Acts 2:31 states that He went to "Hades" (NASB), but "Hades" is not hell. The word "Hades" refers to the realm of the dead, a temporary place where they await the resurrection. Read Revelation 20:11-15 in the *New American Standard Bible* or the *New International Version* and you will see the important distinction. Hell is the permanent and final place of judgment for the lost. Hades is the temporary place. When a Christian dies, he goes to neither place, but to heaven to be with Christ (Phil. 1:20-24).

Our Lord yielded His spirit to the Father, died, and at some time between death and resurrection, visited the realm of the dead where He delivered a message to spirit beings (probably fallen angels; see Jude 6) who were somehow related to the period before the flood. Verse 20 makes this clear. The word translated "preached" simply means "to announce as a herald, to proclaim." It is not the word that means "to preach the Gospel" that Peter used in 1:12 and 4:6. Peter did not tell us *what* Jesus proclaimed to these imprisoned spirits, but it could not be a message of redemption since angels cannot be saved (Heb. 2:16). It was probably a declaration of victory over Satan and his hosts (see 1 Peter 3:22 and Col. 2:15).

How these spirits were related to the pre-flood era, Peter did not explain. Some students believe that "the sons of God" named in Genesis 6:1-4 were fallen angels who cohabited with women and produced a race of giants, but I cannot accept this interpretation. The *good* angels who did not fall are called "sons of God," but not the fallen angels (Job 1:6; 2:1, and note that Satan is distinguished from the "sons of God"). The world before the Flood was unbelievably wicked, and no doubt these spirits had much to do with it (see Gen. 6:5-13 and Rom. 1:18ff).

C. The resurrection of Christ (3:21). Since death comes when the spirit leaves the body (James 2:26), then resurrection involves the spirit *returning* to the body (Luke 8:55). The Father raised Jesus from the

dead (Rom. 6:4; 8:11), but the Son also had authority to raise Himself (John 10:17-18). It was a miracle!
It is because of His resurrection that Christians have
the "living hope" (1 Peter 1:3-4). We shall see later
how the resurrection of Christ relates to the experience of Noah.

We must never minimize the importance of the
resurrection of Jesus Christ. It declares that He is
God (Rom. 1:4), that the work of salvation is completed and accepted by the Father (4:25), and that
death has been conquered (1 Thess. 4:13-18; Rev.
1:17-18). The Gospel message includes the resurrection (1 Cor. 15:1-4), for a dead Saviour can save
nobody. It is the risen Christ who gives us the power
we need on a daily basis for life and service (Gal.
2:20).

D. THE ASCENSION OF CHRIST (3:22). Forty days after
His resurrection, our Lord ascended to heaven to sit
at the right hand of the Father, the place of exalta-
tion (Ps. 110:1; Phil. 2:5-11; Heb. 12:1-3; Acts 2:34-
36). Believers are seated with Him in the heavenlies
(Eph. 2:4-6), and through Him we are able to "reign
in life" (Rom. 5:17). He is ministering to the church
as High Priest (Heb. 7:25; 4:14-16) and Advocate
(1 John 1:9—2:2). He is preparing a place for His
people (John 14:1-6) and will one day come to receive them to Himself.

But the main point Peter wanted to emphasize was
Christ's complete victory over all "angels and authorities and powers" (1 Peter 3:22), referring to the
evil hosts of Satan (Eph. 6:10-12; Col. 2:15). The
unfallen angels were *always* subject to Him. As
Christians, we do not fight *for* victory, but *from*
victory—the mighty victory that our Lord Jesus
Christ won for us in His death, resurrection, and
ascension.

2. The ministry of Noah

The patriarch Noah was held in very high regard among Jewish people in Peter's day, and also among Christians. He was linked with Daniel and Job, two great men, in Ezekiel 14:19-20; and there are many references to the Flood in both the Psalms and the Prophets. Jesus referred to Noah in His prophetic sermon (Matt. 24:37-39, and see Luke 17:26-27), and Peter mentioned him in his second letter (2:5 and see 3:6). He is named with the heroes of faith in Hebrews 11:7.

What relationship did Peter see between his readers and the ministry of Noah? For one thing, Noah was a "preacher of righteousness" (2 Peter 2:5) during a very difficult time in history. In fact, he walked with God and preached God's truth for 120 years (Gen. 6:3), and during that time was certainly laughed at and opposed. The early Christians knew that Jesus had promised that, before His return, the world would become like the "days of Noah" (Matt. 24:37-39); and they were expecting Him soon (2 Peter 3:1-3). As they saw society decay around them, and persecution begin, they would think of our Lord's words.

Noah was a man of faith who kept doing the will of God even when he seemed to be a failure. This would certainly be an encouragement to Peter's readers. If we measured faithfulness by results, then Noah would get a very low grade. Yet God ranked him very high!

But there is another connection: Peter saw in the Flood a picture (type) of a Christian's experience of baptism. No matter what mode of baptism you may accept, it is certain that the early church practiced immersion. It is a picture of our Lord's death, burial, and resurrection. Many people today do not take baptism seriously, but it was a serious matter in the early church. Baptism meant a clean break with the past, and this could include separation from a convert's family, friends, and job. Candidates for baptism were interrogated carefully, for their submission in baptism was a step of consecration, and not just an "initiation rite" to "join the church."

The Flood pictures death, burial, and resurrection. The waters buried the earth in judgment, but they also lifted Noah and his family up to safety. The early church saw in the ark a picture of salvation. Noah and his family were saved by faith because they believed God and entered into the ark of safety. So sinners are saved by faith when they trust Christ and become one with Him.

When Peter wrote that Noah and his family were "saved by water," he was careful to explain that this illustration does not imply salvation by baptism. Baptism is a "figure" of that which does save us, namely, "the resurrection of Jesus Christ" (1 Peter 3:21). Water on the body, or the body placed in water, cannot remove the stains of sin. Only the blood of Jesus Christ can do that (1 John 1:7—2:2). However, baptism does save us from one thing: a bad conscience. Peter had already told his readers that a good conscience was important to a successful witness (see 1 Peter 3:16), and a part of that "good conscience" is being faithful to our commitment to Christ as expressed in baptism.

The word "answer" in verse 21 is a legal term meaning "a pledge, a demand." When a person was signing a contract, he would be asked, "Do you pledge to obey and fulfill the terms of this contract?" His answer had to be "Yes, I do" or he could not sign. When converts were prepared for baptism, they would be asked if they intended to obey God and serve Him, and to break with their sinful past. If they had reservations in their hearts, or deliberately lied, they would not have a good conscience if, under pressure of persecution, they denied the Lord. (Peter knew something about that!) So, Peter reminded them of their baptismal testimony to encourage them to be true to Christ.

It may be worth noting that the chronology of the Flood is closely related to our Lord's day of resurrection. Noah's ark rested on Ararat on the 17th day of the 7th month (Gen. 8:4). The Jewish *civil* year started with October; the religious year started with the Passover in April (Ex. 12:1-2), but that was not instituted until Moses' time. The 7th month from October is April. Our Lord was crucified on the 14th day, Passover (Ex. 12:6), and resurrected after 3 days. This takes us to the 17th day of the month, the date on which the ark rested on Mt. Ararat. So, the illustration of Noah relates closely to Peter's emphasis on the resurrection of the Saviour.

There is a sense in which our Lord's experience on the cross was a baptism of judgment, not unlike the flood. He referred to His sufferings as a baptism (Matt. 20:22; Luke 12:50). He also used Jonah to illustrate His experience of death, burial, and resurrection (Matt. 12:38-41). Jesus could certainly have quoted Jonah 2:3 to describe His own experience: "All Thy billows and Thy waves passed over me."

3. The ministry of Christians today

It is easy to agree on the main lessons Peter was sharing with his readers, lessons which we need today.

First of all, *Christians must expect opposition.* As the coming of Christ draws near, our well-doing will incite the anger and attacks of godless people. Jesus lived a perfect life on earth, and yet He was crucified like a common criminal. If the just One who did no sin was treated cruelly, what right do we who are imperfect have to escape suffering? We must be careful, however, that we suffer because of well-doing, for righteousness' sake, and not because we have disobeyed.

A second lesson is that *Christians must serve God by faith and not trust in results.* Noah served God and kept only seven people from the Flood; yet God honored him. From those seven people, we take courage! Jesus appeared a total failure when He died on the cross, yet His death was a supreme victory. His cause today may seem to fail, but He will accomplish His purposes in this world. The harvest is not the end of a meeting; it is the end of the age.

Third, *we can be encouraged because we are identified with Christ's victory.* This is pictured in baptism, and the doctrine is explained in Romans 6. It is the baptism of the Spirit that identifies a believer with Christ (1 Cor. 12:12-13), and this is pictured in water baptism. It is through the Spirit's power that we live for Christ and witness for Him (Acts 1:8). The opposition of men is energized by Satan, and Christ has already defeated these principalities and powers. He has "all authority in heaven and on earth (Matt. 28:18, NIV), and therefore we can go forth with confidence and victory.

Another practical lesson is that *our baptism is important.* It identifies us with Christ and gives witness that we have broken with the old life (see 1 Peter 4:1-4) and will, by His help, live a new life. The act of baptism is a pledge to God that we shall obey Him. To use Peter's illustration, we are agreeing to the terms of the contract. To take baptism lightly is to sin against God. Some people make too much of baptism by teaching that it is a means of salvation, while others minimize it. Both are wrong. If a believer is to have a good conscience, he must obey God.

Having said this, I want to make it clear that Christians must not make baptism a test of fellowship or of spirituality. There are dedicated believers who disagree on these matters, and we respect them. When General William Booth founded the Salvation Army, he determined not to make it "another church," so he eliminated the ordinances. There are Christian groups, such as the Quakers, who, because of conscience or doctrinal interpretation, do not practice baptism. I have stated my position, but I do not want to give the impression that I make this position a test of anything. "Let us therefore follow after the things which make for peace, and things wherewith one may edify another" (Rom. 14:19). "Let every man be fully persuaded in his own mind" (14:5).

The important thing is that each Christian avow devotion to Christ and make it a definite act of commitment. Most Christians do this in baptism, but even the act of baptism can be minimized or forgotten. It is in taking up our cross daily that we prove we are true followers of Jesus Christ.

Finally, *Jesus Christ is the only Saviour, and the lost world needs to hear His Gospel.* Some people try to use this complex passage of Scripture to prove a "second chance for salvation after death." Our interpretation of "spirits in prison" seems to prove that these were angelic beings, and not the souls of the dead. But even if these "spirits" were those of unsaved people, this passage says nothing about their salvation. And why would Jesus offer salvation (if He did) *only to sinners from Noah's day?* And why did Peter use the verb "proclaim as a herald" instead of the usual word for preaching the Gospel?

Hebrews 9:27 makes it clear that death ends the opportunity for salvation. This is why the church needs to get concerned about evangelism and missions, because people are dying who have never even heard the Good News of salvation, let alone had the opportunity to reject it. It does us no good to quibble about differing interpretations of a difficult passage of Scripture, if what we *do* believe does not motivate us to want to share the Gospel with others.

Peter made it clear that difficult days give us multiplied opportunities for witness.

Are we taking advantage of our opportunities?

Additional Note to 1 Peter 3:19-20
A popular explanation of these verses states that Jesus *by His Spirit* preached through Noah to sinners who (when Peter wrote) were imprisoned in Hades. This explanation ignores the contrast in verse 18 between "in the flesh" and "in the spirit," and, without any biblical authorization, capitalizes the word "spirit." The Greek verb translated "went" in verse 19 means "to make a personal visit." It does not mean "to make a visit by means of a representative or substitute." The simplest view is that Jesus Himself went and did the preaching.

9
The Rest
of Your Time

1 Peter 4:1-11

My wife and I were in Nairobi where I would be ministering to several hundred national pastors at an Africa Inland Mission conference. We were very excited about the conference even though we were a bit weary from the long air journey. We could hardly wait to get started, and the leader of the conference detected our impatience.

"You are in Africa now," he said to me in a fatherly fashion, "and the first thing you want to do is to put away your watch."

In the days that followed, as we ministered in Kenya and Zaire, we learned the wisdom of his words. Unfortunately, when we returned to the States, we found ourselves caught up again in the clockwork prison of deadlines and schedules.

Peter had a great deal to say about *time* (1:5, 11, 17, 20; 4:2-3, 17; 5:6). Certainly the awareness of his own impending martyrdom had something to do with this emphasis (John 21:15-19; 2 Peter 1:12ff). If a person really believes in eternity, then he will make the best use of time. If we are convinced that Jesus is coming, then we will want to live prepared lives. Whether Jesus comes first, or death comes first, we want to make "the rest of the time" count for eternity.

And we can! Peter described four attitudes that a Christian can cultivate in his lifetime ("the rest of his time") if he desires to make his life all that God wants it to be.

1. A militant attitude toward sin (4:1-3)

The picture is that of a soldier who puts on his equipment and arms himself for battle. Our attitudes are weapons, and weak or wrong attitudes will lead us to defeat. Outlook determines outcome, and a believer must have the right attitudes if he is to live a right life.

A friend and I met at a restaurant to have lunch. It was one of those places where the lights are low, and you need a miner's helmet to find your table. We had been seated several minutes before we started looking at the menu, and I remarked that I was amazed how easily I could read it. "Yes," said my friend, "it doesn't take us long to get accustomed to the darkness."

There is a sermon in that sentence: It is easy for Christians to get accustomed to sin. Instead of having a militant attitude that hates and oppose it, we gradually get used to sin, sometimes without even realizing it. The one thing that will destroy "the rest of our time" is sin. A believer living in sin is a terrible weapon in the hands of Satan. Peter presented several arguments to convince us to oppose sin in our lives.

A. THINK OF WHAT SIN DID TO JESUS (4:1). He had to *suffer* because of sin (see 2:21; 3:18). How can we enjoy that which made Jesus suffer and die on the cross? If a vicious criminal stabbed your child to death, would you preserve that knife in a glass case on your mantle? I doubt it. You would never want to see that knife again.

Our Lord came to earth to deal with sin and to conquer it forever. He dealt with the ignorance of sin by teaching the truth and by living it before men's eyes. He dealt with the consequences of sin by healing and forgiving; and, on the cross, He dealt the final deathblow to sin itself. He was armed, as it were, with a militant attitude toward sin, even though He had great compassion for lost sinners.

Our goal in life is to "cease from sin." We will not reach this goal until we die, or are called Home when the Lord returns; but this should not keep us from striving (1 John 2:28—3:9). Peter did not say that suffering *of itself* would cause a person to stop sinning. Pharaoh in Egypt went through great suffering in the plagues, and yet he sinned even more! I have visited suffering people who cursed God and grew more and more bitter because of their pain.

Suffering, *plus Christ in our lives,* can help us have victory over sin. But the central idea here seems to be the same truth taught in Romans 6: We are identified with Christ in His suffering and death, and therefore can have victory over sin. As we yield ourselves to God, and have the same attitude toward sin that Jesus had, we can overcome the old life and manifest the new life.

B. ENJOY THE WILL OF GOD (4:2). The contrast is between the desires of men and the will of God. Our longtime friends cannot understand the change in our lives, and they want us to return to the same "excess of riot" that we used to enjoy. But the will of God is so much better! If we do the will of God, then we will *invest* "the rest of our time" in that which is lasting and satisfying; but if we give in to the world around us, we will *waste* "the rest of our time" and regret it when we stand before Jesus.

The will of God is not a burden that the Father places on us. Rather it is the divine enjoyment and enablement that makes all burdens light. The will of God comes from the heart of God (Ps. 33:11) and therefore is an expression of the love of God. We may not always understand what He is doing, but we know that He is doing what is best for us. We do not live on explanations; we live on promises.

C. REMEMBER WHAT YOU WERE BEFORE YOU MET CHRIST (4:3). There are times when looking back at your past life would be wrong, because Satan could use those memories to discourage you. But God urged Israel to remember that they had once been slaves in Egypt (Deut. 5:15). Paul remembered that he had been a persecutor of believers (1 Tim. 1:12ff), and this encouraged him to do even more for Christ. We sometimes forget the bondage of sin and remember only the passing pleasures of sin.

"The will of the Gentiles" means "the will of the unsaved world" (see 1 Peter 2:12). Lost sinners imitate each other as they conform to the fashions of this world (Rom. 12:2; Eph. 3:1-3). "Lasciviousness" and "lusts" describe all kinds of evil appetites and not just sexual sins. "Revelings and banquetings" refer to pagan orgies where the wine flowed freely. Of course, all of this could be a part of pagan worship, since "religious prostitution" was an accepted thing. Even though these practices were forbidden by law ("abominable" = illegal), they were often practiced in secret.

We may not have been guilty of such gross sins in our preconversion days, but we were still sinners— and our sins helped to crucify Christ. How foolish to go back to that kind of life!

2. A patient attitude toward the lost (4:4-6)

Unsaved people do not understand the radical change that their friends experience when they trust Christ and become children of God. They do not think it strange when people wreck their bodies, destroy their homes, and ruin their lives by running from one sin to another! But let a drunkard become sober, or an immoral person pure, and the family thinks he has lost his mind! Festus told Paul, "You are out of your mind!" (Acts 26:24, NASB); and people even thought the same thing of our Lord (Mark 3:21).

We must be patient toward the lost, even though we do not agree with their lifestyles or participate in their sins. After all, unsaved people are blind to spiritual truth (2 Cor. 4:3-4) and dead to spiritual enjoyment (Eph. 2:1). In fact, our contact with the lost is important *to them* since we are the bearers of the truth that they need. When unsaved friends attack us, this is our opportunity to witness to them (1 Peter 3:15).

The unsaved may judge us, but one day, God will judge them. Instead of arguing with them, we should pray for them, knowing that the final judgment is with God. This was the attitude that Jesus took (2:23), and also the Apostle Paul (2 Tim. 4:6-8).

We must not interpret verse 6 apart from the context of suffering; otherwise, we will get the idea that there is a second chance for salvation after death. Peter was reminding his readers of the Christians who had been martyred for their faith. They had been falsely judged by men, but now, in the presence of God, they received their true judgment. "Them that are dead" means "them that are *now* dead" at the time Peter was writing. The Gospel is preached only to the living (1 Peter 1:25) because there is no opportunity for salvation after death (Heb. 9:27).

Unsaved friends may speak evil of us and even oppose us, but the final Judge is God. We may sacrifice our lives in the midst of persecution, but God will honor and reward us. We must fear God and not men (1 Peter 3:13-17; and see Matt. 10:24-33). While we are in these human bodies ("in the flesh"), we are judged by human standards. One day, we shall be with the Lord ("in the spirit") and receive the true and final judgment.

3. An expectant attitude toward Christ (4:7)

Christians in the early church expected Jesus to return in their lifetime (Rom. 13:12; 1 John 2:18). The fact that He did not return does not invalidate His promise (2 Peter 3; Rev. 22:20). No matter what interpretation we give to the prophetic Scriptures, we must all live in expectancy. The important thing is that we shall see the Lord one day and stand before Him. How we live and serve today will determine how we are judged and rewarded on that day.

This attitude of expectancy must not turn us into lazy dreamers (2 Thes. 3:6ff) or zealous fanatics. Peter gave "ten commandments" to his readers to keep them in balance as far as the Lord's return was concerned:

1. Be sober—v. 7
2. Watch unto prayer—v. 7
3. Have fervent love—v. 8
4. Use hospitality—v. 9
5. Minister your spiritual gifts—vv. 10-11
6. Think it not strange—v. 12
7. Rejoice—v. 13

8. Do not be ashamed—vv. 15-16
9. Glorify God—vv. 16-18
10. Commit yourself to God—v. 19

The phrase "be sober" means "be sober-minded, keep your mind steady and clear." Perhaps a modern equivalent would be "keep cool." It was a warning against wild thinking about prophecy that could lead to an unbalanced life and ministry. Often we hear of sincere people who go "off balance" because of an unbiblical emphasis on prophecy or a misinterpretation of prophecy. There are people who set dates for Christ's return, contrary to His warning (Matt. 25:13, and see Acts 1:6-8); or they claim to know the name of the beast of Revelation 13. I have books in my library, written by sincere and godly men, in which all sorts of claims are made, only to the embarrassment of the writers.

The opposite of "be sober-minded" is "frenzy, madness." It is the Greek word *mania*, which has come into our English vocabulary via psychology. If we are sober-minded, we will be intellectually sound and not off on a tangent because of some "new" interpretation of the Scriptures. We will also face things realistically and be free from delusions. The sober-minded saint will have a purposeful life and not be drifting, and he will exercise restraint and not be impulsive. He will have "sound judgment" not only about doctrinal matters, but also about the practical affairs of life.

Ten times in the pastoral epistles, Paul admonished people to "be sober-minded." It is one of the qualifications for pastors (1 Tim. 3:2) and for the members of the church (Titus 2:1-6). In a world that is susceptible to wild thinking, the church must be sober-minded.

Early in my ministry, I gave a message on prophecy that sought to explain everything. I have since filed away that outline and will probably never look at it (except when I need to be humbled). A pastor friend who suffered through my message said to me after the service, "Brother, you must be on the planning committee for the return of Christ!" I got his point, but he made it even more pertinent when he said quietly, "I've moved from the program committee to the welcoming committee."

I am not suggesting that we not study prophecy, or that we become timid about sharing our interpretations. What I am suggesting is that we not allow ourselves to get out of balance because of an abuse of prophecy. There is a practical application to the prophetic Scriptures. Peter's emphasis on hope and the glory of God ought to encourage us to be faithful *today* in whatever work God has given us to do (see Luke 12:31-48).

If you want to make the best use of "the rest of your time," live in the light of the return of Jesus Christ. All Christians may not agree on the details of the event, but we can agree on the demands of the experience. We shall stand before the Lord! Read Romans 14:10-23 and 2 Corinthians 5:1-21 for the practical meaning of this.

If we are sober-minded, we will "watch unto prayer." If our prayer life is confused, it is because the mind is confused. Dr. Kenneth Wuest, in his translation, shows the important relationship between the two: "Be calm and collected in spirit with a view to giving yourself to prayer." The word "watch" carries with it the idea of alertness and self-control. It is the opposite of being drunk or asleep (1 Thess. 5:6-8). This admonition had special meaning to Peter, because he went to sleep when he should have been "watching unto prayer" (Mark 14:37-40).

You find the phrase "watch and pray" often in the *Authorized Version* of the New Testament (Mark 13:33; 14:38; Eph. 6:18; Col. 4:2). It simply means to "be alert in our praying, to be controlled." There is no place in the Christian life for lazy, listless routine praying. We must have an alert attitude and be on guard, just like the workers in Nehemiah's day (Neh. 4:9).

An expectant attitude toward Christ's return involves a serious, balanced mind and an alert, awake prayer life. The test of our commitment to the doctrine of Christ's return is not our ability to draw charts or discern signs, but our thinking and praying. If our thinking and praying are right, our living should be right.

4. A fervent attitude toward the saints (4:8-11)

If we really look for the return of Christ, then we shall think of others and properly relate to them. Love for the saints is important, "above [before] all things." Love is the badge of a believer in this world (John 13:34-35). Especially in times of testing and persecution, Christians need to love one another and be united in heart.

This love should be "fervent." The word pictures an athlete straining to reach the goal. It speaks of eagerness and intensity. Christian love is something we have to work at, just the way an athlete works on his skills. It is not a matter of emotional feeling, though that is included, but of dedicated will. Christian love means that we treat others the way God treats us, obeying His commandments in the Word. It is even possible to love people that we do not like!

Christian love is forgiving. Peter quoted from Proverbs 10:12—"Hatred stirreth up strifes: but love covereth all sins." This verse is alluded to in James 5:20 and 1 Corinthians 13:4 and 7. Love does not *condone* sin; for, if we love somebody, we will be grieved to see him sin and hurt himself and others. Rather, love *covers* sin in that love motivates us to hide the sin from others and not spread it abroad. Where there is hatred, there is malice; and malice causes a person to want to tear down the reputation of his enemy. This leads to gossip and slander (Prov. 11:13; 17:9, and see 1 Peter 2:1). Sometimes we try to make our gossip sound "spiritual" by telling people things "so they might pray more intelligently."

No one can hide his sins from God, but believers ought to try, in love, to cover each other's sins at least from the eyes of the unsaved. After all, if the unsaved crowd finds ammunition for persecuting us because of our *good* words and works (1 Peter 2:19-20; 3:14), what would they do if they knew the *bad* things that Christians say and do!

Genesis 9:18-27 gives us a beautiful illustration of this principle. Noah got drunk and shamefully uncovered himself. His son Ham saw his father's shame and told the matter to the family. In loving concern, Ham's two brothers covered their father and his shame. It should not be too difficult for us to cover the sins of others; after all, Jesus Christ died that *our* sins might be washed away.

Our Christian love should not only be fervent and forgiving, but it should also be practical. We should share our homes with others in generous (and uncomplaining) hospitality, and we should use our spiritual gifts in ministry to one another. In New Testament times hospitality was an important thing, because there were few inns and poor Christians could not afford to stay at them anyway. Persecuted saints in particular would need places to stay where they could be assisted and encouraged.

Hospitality is a virtue that is commanded and commended throughout the Scriptures. Moses included it in the Law (Ex. 22:21; Deut. 14:28-29). Jesus enjoyed hospitality when He was on earth, and so did the apostles in their ministry (Acts 28:7; Phile. 22). Human hospitality is a reflection of God's hospitality to us (Luke 14:16ff). Christian leaders in particular should be "given to hospitality" (1 Tim. 3:2; Titus 1:8).

Abraham was hospitable to three strangers, and discovered that he had entertained the Lord and two angels (Gen. 18; Heb. 13:2). We help to promote the truth when we open our homes to God's servants (3 John 5-8). In fact, when we share with others, we share with Christ (Matt. 25:35, 43). We should not open our homes to others just so that others will invite us over (Luke 14:12-14). We should do it to glorify the Lord.

In my own itinerant ministry, I have often had the joy of staying in Christian homes. I have appreciated the kindness and (in some cases) sacrifice of dear saints who loved Christ and wanted to share with others. My wife and I have made new friends in many countries, and our children have been blessed, because we have enjoyed and practiced Christian hospitality.

Finally, Christian love must result in service. Each Christian has at least one spiritual gift that he must use to the glory of God and the building up of the church (see Rom. 12:1-13; Eph. 4:1-16; and 1 Cor. 12). We are stewards. God has entrusted these gifts to us that we might use them for the good of His church. He even gives us the spiritual ability to develop our gifts and be faithful servants of the church.

There are speaking gifts and there are serving gifts, and both are important to the church. Not everybody is a teacher or preacher, though all can be witnesses for Christ. There are those "behind-the-scenes" ministries that help to make the public ministries possible. God gives us the gifts, the abilities, and the opportunities to use the gifts, and He alone must get the glory.

The phrase "oracles of God" in 1 Peter 4:11 does not suggest that everything a preacher or teacher says today is God's truth, because human speakers are fallible. In the early church, there were prophets who had the special gift of uttering God's Word, but we do not have this gift today since the Word of God has been completed. Whoever shares God's Word must be careful about what he says and how he says it, and all must conform to the written Word of God.

While on our way home from the African trip I mentioned at the beginning of this chapter, we were delayed in London by a typical English fog. London is one of my favorite places, so I was not disturbed a bit! But the delay gave my wife and me the opportunity to show London to a couple who were traveling with us. Imagine trying to see that marvelous city in one day!

We had to make the most of the time—and we did! Our friends saw many exciting sites in the city.

How long is "the rest of your time"? Only God knows.

Don't waste it! Invest it by doing the will of God.

10
Facts about Furnaces

1 Peter 4:12-19

Every Christian who lives a godly life experiences a certain amount of persecution. On the job, in school, in the neighborhood, perhaps even in the family, there are people who resist the truth and oppose the Gospel of Christ. No matter what a believer says or does, these people find fault and criticize. Peter dealt with this kind of "normal persecution" in the previous part of his letter.

But in this section, Peter explained about a special kind of persecution—a "fiery trial"—that was about to overtake the entire church. It would not be occasional personal persecution from those around them, but *official* persecution from those above them. Thus far, Christianity had been tolerated by Rome because it was considered a "sect" of Judaism, and the Jews were permitted to worship freely. That attitude would change and the fires of persecution would be ignited, first by Nero, and then by the emperors that followed.

Peter gave the believers four instructions to follow in the light of the coming "fiery trial."

1. Expect suffering (4:12)

Persecution is not something that is alien to the Christian life. Throughout history the people of God have suffered at the hands of the unbelieving world. Christians are different from unbelievers (2 Cor. 6:14-18), and this different kind of life produces a different kind of lifestyle. Much of what goes on in the world depends on lies, pride, pleasure, and the desire to "get more." A dedicated Christian builds his life on truth, humility, holiness, and the desire to glorify God.

This conflict is illustrated throughout the Bible. Cain was a religious man, yet he hated his brother and killed him (Gen. 4:1-8). The world does not persecute "religious people," but it does persecute righteous people. Why Cain killed Abel is explained in 1 John 3:12: "Because his own works were evil, and his brother's righteous." The Pharisees and Jewish leaders were religious people, yet they crucified Christ and persecuted the early church. "But beware of men," Jesus warned His disciples, "for they will deliver you up to the councils, and they will scourge you in their synagogues" (Matt. 10:17). Imagine scourging the servants of God in the very house of God!

God declared war on Satan after the Fall of man (Gen. 3:15), and Satan has been attacking God through His people ever since. Christians are "strangers and pilgrims" in an alien world where Satan is the god and prince (John 14:30; 2 Cor. 4:3-4). Whatever glorifies God will anger the enemy, and he will attack. For believers, persecution is not a strange thing. The *absence* of Satanic opposition would be strange!

Jesus explained to his disciples that they should expect opposition and persecution from the world

(John 15:17—16:4). But He also gave them an encouraging promise: "In the world ye shall have tribulation: but be of good cheer; I have overcome the world" (16:33). It was through His death on the cross of Calvary, plus His resurrection, that He overcame sin and the world (John 12:23-33; and see Gal. 6:14).

The image of "fire" is often applied to testing or persecution even in modern conversation. "He is really going through the fire," is a typical statement to describe someone experiencing personal difficulties. In the Old Testament, fire was a symbol of the holiness of God and the presence of God. The fire on the altar consumed the sacrifice (Heb. 12:28-29). But Peter saw in the image of fire *a refining process* rather than a divine judgment (see 1 Peter 1:7; Job 23:10).

It is important to note that not all of the difficulties of life are necessarily fiery trials. There are some difficulties that are simply a part of human life and almost everybody experiences them. Unfortunately, there are some difficulties that we bring on ourselves because of disobedience and sin. Peter mentioned these in 2:18-20 and 3:13-17. The fiery trial he mentioned in 4:12 comes because we are faithful to God and stand up for that which is right. It is because we bear the name of Christ that the lost world attacks us. Christ told His disciples that people would persecute them, as they had Him, because their persecutors did not know God (John 15:20-21).

The word "happened" is important; it means "to go together." Persecution and trials do not just "happen," in the sense of being accidents. They are a part of God's plan, and He is in control. They are a part of Romans 8:28 and will work out for good if we let God have His way.

2. Rejoice in suffering (4:13-14)

Literally, Peter wrote, "Be constantly rejoicing!" In fact, he mentioned joy in one form or another *four times* in these two verses! "Rejoice . . . be glad also with exceeding joy . . . .happy are ye!" The world cannot understand how difficult circumstances can produce exceeding joy, because the world has never experienced the grace of God (see 2 Cor. 8:1-5). Peter named several privileges that we share that encourage us to rejoice in the midst of the fiery trial.

A. OUR SUFFERING MEANS FELLOWSHIP WITH CHRIST (4:13). It is an honor and a privilege to suffer *with* Christ and be treated by the world the way it treated Him. "The fellowship of His sufferings" is a gift from God (Phil. 1:29; 3:10). Not every believer grows to the point where God can trust him with this kind of experience, so we ought to rejoice when the privilege comes to us. "And they [the apostles] departed from the presence of the council, rejoicing that they were counted worthy to suffer shame for His name" (Acts 5:41).

Christ is with us in the furnace of persecution (Isa. 41:10; 43:2). When the three Hebrew children were cast into the fiery furnace, they discovered they were not alone (Dan. 3:23-25). The Lord was with Paul in all of his trials (Acts 23:11; 27:21-25; 2 Tim. 4:9-18), and He promises to be with us "to the end of the age" (Matt. 28:20, NASB). In fact, when sinners persecute us, they are really persecuting Jesus Christ (Acts 9:4).

B. OUR SUFFERING MEANS GLORY IN THE FUTURE (4:13). "Suffering" and "glory" are twin truths that are woven into the fabric of Peter's letter. The world believes that the *absence* of suffering means glory, but a Christian's outlook is different. The trial of our faith today is the assurance of glory when Jesus returns (1 Peter 1:7-8). This was the experience of our Lord (5:1), and it shall also be our experience.

But it is necessary to understand that God is not going to *replace* suffering with glory; rather He will *transform* suffering into glory. Jesus used the illustration of a woman giving birth (John 16:20-22). The same baby that gave her pain also gave her joy. The pain was *transformed* into joy by the birth of the baby. The thorn in the flesh that gave Paul difficulty also gave him power and glory (2 Cor. 12:7-10). The cross that gave Jesus shame and pain also brought power and glory.

Mature people know that life includes some "postponed pleasures." We pay a price *today* in order to have enjoyments in the *future*. The piano student may not enjoy practicing scales by the hour, but he looks forward to the pleasure of playing beautiful music one day. The athlete may not enjoy exercising and practicing his skills, but he looks forward to winning the game by doing his best. Christians have something even better: our very sufferings will one day be transformed into glory, and we will be "glad also with exceeding joy." (See Rom. 8:17 and 2 Tim. 3:11.)

C. Our suffering brings to us the ministry of the Holy Spirit (4:14). He is the Spirit of glory and He has a special ministry to those who suffer for the glory of Jesus Christ. This verse can be translated "for the presence of the glory, even the Spirit, rests on you." The reference is to the Shekinah glory of God that dwelt in the tabernacle and in the temple (Ex. 40:34; 1 Kings 8:10-11). When the people stoned Stephen, he saw Jesus in heaven and experienced God's glory (Acts 6:15; 7:54-60). This is the "joy unspeakable and full of glory" that Peter wrote about in 1:7-8.

In other words, suffering Christians do not have to wait for heaven in order to experience His glory. Through the Holy Spirit, *they can have the glory now.* This explains how martyrs could sing praises to God while bound in the midst of blazing fires. It also explains how persecuted Christians (and there are many in today's world) can go to prison and to death without complaining or resisting their captors.

D. OUR SUFFERING ENABLES US TO GLORIFY HIS NAME (4:14). We suffer because of His name (John 15:21). You can tell your unsaved friends that you are Baptist, a Presbyterian, a Methodist, or even an agnostic, and there will be no opposition; but tell them you are *a Christian*—bring Christ's name into the conversation—and things will start to happen. Our authority is in the name of Jesus, and Satan hates that name. Every time we are reproached for the name of Christ, we have the opportunity to bring glory to that name. The world may speak against His name, but we will so speak and live that His name will be honored and God will be pleased.

The word "Christian" is found only three times in the entire New Testament (1 Peter 4:16; Acts 11:26; 26:28). The name was originally given by the enemies of the church as a term of reproach; but in time, it became an honored name. Of course, in today's world, the word "Christian" means to most people the opposite of "pagan." But the word carries the idea of "a Christ one, belonging to Christ." Certainly it is a privilege to bear the name and to suffer for His name's sake (Acts 5:41).

Polycarp was the Bishop of Smyrna about the middle of the second century. He was arrested for his faith and threatened with death if he did not recant. "Eighty and six years have I served Him," the saintly Bishop replied, "and He never did me any injury. How can I blaspheme my King and my Saviour?"

"I have respect for your age," said the Roman officer. "Simply say, 'Away with the atheists!' and be set free." By "the atheists" he meant the Christians who would not acknowledge that Caesar was "lord."

The old man pointed to the crowd of Roman pagans surrounding him, and cried, "Away with the atheists!" He was burned at the stake and in his martyrdom brought glory to the name of Jesus Christ.

3. Examine your life (4:15-18)

In the furnace of persecution and suffering, we often have more light by which we can examine our lives and ministries. The fiery trial is a refining process, by which God removes the dross and purifies us. One day, a fiery judgment will overtake the whole world (2 Peter 3:7-16). Meanwhile, God's judgment begins "at the house of God," the church (1 Peter 2:5). This truth ought to motivate us to be as pure and obedient as possible. (See Ezekiel 9 for an Old Testament illustration of this truth.)

There are several questions we should ask ourselves as we examine our own lives.

A. WHY AM I SUFFERING? (4:15) We noted before that not all suffering is a "fiery trial" from the Lord. If a professed Christian breaks the law and gets into trouble, or becomes a meddler into other people's lives, then he *ought* to suffer! The fact that we are Christians is not a guarantee that we escape the normal consequences of our misdeeds. We may not be guilty of murder (though anger can be the same as murder in the heart, Matt. 5:21-26), but what about stealing, or meddling? When Abraham, David,

Peter, and other Bible "greats" disobeyed God, they suffered for it; so, who are we that we should escape? Let's be sure we are suffering because we are Christians and not because we are criminals.

B. AM I ASHAMED, OR GLORIFYING CHRIST? (4:16) This statement must have reminded Peter of his own denial of Christ (Luke 22:54-62). Jesus Christ is not ashamed of us (Heb. 2:11)—though many times He surely could be! The Father is not ashamed to be called our God (11:16). On the cross Jesus Christ despised shame for us (12:2), so surely we can bear reproach for Him and not be ashamed. The warning in Mark 8:38 is worth pondering.

"Not be ashamed" is negative; "glorify God" is positive. It takes both for a balanced witness. If we seek to glorify God, then we will not be ashamed of the name of Jesus Christ. It was this determination not to be ashamed that encouraged Paul when he went to Rome (Rom. 1:16), when he suffered in Rome (Phil. 1:20-21), and when he faced martyrdom in Rome (2 Tim. 1:12).

C. AM I SEEKING TO WIN THE LOST? (4:17-18) Note the words that Peter used to describe the lost: "Them that obey not the Gospel . . . . the ungodly and the sinner." The argument of this verse is clear: If God sends a "fiery trial" to His own children, and they are saved "with difficulty," what will happen to lost sinners when God's fiery judgment falls?

When a believer suffers, he experiences glory and knows that there will be greater glory in the future. But a sinner who causes that suffering is only filling up the measure of God's wrath more and more (Matt. 23:29-33). Instead of being concerned only about ourselves, we need to be concerned about the lost sinners around us. Our present "fiery trial" is nothing compared with the "flaming fire" that shall punish the lost when Jesus returns in judgment (2 Thes. 1:7-10). The idea is expressed in Proverbs 11:31—"If the righteous receive their due on earth, how much more the ungodly and the sinner!" (NIV)

The phrase "scarcely be saved" means "saved with difficulty," but it does not suggest that God is too weak to be able to save us. The reference is probably to Genesis 19:15-26, when God sought to rescue Lot from Sodom before the city was destroyed. God was able—but Lot was unwilling! He lingered, argued with the angels, and finally had to be taken by the hand and dragged out of the city! Lot was "saved as by fire" and everything he lived for went up in smoke (see 1 Cor. 3:9-15).

Times of persecution are times of opportunity for a loving witness to those who persecute us (see Matt. 5:10-12, 43-48). It was not the earthquake that brought that Philippian jailer to Christ, because that frightened him into almost committing suicide! No, it was Paul's loving concern for him that brought the jailer to faith in Christ. As Christians, we do not seek for vengeance on those who have hurt us. Rather, we pray for them and seek to lead them to Jesus Christ.

4. Commit yourself to God (4:19)

When we are suffering in the will of God, we can commit ourselves into the care of God. Everything else that we do as Christians depends on this. The word is a banking term; it means "to deposit for safe keeping" (see 2 Tim. 1:12). Of course, when you deposit your life in God's bank, you always receive eternal dividends on your investment.

This picture reminds us that we are valuable to God. He made us, redeemed us, lives in us, guards, and protects us. I saw a savings and loan association advertisement in the newspaper, reaffirming the financial stability of the firm and the backing of the Federal Deposit Insurance Corporation. In days of financial unsteadiness, such assurances are necessary to depositors. But when you "deposit" your life with God, you have nothing to fear; for He is able to keep you.

This commitment is not a single action but a constant attitude. "Be constantly committing" is the force of the admonition. How do we do this? "By means of well-doing." As we return good for evil and do good even though we suffer for it, we are committing ourselves to God so that He can care for us. This commitment involves every area of our lives and every hour of our lives.

If we really have hope, and believe that Jesus is coming again, then we will obey His Word and start laying up treasures and glory in heaven. Unsaved people have a present that is controlled by their past, but Christians have a present that is controlled by the future (Phil. 3:12-21). In our very serving, we are committing ourselves to God and making investments for the future.

There is a striking illustration of this truth in Jeremiah 32. The Prophet Jeremiah had been telling the people that one day their situation would change and they would be restored to their land. But at that time, the Babylonian army occupied the land and was about to take Jerusalem. Jeremiah's cousin, Hanamel, gave Jeremiah an option to purchase the family land *which was now occupied by enemy soldiers.* The prophet had to "put his money where his mouth is." And he did it! As an act of faith, he purchased the land and became, no doubt, the laughingstock of the people in Jerusalem. But God honored his faith because Jeremiah lived according to the Word that he preached.

Why did Peter refer to God as "a faithful Creator" rather than "a faithful Judge" or even "a faithful Saviour"? Because God the Creator meets the needs of His people (Matt. 6:24-34). It is the Creator who provides food and clothing to persecuted Christians, and who protects them in times of danger. When the early church was persecuted, they met together for prayer and addressed the Lord as the "God, which has made heaven, and earth, and the sea, and all that in them is" (Acts 4:24). They prayed to the Creator!

Our heavenly Father is "the Lord of heaven and earth" (Matt. 11:25). With that kind of a Father, we have no need to worry! He is the *faithful* Creator, and His faithfulness will not fail.

Before God pours out His wrath upon this evil world, a "fiery trial" will come to God's church, to unite and purify it, that it might be a strong witness to the lost. There is nothing for us to fear if we are suffering in the will of God. Our faithful Father-Creator will victoriously see us through!

11
How to Be
a Good Shepherd

1 Peter 5:1-4

Times of persecution demand that God's people have adequate spiritual leadership. If judgment is to begin at God's house (1 Peter 4:17), then that house had better be in order, or it will fall apart! This explains why Peter wrote this special message to the leaders of the church, to encourage them to do their work faithfully. Leaders who run away in times of difficulty are only proving that they are hirelings and not true shepherds (John 10:12-14).

The New Testament assemblies were organized under the leadership of elders and deacons (1 Tim. 3). The words "elder" and "bishop" refer to the same office (Acts 20:17, 28). The word "bishop" is often translated "overseer" (see 1 Peter 5:2, and note that this title is applied to Christ in 2:25). "Elder" refers to the maturity of the officer, and "bishop" to the responsibility of the office. The word "pastor" (which means "shepherd") is another title for this same office (Eph. 4:11). The elders were appointed to office (Acts 14:23, where the verb "ordain" means "to appoint by the raising of hands"). Apparently each congregation had the privilege of voting on qualified men.

Peter was concerned that the leadership in the local churches be at its best. When the fiery trial would come, the believers in the assemblies would look to their elders for encouragement and direction. What are the personal qualities that make for a successful pastor?

1. A vital personal experience with Christ (5:1)

Peter did not introduce himself in this letter as an apostle or a great spiritual leader, but simply as another elder. However, he did mention the fact that he had personally witnessed Christ's sufferings (see Matt. 26:36ff). The Greek word translated "witness" gives us our English word "martyr." We think of a "martyr" only as one who gives his life for Christ, and Peter did that; but basically, a "martyr" is a witness who tells what he has seen and heard.

It is interesting to read 1 Peter 5 in the light of Peter's personal experiences with Christ. Verse 1 takes us to Gethsemane and Calvary. "The glory that shall be revealed" reminds us of Peter's experience with Christ on the Mount of Transfiguration (2 Peter 1:15-18; Matt. 17:1-5). The emphasis in verse 2 on the shepherd and the sheep certainly brings to mind John 10 and our Lord's admonition to Peter in John 21:15-17.

The warning in verse 3 about "lording it over" the saints reminds us of Christ's lesson about true greatness in Luke 22:24-30, as well as the other times that He taught His disciples about humility and service. The phrase in verse 5, "be clothed with humility," takes us back to the Upper Room where Jesus put on the towel and washed the disciples' feet (John 13:1-17).

The warning about Satan in verse 8 parallels our Lord's warning to Peter that Satan was going to "sift" him and the other apostles (Luke 22:31). Peter did not heed that warning, and he ended up denying his Lord three times.

It is interesting to note that the verb "make you perfect" (v. 10) is translated "mending their nets" in Matthew 4:21, the account of the call of the four fishermen into the Lord's service.

In other words, Peter wrote these words, inspired by the Spirit of God, out of his own personal experience with Jesus Christ. He had a vital and growing relationship with Christ, and this made it possible for him to minister effectively to God's people.

The pastor of the local assembly must be a man who walks with God and who is growing in his spiritual life. Paul admonished young Timothy: "Be diligent in these matters; give yourself wholly to them, so that everyone may see your progress" (1 Tim. 4:15, NIV). The word "progress" in the original means "pioneer advance." The elders must constantly be moving into new territories of study, achievement, and ministry. If the leaders of the church are not moving forward, the church will not move forward.

"We love our pastor," a fine church member said to me during a conference, "but we get tired of the same thing all the time. He repeats himself and doesn't seem to know that there are other books in the Bible beside Psalms and Revelation." That man needed to become a "spiritual pioneer" and move into new territory, so that he might lead his people into new blessings and challenges.

Sometimes God permits trials to come to a church so that the people will be *forced* to grow and discover new truths and new opportunities. Certainly Peter

126 / Be Hopeful

grew in his spiritual experience as he suffered for
Christ in the city of Jerusalem. He was not perfect by
any means; in fact, Paul had to rebuke him once for
inconsistency (Gal. 2:11-21). But Peter was yielded
to Christ and willing to learn all that God had for
him.

If I have any counsel for God's shepherds today, it
is this: cultivate a growing relationship with Jesus
Christ, and share what He gives you with your people. That way, you will grow, and they will grow with
you.

2. A loving concern for God's sheep (5:2-3)

The image of the flock is often used in the Bible, and
it is a very instructive one. (See Ps. 23 and 100; Isa.
40:11; Luke 15:4-6; John 10; Acts 20:28; Heb.
13:20-21; 1 Peter 2:25; Rev. 7:17.) We were once
stray sheep, wandering toward ruin; but the Good
Shepherd found us and restored us to the fold.

Sheep are clean animals, unlike dogs and pigs
(2 Peter 2:20-22). Sheep tend to flock together, and
God's people need to be together. Sheep are no-
toriously ignorant and prone to wander away if they
do not follow the shepherd. Sheep are defenseless,
for the most part, and need their shepherd to protect
them (Ps. 23:4).

Sheep are very useful animals. Jewish shepherds
tended their sheep, not for the meat (which would
have been costly) but for the wool, milk, and lambs.
God's people should be useful to Him and certainly
ought to "reproduce" themselves by bringing others
to Christ. Sheep were used for the sacrifices, and we
ought to be "living sacrifices," doing the will of God
(Rom. 12:1-2).

Peter reminded the shepherd-elders of their God-
given responsibilities.

A. FEED THE FLOCK OF GOD (5:2). The word "feed" means "shepherd, care for." The shepherd had many tasks to perform in caring for the flock. He had to protect the sheep from thieves and marauders, and the pastor must protect God's people from those who want to spoil the flock (Acts 20:28-35). Sometimes the sheep do not like it when their shepherd rebukes or warns them, but this ministry is for their own good.

A faithful shepherd not only protected his flock, but he also led them from pasture to pasture so that they might be adequately fed. The shepherd always went before the flock and searched out the land so that there would be nothing there to harm his flock. He would check for snakes, pits, poisonous plants, and dangerous animals. How important it is for pastors to lead their people into the green pastures of the Word of God so that they might feed themselves and grow.

Sometimes it was necessary for a shepherd to seek out a wayward sheep and give it personal attention. Some pastors today are interested only in the crowds; they have no time for individuals. Jesus preached to great multitudes, but He took time to chat with Nicodemus (John 3), the woman at the well (John 4), and others who had spiritual needs. Paul ministered to people *personally* in Thessalonica (1 Thes. 2:11) and loved them dearly.

If a sheep is too rebellious, the shepherd may have to discipline him in some way. If a sheep has a special need, the shepherd might carry it in his arms, next to his heart. At the close of each day, the faithful shepherd would examine each sheep to see if it needed special attention. He would anoint the bruises with healing oil, and remove the briars from the wool. A good shepherd would know each of his sheep by name and would understand the special traits of each one.

It is not an easy thing to be a faithful shepherd of God's sheep! It is a task that never ends and that demands the supernatural power of God if it is to be done correctly. What makes it even more challenging is the fact that the flock is not the shepherd's; it is God's. I sometimes hear pastors say, "Well, at *my* church . . ." and I know what they mean; but strictly speaking, it is *God's* flock, purchased by the precious blood of His Son (Acts 20:28). We pastors must be careful how we minister to *God's* sheep, because one day we will have to give an account of our ministry. But the sheep will also one day give an account of how they have obeyed their spiritual leaders (Heb. 13:17), so both shepherds and sheep have a great responsibility to each other.

B. TAKE THE OVERSIGHT (5:2). The word "bishop" means "over-seer, one who looks over for the purpose of leading." You will notice that the shepherd is both "among" and "over," and this can create problems if the sheep do not understand. Because he is one of the sheep, the pastor is "among" the members of the flock. But because he is called to be a leader, the pastor is "over" the flock. Some people try to emphasize the "among" relationship and refuse to follow the authority of the shepherd. Others want to put the pastor on a pedestal and make him a "super saint" who never mixes with the people.

The effective pastor needs both relationships. He must be "among" his people so that he can get to know them, their needs and problems; and he needs to be "over" his people so he can lead them and help them solve their problems. There must be no conflict between *pastoring* and *preaching,* because they are both ministries of a faithful shepherd. The preacher needs to be a pastor so he can apply the Word to the needs of the people. The pastor needs to be a preacher so that he can have authority when he shares in their daily needs and problems. The pastor is not a religious lecturer who weekly passes along information about the Bible. He is a shepherd who knows his people and seeks to help them through the Word.

Being the spiritual leader of a flock has its dangers, and Peter pointed out some of the sins that the elders must avoid. The first was *laziness*—"not by constraint but willingly." His ministry must not be a job that he has to perform. He should do God's will from his heart (Eph. 6:6). Dr. George W. Truett was pastor of First Baptist Church in Dallas, Texas, for nearly fifty years. Often he was asked to accept other positions, and he refused, saying, "I have sought and found a pastor's heart." When a man has a pastor's heart, he loves the sheep and serves them because he *wants* to, not because he *has* to.

If a man has no conscience, the ministry is a good place to be lazy. Church members rarely ask what their pastor is doing with his time, and he can "borrow" sermons from other preachers and use them as his own. I met one pastor who spent most of his week on the golf course; then on Saturday he listened to tapes of other preachers and used their sermons on Sunday. He seems to be getting away with it, but what will he say when he meets the Chief Shepherd?

Next to laziness, the shepherd must beware of *covetousness*—"not for filthy lucre, but of a ready mind." It is perfectly proper for the church to pay the pastor (1 Cor. 9; 1 Tim. 5:17-18), and they ought to be as fair and generous as possible. But making money must not be the main motive for his ministry.

Paul stresses this in his qualifications for an elder: "not greedy of filthy lucre" (1 Tim. 3:3); "not given to filthy lucre" (Titus 1:7). He must not be a lover of money nor devote himself to pursuing money.

Because of family or church situations, some pastors have to engage in outside employment. Paul was a tentmaker, so there is no disgrace in "moonlighting." But, as soon as possible, the members of the church ought to relieve their pastor of outside employment so he can devote himself fully to the ministry of the Word. Pastors need to beware of getting involved in money-making schemes that detour them from their ministry. "No one serving as a soldier gets involved in civilian affairs—he wants to please his commanding officer" (2 Tim. 2:4, NIV).

The phrase "a ready mind" means "an eager mind." It is the same word Paul used in Romans 1:15—"I am so eager to preach the gospel" (NIV). It means a willingness to serve because of a readiness and an eagerness within the heart. This is the difference between a true shepherd and a hireling: a hireling works because he is paid for it, but a shepherd works because he loves the sheep and has a heart devoted to them. Read Acts 20:17-38 for a description of the heart and ministry of a true shepherd.

C. BE AN EXAMPLE TO THE FLOCK (5:3). The contrast is between *dictatorship* and *leadership*. You cannot drive sheep; you must go before them and lead them. It has been well said that the church needs leaders who serve and servants who lead. A Christian leader said to me, "The trouble today is that we have too many celebrities and not enough servants."

It is by being an example that the shepherd solves the tension between being "among" the sheep and "over" the sheep. People are willing to follow a leader who practices what he preaches and gives them a good example to imitate. I know of a church that was constantly having financial problems, and no one could understand why. After the pastor left, it was discovered that he had not himself contributed to the work of the church but had preached sermons telling others to contribute. We cannot lead people where we have not been ourselves.

Peter was not changing the image when he called the church "God's heritage." The people of God are certainly His priceless possession (Deut. 32:9; Ps. 33:12). This word means "to be chosen by lot," as the dividing up of land (Num. 26:55). Each elder has his own flock to care for, but the sheep all belong to the one flock of which Jesus Christ is the Chief Shepherd. The Lord assigns His workers to the places of His choosing, and we must all be submissive to Him. There is no competition in the work of God when you are serving in the will of God. Therefore, nobody has to act important and "lord it over" God's people. Pastors are to be "overseers" and not "over-lords."

3. A desire to please Christ alone (5:4)
Since this is the epistle of hope, Peter brought in once again the promise of the Lord's return. His coming is an encouragement in suffering (1:7-8) and a motivation for faithful service. If a pastor ministers to please himself, or to please people, he will have a disappointing and difficult ministry. "It must be hard to keep all these people happy," a visitor said to me after a church service. "I don't even try to keep them happy," I replied with a smile. "I try to please the Lord, and I let Him take care of the rest."

Jesus Christ is the *Good* Shepherd who died for the sheep (John 10:11), the *Great* Shepherd who lives for the sheep (Heb. 13:20-21), and the *Chief*

Shepherd who comes for the sheep (1 Peter 5:4). As the Chief Shepherd, He alone can assess a man's ministry and give him the proper reward. Some who appear to be first may end up last when the Lord examines each man's ministry.

One summer day, I stood amid the ruins of a church near Anworth in Scotland. The building at one time seated perhaps 150 people. By modern standards, it would not have been a successful church. But the man who pastored that flock was the saintly Samuel Rutherford, whose *Letters of Samuel Rutherford* is a spiritual classic. His ministry continues, though today his church building is in ruins. The Chief Shepherd has rewarded him for his faithful labors, which included a great deal of persecution and physical suffering.

There were several kinds of "crowns" in those days. The one Peter mentioned was the athlete's crown, usually a garland of leaves or flowers that would quickly fade away. The faithful pastor's crown is a crown of glory, a perfect reward for an *inheritance* that will never fade away (1:4).

Today a Christian worker may labor for many different kinds of rewards. Some work hard to build personal empires; others strive for the applause of men; still others seek promotion in their denomination. All of these things will fade one day. The only reward we ought to strive for is the "Well done!" of the Saviour and the unfading crown of glory that goes with it. What a joy it will be to place the crown at His feet (Rev. 4:10) and acknowledge that all we did was because of His grace and power (1 Cor. 15:10; 1 Peter 4:11). We will have no desire for personal glory when we see Jesus Christ face to face.

Everything in the local church rises or falls with leadership. No matter how large or small a fellowship might be, the leaders must be Christians, each with a vital personal relationship with Christ, a loving concern for their people, and a real desire to please Jesus Christ.

We lead by serving, and we serve by suffering.

This is the way Jesus did it, and this is the only way that truly glorifies Him.

12
From Grace to Glory!

1 Peter 5:5-11

When World War II was being fought, I was a junior high school student, and the fighting seemed very far away from our northern Indiana city. But then the city began to organize Civil Defense units in each neighborhood, and officials appointed my father an assistant block captain. Often I went with him to watch the training films and listen to the speakers. (The best part of the evening was stopping for an ice cream cone!) But, no matter how many films we watched, we somehow didn't feel that our neighborhood was in danger of being bombed. Our philosophy was, "It can't happen here."

Peter knew that a "fiery trial" was about to occur, and he wanted the entire church family to be prepared. As he closed his letter, Peter gave the church three important admonitions to obey if they were to glorify God in this difficult experience.

1. Be humble (5:5-7)
He had already admonished the saints to be submissive to government authorities (2:13-17), the slaves to submit to their masters (2:18-25), and the

wives to their husbands (3:1-7). Now he commanded all of the believers to submit to God and to each other.

The younger believers should submit to the older believers, not only out of respect for their age, but also out of respect for their spiritual maturity. Not every "senior saint" is a mature Christian, of course, because quantity of years is no guarantee of quality of experience. This is not to suggest that the older church members "run the church" and never listen to the younger members! Too often there is a generation war in the church, with the older people resisting change, and the younger people resisting the older people!

The solution is two-fold: (1) all believers, young and old, should submit to each other; (2) all should submit to God. "Be clothed with humility" is the answer to the problem. Just as Jesus laid aside His outer garments and put on a towel to become a servant, so each of us should have a servant's attitude and minister to each other. True humility is described in Philippians 2:1-11. Humility is not demeaning ourselves and thinking poorly of ourselves. It is simply not thinking of ourselves at all!

We can never be submissive to each other until we are first submissive to God. Peter quoted Proverbs 3:34 to defend his point, a verse that is also quoted in James 4:6. It takes grace to submit to another believer, but God can give that grace *if* we humble ourselves before Him.

God resists the proud because God hates the sin of pride (Prov. 6:16-17; 8:13). It was pride that turned Lucifer into Satan (Isa. 14:12-15). It was pride—a desire to be like God—that stirred Eve to take the forbidden fruit. "The pride of life" is an evidence of worldliness (1 John 2:16). The only antidote to pride is the grace of God, and we receive that grace when we yield ourselves to Him. The evidence of that grace is that we yield to one another.

Submission is an act of faith. We are trusting God to direct in our lives and to work out His purposes in His time. After all, there is a danger in submitting to others; they might take advantage of us—but not if we trust God and if we are submitted to one another! A person who is truly yielded to God, and who wants to serve his fellow Christians, would not even think of taking advantage of someone else, saved or unsaved. The "mighty hand of God" that directs our lives can also direct in the lives of others.

The key, of course, is the phrase "in due time." God never exalts anyone until that person is ready for it. First the cross, then the crown; first the suffering, then the glory. Moses was under God's hand for forty years before God sent him to deliver the Jews from Egypt. Joseph was under God's hand for at least thirteen years before God lifted him to the throne. One of the evidences of our pride is our impatience with God, and one reason for suffering is that we might learn patience (James 1:1-6). Here Peter was referring to words he heard the Master say: "For whosoever exalteth himself shall be abased; and he that humbleth himself shall be exalted" (Luke 14:11).

One of the benefits of this kind of relationship with God is the privilege of letting Him take care of our burdens. Unless we meet the conditions laid down in 1 Peter 5:5-6, we cannot claim the wonderful promise of verse 7. The word translated "care" means "anxiety, the state of being pulled apart." When circumstances are difficult, it is easy for us to be anxious and worried; but if we are, we will miss God's blessing and become poor witnesses to the lost. We need His inward peace if we are going to triumph in the fiery trial and bring glory to His name. Dr. George Morrison said, "God does not make His children carefree in order that they be careless."

According to 1 Peter 5:7, we must *once and for all* give all of our cares—past, present, and future—to the Lord. We must not hand them to Him piecemeal, keeping those cares that we think we can handle ourselves. If we keep "the little cares" for ourselves, they will soon become big problems! Each time a new burden arises, we must by faith remind the Lord (and ourselves) that we have already turned it over to Him.

If anybody knew from experience that God cares for His own, it was Peter! When you read the four Gospels, you discover that Peter shared in some wonderful miracles. Jesus healed Peter's mother-in-law (Mark 1:29-31), gave him a great catch of fish (Luke 5:1-11), helped him pay his temple tax (Matt. 17:24-27), helped him walk on the water (14:22-33), repaired the damage he did to the ear of Malchus (Luke 22:50-51; John 18:10-11), and even delivered Peter from prison (Acts 12).

How does God show His love and care for us when we give our cares to Him? I believe that He performs four wonderful ministries on our behalf. (1) He gives us the courage to face our cares honestly and not run away (Isa. 41:10). (2) He gives us the wisdom to understand the situation (James 1:5). (3) He gives us the strength to do what we must do (Phil. 4:13). And (4) He gives us the faith to trust Him to do the rest (Ps. 37:5).

Some people give God their burdens and expect Him to do everything! It is important that we let Him work *in* us as well as work *for* us, so that we will be prepared when the answer comes. "Cast thy burden upon the Lord, and He shall sustain thee" (Ps. 55:22).

2. Be watchful (5:8-9)

One reason we have cares is because we have an enemy. As the serpent, Satan deceives (2 Cor. 11:3); and as the lion, Satan devours. The word "Satan" means "adversary," and the word "devil" means "the accuser, the slanderer." The recipients of this letter had already experienced the attacks of the slanderer (1 Peter 4:4, 14), and now they would meet "the lion" in their fiery trial. Peter gave them several practical instructions to help them get victory over their adversary.

A. RESPECT HIM—HE IS DANGEROUS. Since I have no mechanical ability, I admire people who can build and repair things. During a church building program, I was watching an electrician install a complex control panel. I said to the man, "It just amazes me how you fellows can calmly work on those lines with all of that power there. How do you do it?" The electrician smiled and said, "Well, the first thing you have to do is respect it. Then you can handle it."

Satan is a dangerous enemy. He is a serpent who can bite us when we least expect it. He is a destroyer (Rev. 12:11; "Abaddon" and "Apollyon" both mean "destruction") and an accuser (Rev. 12:9-11, Zech. 3:1-5). He has great power and intelligence, and a host of demons who assist him in his attacks against God's people (Eph. 6:10ff). He is a formidable enemy; we must never joke about him, ignore him, or underestimate his ability. We must "be sober" and have our minds under control when it comes to our conflict with Satan.

A part of this soberness includes not blaming

everything on the devil. Some people see a demon behind every bush and blame Satan for their headaches, flat tires, and high rent. While it is true that Satan can inflict physical sickness and pain (Luke 13:16, and the Book of Job), we have no biblical authority for casting out "demons of headache" or "demons of backache." One lady phoned me long distance to inform me that Satan had caused her to shrink seven and a half inches. While I have great respect for the wiles and powers of the devil, I still feel we must get our information about him from the Bible and not from our own interpretation of experiences.

B. RECOGNIZE HIM—HE IS A GREAT PRETENDER (2 Cor. 11:13-15; John 8:44). Because he is a subtle foe, we must "be vigilant" and always on guard. His strategy is to counterfeit whatever God does. According to the Parable of the Tares, wherever God plants a true Christian, Satan seeks to plant a counterfeit (Matt. 13:24-30, 36-43). He would deceive us were it not for the Word of God and the Spirit of God (1 John 2:18-27). The better we know God's Word, the keener our spiritual senses will be to detect Satan at work. We must be able to "try the spirits" and know the true from the false (4:1-6).

C. RESIST HIM. This means that we take our stand on the Word of God and refuse to be moved. Ephesians 6:10-13 instructs us to "stand . . . withstand . . . stand." Unless we stand, we cannot withstand. Our weapons are the Word of God and prayer (Eph. 6:17-18) and our protection is the complete armor God has provided. We resist him "in the faith," that is, our faith in God. Just as David took his stand against Goliath, and trusted in the name of Jehovah, so we take our stand against Satan in the victorious name of Jesus Christ.

A word of caution here: never discuss things with Satan or his associates. Eve made this mistake, and we all know the sad consequences. Also, never try to fight Satan in your own way. Resist him the way Jesus did, with the Word of God (Matt. 4:1-11). Never get the idea that you are the only one going through these battles, because "your brethren that are in the world" are facing the same trials. We must pray for one another and encourage each other in the Lord. And we must remember that our personal victories will help others, just as their victories will help us.

Had Peter obeyed these three instructions the night Jesus was arrested, he would not have gone to sleep in the Garden of Gethsemane, attacked Malchus, or denied the Lord. He did not take the Lord's warning seriously; in fact, he argued with Him! Nor did he recognize Satan when the adversary inflated his ego with pride, told him he did not have to "watch and pray," and then incited him to use his sword. Had Peter listened to the Lord and resisted the enemy, he would have escaped all those failures.

Both Peter and James give us the same formula for success: "Submit yourselves therefore to God. Resist the devil, and he will flee from you" (James 4:7). Before we can stand before Satan, we must bow before God. Peter resisted the Lord and ended up submitting to Satan!

3. Be hopeful (5:10-11)

Peter closed on a positive note and reminded his readers that God knew what He was doing and was in complete control. No matter how difficult the fiery trial may become, a Christian always has hope. Peter gave several reasons for this hopeful attitude.

A. WE HAVE GOD'S GRACE. Our salvation is because

of His grace (1 Peter 1:10). He called us before we called on Him (1:2). We have "tasted that the Lord is gracious" (2:3), so we are not afraid of anything that He purposes for us. His grace is "manifold" (4:10) and meets every situation of life. As we submit to Him, He gives us the grace that we need. In fact, He is "the God of all grace." He has grace to help in every time of need (Heb. 4:16). "He giveth more grace" (James 4:6), and we must stand in that grace (1 Peter 5:12, and see Rom. 5:2).

B. WE KNOW WE ARE GOING TO GLORY. He has "called us unto His eternal glory by Christ Jesus." This is the wonderful inheritance into which we were born (1 Peter 1:4). Whatever begins with God's grace will always lead to God's glory (Ps. 84:11). If we depend on God's grace when we suffer, that suffering will result in glory (1 Peter 4:13-16). The road may be difficult, but it leads to glory, and that is all that really counts.

C. OUR PRESENT SUFFERING IS ONLY FOR A WHILE. Our various trials are only "for a season" (1 Peter 1:6), but the glory that results is *eternal*. Paul had this same thought in mind when he wrote 2 Corinthians 4:17—"These little troubles (which are really so transitory) are winning for us a permanent, glorious, and solid reward out of all proportion to our pain" (Ph.).

D. WE KNOW THAT OUR TRIALS ARE BUILDING CHRISTIAN CHARACTER. The Greek word translated "make you perfect" means "to equip, to adjust, to fit together." It is translated "mending nets" in Matthew 4:21. God has several tools which He uses to equip His people for life and service, and suffering is one of them. The Word of God is another tool (2 Tim. 3:16-17, where "thoroughly furnished" means "fully equipped"). He also uses the fellowship and ministry of the church (Eph. 4:11-16). Our Saviour in heaven is perfecting His children so that they will do His will and His work (Heb. 13:20-21).

Peter used three words to describe the kind of character God wants us to have.

Establish means "to fix firmly, to set fast." Christians must not be unsteady in their stand for Christ. Our hearts need to be established (1 Thes. 3:13; James 5:8), and this is accomplished by God's truth (2 Peter 1:12). The believer who is established will not be moved by persecution, or led away by false doctrine (3:17).

Strengthen means just that: God's strength given to us to meet the demands of life. What good is it to stand on a firm foundation if we do not have power to act?

Settle is the translation of a word that means "to lay a foundation." It is used this way in Hebrews 1:10. The house founded on the rock withstood the storm (Matt. 7:24-27). A believer who is equipped by God will "continue in the faith grounded and settled" (Col. 1:23). He will not be "tossed to and fro, and carried about with every wind of doctrine" (Eph. 4:14).

When an unbeliever goes through suffering, he loses his hope; but for a believer, suffering only increases his hope. "Not only so, but we also rejoice in our sufferings, because we know that suffering produces perseverance; perseverance, character; and character, hope" (Rom. 5:3-4, NIV). God builds character and brightens hope when a believer trusts Him and depends on His grace. The result is that God receives the glory forever and ever.

We have already considered verses 12 and 13 in our introductory chapter.

Paul always ended his letters with a benediction of

grace (2 Thes. 3:17-18). Peter closed this epistle with a benediction of peace. He opened the letter with a greeting of peace (1 Peter 1:2), so the entire epistle points to "God's peace" from beginning to end. What a wonderful way to end a letter that announced the coming of a fiery trial!

Four times in the New Testament we will find the admonition about "a holy kiss" (Rom. 16:16; 1 Cor. 16:20; 2 Cor. 13:12; and 1 Thes. 5:26). Peter called it "a kiss of love." Keep in mind that the men kissed the men and the women kissed the women. It was a standard form of greeting or farewell in that part of the world at that time, just as it is in many Latin countries today. How wonderful that Christian slaves and masters would so greet each other "in Jesus Christ"!

Peter has given to us a precious letter that encourages us to hope in the Lord no matter how trying the times may be. Down through the centuries, the church has experienced various fiery trials, and yet Satan has not been able to destroy it. The church today is facing a fiery trial, and we must be prepared.

But, whatever may come, Peter is still saying to each of us—BE HOPEFUL! The glory is soon to come!

THE VOYAGE OF
THE *DAWN TREADER*

Having to spend the summer holidays with their odious cousin Eustace was about the end for Edmund and Lucy. They were looking dejectedly at the picture of the ship with the dragon prow when slowly it began to rock and the wind to blow. In a flash the frame dissolved and the three children were flung into the sea. Grasping at the ropes thrown out to them, they clambered to safety aboard the boat.

Settled into her cabin, Lucy felt sure they were in for a lovely time. And so they were, for they had joined Prince Caspian in his search for the seven friends of his father long since lost on a dangerous voyage to the Eastern Islands.

THE CHRONICLES OF NARNIA
are all available in Lions

In reading order
The Magician's Nephew
The Lion, The Witch and the Wardrobe
The Horse and his Boy
Prince Caspian
The Voyage of the *Dawn Treader*
The Silver Chair
The Last Battle

C. S. LEWIS

The Voyage of the *Dawn Treader*

Illustrated by
Pauline Baynes

LIONS

to Geoffrey Corbett

First published 1955 by Geoffrey Bles
First published in Lions 1980
Twenty-fifth impression August 1990

Lions is an imprint of
the Children's Division, part of
Harper Collins Publishers,
8 Grafton Street, London W1X 3LA

Printed and bound in Great Britain by
William Collins Sons & Co. Ltd, Glasgow

CONTENTS

CHAPTER ONE

THE PICTURE IN THE BEDROOM

THERE was a boy called Eustace Clarence Scrubb, and he almost deserved it. His parents called him Eustace Clarence and masters called him Scrubb. I can't tell you how his friends spoke to him, for he had none. He didn't call his Father and Mother "Father" and "Mother", but Harold and Alberta. They were very up-to-date and advanced people. They were vegetarians, non-smokers and tee-totallers and wore a special kind of underclothes. In their house there was very little furniture and very few clothes on beds and the windows were always open.

Eustace Clarence liked animals, especially beetles, if they were dead and pinned on a card. He liked books if they were books of information and had pictures of grain elevators or of fat foreign children doing exercises in model schools.

Eustace Clarence disliked his cousins the four Pevensies, Peter, Susan, Edmund and Lucy. But he was quite glad when he heard that Edmund and Lucy were coming to stay. For deep down inside him he liked bossing and bullying; and, though he was a puny little person who couldn't have stood up even to Lucy, let alone Edmund, in a fight, he knew that there are dozens of ways to give people a bad time if you are in your own home and they are only visitors.

Edmund and Lucy did not at all want to come and stay with Uncle Harold and Aunt Alberta. But it really couldn't be helped. Father had got a job lecturing in America for sixteen weeks that summer, and Mother was to go with him because she hadn't had a real holiday for ten years. Peter was working very hard for an exam and he was to spend the holidays being coached by old Professor Kirke in whose house these four children had had wonderful adventures long ago in the war years. If he had still been in that house he would have had them all to stay. But he had somehow become poor since the old days and was living in a small cottage with only one bedroom to spare. It would have cost too much money to take the other three all to America, and Susan had gone.

Grown-ups thought her the pretty one of the family and she was no good at school work (though otherwise very old

for her age) and Mother said she "would get far more out of a trip to America than the youngsters". Edmund and Lucy tried not to grudge Susan her luck, but it was dreadful having to spend the summer holidays at their Aunt's. "But it's far worse for me," said Edmund, "because you'll at least have a room of your own and I shall have to share a bedroom with that record stinker, Eustace."

The story begins on an afternoon when Edmund and Lucy were stealing a few precious minutes alone together. And of course they were talking about Narnia, which was the name of their own private and secret country. Most of us, I suppose, have a secret country but for most of us it is only an imaginary country. Edmund and Lucy were luckier than other people in that respect. Their secret country was real. They had already visited it twice; not in a game or a dream but in reality. They had got there of course by Magic, which is the only way of getting to Narnia. And a promise, or very nearly a promise, had been made them in Narnia itself that they would some day get back. You may imagine that they talked about it a good deal, when they got the chance.

They were in Lucy's room, sitting on the edge of her bed and looking at a picture on the opposite wall. It was the only picture in the house that they liked. Aunt Alberta didn't like it at all (that was why it was put away in a little back room upstairs), but she couldn't get rid of it because it had been a wedding present from someone she did not want to offend.

It was a picture of a ship – a ship sailing straight towards you. Her prow was gilded and shaped like the head of a dragon with wide-open mouth. She had only one mast and one large, square sail which was a rich purple. The sides of the ship – what you could see of them where the gilded wings of the dragon ended – were green. She had just run up to the top of one glorious blue wave, and the nearer slope of that wave came down towards you, with streaks and bubbles on it. She was obviously running fast before a gay wind, listing over a little on her port side. (By the way, if you are going to read this story at all, and if you don't know already, you had better get it into your head that the left of a ship when you are looking ahead, is *port*, and the right is *starboard*.) All the sunlight fell on her from that side, and the water on that side was full of greens and purples. On the other, it was darker blue from the shadow of the ship.

"The question is," said Edmund, "whether it doesn't make things worse, *looking* at a Narnian ship when you can't get there."

"Even looking is better than nothing," said Lucy. "And she is such a very Narnian ship."

"Still playing your old game?" said Eustace Clarence, who had been listening outside the door and now came grinning into the room. Last year, when he had been staying with the Pevensies, he had managed to hear them all talking of Narnia and he loved teasing them about it. He thought of course that they were making it all up; and as he was far too stupid to make anything up himself, he did not approve of that.

"You're not wanted here," said Edmund curtly.

"I'm trying to think of a limerick," said Eustace. "Something like this:

> "Some kids who played games about Narnia
> Got gradually balmier and balmier –"

"Well *Narnia* and *balmier* don't rhyme, to begin with," said Lucy.

"It's an assonance," said Eustace.

"Don't ask him what an assy-thingummy is," said Edmund. "He's only longing to be asked. Say nothing and perhaps he'll go away."

Most boys, on meeting a reception like this, would either have cleared out or flared up. Eustace did neither. He just hung about grinning, and presently began talking again.

"Do you like that picture?" he asked.

"For heaven's sake don't let him get started about Art and all that," said Edmund hurriedly, but Lucy, who was very truthful, had already said, "Yes, I do. I like it very much."

"It's a rotten picture," said Eustace.

"You won't see it if you step outside," said Edmund.

"Why do you like it?" said Eustace to Lucy.

"Well, for one thing," said Lucy, "I like it because the ship looks as if it was really moving. And the water looks as if it was really wet. And the waves look as if they were really going up and down."

Of course Eustace knew lots of answers to this, but he didn't say anything. The reason was that at that very moment he looked at the waves and saw that they did look very much indeed as if they were going up and down. He had only once been in a ship (and then only as far as the Isle of Wight) and had been horribly seasick. The look of the waves in the picture made him feel sick again. He turned rather green and tried another look. And then all three children were staring with open mouths.

What they were seeing may be hard to believe when you read it in print, but it was almost as hard to believe when you saw it happening. The things in the picture were moving. It didn't look at all like a cinema either; the colours were too real and clean and out-of-doors for that. Down went the prow of the ship into the wave and up went a great shock of spray. And then up went the wave behind her, and her stern and her deck became visible for the first time, and then disappeared as the next wave came to meet her and her bows went up again. At the same moment an exercise book which had been lying beside Edmund on the bed flapped, rose and sailed through the air to the wall behind him, and Lucy felt all her hair whipping round her face as it does on a windy day. And this was a windy day; but the wind was blowing out of the picture towards them. And suddenly with the wind came the noises – the swishing of waves and the slap of water against the ship's sides and the creaking and the over-all high steady roar of air and water. But it was the smell, the wild, briny smell, which really convinced Lucy that she was not dreaming.

"Stop it," came Eustace's voice, squeaky with fright and bad temper. "It's some silly trick you two are playing. Stop it. I'll tell Alberta – Ow!"

The other two were much more accustomed to adventures, but, just exactly as Eustace Clarence said "Ow," they both said "Ow" too. The reason was that a great cold, salt splash had broken right out of the frame and they were breathless from the smack of it, besides being wet through.

"I'll smash the rotten thing," cried Eustace; and then several things happened at the same time. Eustace rushed towards the picture. Edmund, who knew something about magic, sprang after him, warning him to look out and not to be a fool. Lucy grabbed at him from the other side and was dragged forward. And by this time either they had grown much smaller or the picture had grown bigger. Eustace jumped to try to pull it off the wall and found himself standing on the frame; in front of him was not glass but real sea, and wind and waves rushing up to the frame as they might to a rock. He lost his head and clutched at the other two who had jumped up beside him. There was a second of struggling and shouting, and just as they thought they had got their balance a great blue roller surged up round them, swept them off their feet, and drew them down into the sea. Eustace's despairing cry suddenly ended as the water got into his mouth.

Lucy thanked her stars that she had worked hard at her swimming last summer term. It is true that she would have got on much better if she had used a slower stroke, and also that the water felt a great deal colder than it had looked while it was only a picture. Still, she kept her head and kicked her shoes off, as everyone ought to do who falls into deep water in their clothes. She even kept her mouth shut and her eyes open. They were still quite near the ship; she saw its green side towering high above them, and people looking at her from the deck. Then, as one might have

expected, Eustace clutched at her in a panic and down they both went.

When they came up again she saw a white figure diving off the ship's side. Edmund was close beside her now, treading water, and had caught the arms of the howling Eustace. Then someone else, whose face was vaguely familiar, slipped an arm under her from the other side. There was a lot of shouting going on from the ship, heads crowding together above the bulwarks, ropes being thrown. Edmund and the stranger were fastening ropes round her. After that followed what seemed a very long delay during which her face got blue and her teeth began chattering. In reality the delay was not very long; they were waiting till the moment when she could be got on board the ship without being dashed against its side. Even with all their best endeavours she had a bruised knee when she finally stood, dripping and shivering, on the deck. After her Edmund was heaved up, and then the miserable Eustace. Last of all came the stranger — a golden-headed boy some years older than herself.

"Ca – Ca – Caspian!" gasped Lucy as soon as she had breath enough. For Caspian it was; Caspian, the boy king of Narnia whom they had helped to set on the throne during their last visit. Immediately Edmund recognized him too. All three shook hands and clapped one another on the back with great delight.

"But who is your friend?" said Caspian almost at once, turning to Eustace with his cheerful smile. But Eustace was crying much harder than any boy of his age has a right to cry when nothing worse than a wetting has happened to him, and would only yell out, "Let me go. Let me go back. I don't *like* it."

"Let you go?" said Caspian. "But where?"

Eustace rushed to the ship's side, as if he expected to see the picture frame hanging above the sea, and perhaps a glimpse of Lucy's bedroom. What he saw was blue waves flecked with foam, and paler blue sky, both spreading without a break to the horizon. Perhaps we can hardly blame him if his heart sank. He was promptly sick.

"Hey! Rynelf," said Caspian to one of the sailors. "Bring

spiced wine for their Majesties. You'll need something to
warm you after that dip." He called Edmund and Lucy their
Majesties because they and Peter and Susan had all been
Kings and Queens of Narnia long before his time. Narnian
time flows differently from ours. If you spent a hundred
years in Narnia, you would still come back to our world at
the very same hour of the very same day on which you left.
And then, if you went back to Narnia after spending a week
here, you might find that a thousand Narnian years had

passed, or only a day, or no time at all. You never know till
you get there. Consequently, when the Pevensie children
had returned to Narnia last time for their second visit, it was
(for the Narnians) as if King Arthur came back to Britain, as
some people say he will. And I say the sooner the better.

Rynelf returned with the spiced wine steaming in a flagon
and four silver cups. It was just what one wanted, and as
Ludy and Edmund sipped it they could feel the warmth
going right down to their toes. But Eustace made faces and
spluttered and spat it out and was sick again and began to
cry again and asked if they hadn't any Plumptree's
Vitaminized Nerve Food and could it be made with distilled
water and anyway he insisted on being put ashore at the
next station.

"This is a merry shipmate you've brought us, Brother," whispered Caspian to Edmund with a chuckle; but before he could say anything more Eustace burst out again.

"Oh! Ugh! What on earth's *that*! Take it away, the horrid thing."

He really had some excuse this time for feeling a little surprised. Something very curious indeed had come out of the cabin in the poop and was slowly approaching them. You might call it – and indeed it was – a Mouse. But then it

was a Mouse on its hind legs and stood about two feet high. A thin band of gold passed round its head under one ear and over the other and in this was stuck a long crimson feather. (As the Mouse's fur was very dark, almost black, the effect was bold and striking.) Its left paw rested on the hilt of a sword very nearly as long as its tail. Its balance, as it paced gravely along the swaying deck, was perfect, and its manners courtly. Lucy and Edmund recognized it at once – Reepicheep, the most valiant of all the Talking Beasts of Narnia, and the Chief Mouse. It had won undying glory in the second Battle of Beruna. Lucy longed, as she had always done, to take Reepicheep up in her arms and cuddle him. But this, as she well knew, was a pleasure she could never have:

it would have offended him deeply. Instead, she went down on one knee to talk to him.

Reepicheep put forward his left leg, drew back his right, bowed, kissed her hand, straightened himself, twirled his whiskers, and said in his shrill, piping voice:

"My humble duty to your Majesty. And to King Edmund, too." (Here he bowed again.) "Nothing except your Majesties' presence was lacking to this glorious venture."

"Ugh, take it away," wailed Eustace. "I hate mice. And I never could bear performing animals. They're silly and vulgar and – and sentimental."

"Am I to understand," said Reepicheep to Lucy after a long stare at Eustace, "that this singularly discourteous person is under your Majesty's protection? Because, if not –"

At this moment Lucy and Edmund both sneezed.

"What a fool I am to keep you all standing here in your wet things," said Caspian. "Come on below and get changed. I'll give you my cabin of course, Lucy, but I'm afraid we have no women's clothes on board. You'll have to make do with some of mine. Lead the way, Reepicheep, like a good fellow."

"To the convenience of a lady," said Reepicheep, "even a question of honour must give way – at least for the moment –" and here he looked very hard at Eustace. But Caspian hustled them on and in a few minutes Lucy found herself passing through the door into the stern cabin. She fell in love with it at once – the three square windows that looked out on the blue, swirling water astern, the low cushioned benches round three sides of the table, the swinging silver lamp overhead (Dwarfs' work, she knew at once by its exquisite delicacy) and the flat gold image of Aslan the Lion on the forward wall above the door. All this she took in in a flash, for Caspian immediately opened a door on the starboard side, and said, "This'll be your room, Lucy. I'll just get some dry things for myself –" he was rummaging in one of the lockers while he spoke – "and then leave you to change. If you'll fling your wet things outside the door I'll get them taken to the galley to be dried."

Lucy found herself as much at home as if she had been in Caspian's cabin for weeks, and the motion of the ship did not worry her, for in the old days when she had been a queen in Narnia she had done a good deal of voyaging. The cabin was very tiny but bright with painted panels (all birds and beasts and crimson dragons and vines) and spotlessly clean. Caspian's clothes were too big for her, but she could manage. His shoes, sandals and sea-boots were hopelessly big but she did not mind going barefoot on board ship. When she had finished dressing she looked out of her window at the water rushing past and took a long deep breath. She felt quite sure they were in for a lovely time.

CHAPTER TWO

ON BOARD THE *DAWN TREADER*

"Ah, there you are, Lucy," said Caspian. "We were just waiting for you. This is my captain, the Lord Drinian."

A dark-haired man went down on one knee and kissed her hand. The only others present were Reepicheep and Edmund.

"Where is Eustace?" asked Lucy.

"In bed," said Edmund, "and I don't think we can do anything for him. It only makes him worse if you try to be nice to him."

"Meanwhile," said Caspian, "we want to talk."

"By Jove, we do," said Edmund. "And first, about time. It's a year ago by our time since we left you just before your coronation. How long has it been in Narnia?"

"Exactly three years," said Caspian.

"All going well?" asked Edmund.

"You don't suppose I'd have left my kingdom and put to sea unless all was well," answered the King. "It couldn't be better. There's no trouble at all now between Telmarines, Dwarfs, Talking Beasts, Fauns and the rest. And we gave those troublesome giants on the frontier such a good beating last summer that they pay us tribute now. And I had an excellent person to leave as Regent while I'm away – Trumpkin, the Dwarf. You remember him?"

"Dear Trumpkin," said Lucy, "of course I do. You couldn't have made a better choice."

"Loyal as a badger, Ma'am, and valiant as – as a Mouse," said Drinian. He had been going to say "as a lion" but had noticed Reepicheep's eyes fixed on him.

"And where are we heading for?" asked Edmund.

"Well," said Caspian, "that's rather a long story. Perhaps you remember that when I was a child my usurping uncle Miraz got rid of seven friends of my father's (who might have taken my part) by sending them off to explore the unknown Eastern Seas beyond the Lone Islands."

"Yes," said Lucy, "and none of them ever came back."

"Right. Well, on my coronation day, with Aslan's approval, I swore an oath that, if once I established peace in Narnia, I would sail east myself for a year and a day to find my father's friends or to learn of their deaths and avenge them if I could. These were their names – the Lord Revilian, the Lord Bern, the Lord Argoz, the Lord Mavramorn, the Lord Octesian, the Lord Restimar, and – oh, that other one who's so hard to remember."

"The Lord Rhoop, Sire," said Drinian.

"Rhoop, Rhoop, of course," said Caspian. "That is my main intention. But Reepicheep here has an even higher hope." Everyone's eyes turned to the Mouse.

"As high as my spirit," it said. "Though perhaps as small as my stature. Why should we not come to the very eastern end of the world? And what might we find there? I expect to find Aslan's own country. It is always from the east, across the sea, that the great Lion comes to us."

"I say, that *is* an idea," said Edmund in an awed voice.

"But do you think," said Lucy, "Aslan's country would be that sort of country – I mean, the sort you could ever *sail* to?"

"I do not know, Madam," said Reepicheep. "But there is this. When I was in my cradle, a wood woman, a Dryad, spoke this verse over me:

"Where sky and water meet,
Where the waves grow sweet,
Doubt not, Reepicheep,
To find all you seek,
There is the utter East.

"I do not know what it means. But the spell of it has been on me all my life."

After a short silence Lucy asked, "And where are we now, Caspian?"

"The Captain can tell you better than I," said Caspian, so Drinian got out his chart and spread it on the table.

"That's our position," he said, laying his finger on it. "Or was at noon today. We had a fair wind from Cair Paravel and stood a little north for Galma, which we made on the next day. We were in port for a week, for the Duke of Galma made a great tournament for His Majesty and there he unhorsed many knights –"

"And got a few nasty falls myself, Drinian. Some of the bruises are there still," put in Caspian.

"– And unhorsed many knights," repeated Drinian with a grin. "We thought the Duke would have been pleased if the King's Majesty would have married his daughter, but nothing came of that –"

"Squints, and has freckles," said Caspian.

"Oh, poor girl," said Lucy.

"And we sailed from Galma," continued Drinian, "and ran into a calm for the best part of two days and had to row, and then had wind again and did not make Terebinthia till the fourth day from Galma. And there their King sent out a warning not to land for there was sickness in Terebinthia, but we doubled the cape and put in at a little creek far from the city and watered. Then we had to lie off for three days before we got a south-east wind and stood out for Seven Isles. The third day out a pirate (Terebinthian by her rig) overhauled us, but when she saw us well armed she stood off after some shooting of arrows on either part –"

"And we ought to have given her chase and boarded her and hanged every mother's son of them," said Reepicheep.

"– And in five days more we were in sight of Muil, which, as you know, is the westernmost of the Seven Isles. Then we rowed through the straits and came about sundown into Redhaven on the isle of Brenn, where we were very lovingly feasted and had victuals and water at will. We left Redhaven six days ago and have made marvellously good speed, so that I hope to see the Lone Islands the day after tomorrow. The sum is, we are now nearly thirty days at sea and have sailed more than four hundred leagues from Narnia."

"And after the Lone Islands?" said Lucy.

"No one knows, your Majesty," answered Drinian. "Unless the Lone Islanders themselves can tell us."

"They couldn't in our days," said Edmund.

"Then," said Reepicheep, "it is after the Lone Islands that the adventure really begins."

Caspian now suggested that they might like to be shown over the ship before supper, but Lucy's conscience smote her and she said, "I think I really must go and see Eustace. Seasickness is horrid, you know. If I had my old cordial with me I could cure him."

"But you have," said Caspian. "I'd quite forgotten about it. As you left it behind I thought it might be regarded as one of the royal treasures and so I brought it – if you think it ought to be wasted on a thing like seasickness."

"It'll only take a drop," said Lucy.

Caspian opened one of the lockers beneath the bench and brought out the beautiful little diamond flask which

Lucy remembered so well. "Take back your own, Queen," he said. They then left the cabin and went out into the sunshine.

In the deck there were two large, long hatches, fore and aft of the mast, and both open, as they always were in fair weather, to let light and air into the belly of the ship. Caspian led them down a ladder into the after hatch. Here they found themselves in a place where benches for rowing ran from side to side and the light came in through the oar-holes and danced on the roof. Of course Caspian's ship was not that horrible thing, a galley rowed by slaves. Oars were used only when wind failed or for getting in and out of harbour and everyone (except Reepicheep whose legs were too short) had often taken a turn. At each side of the ship the space under the benches was left clear for the rowers' feet, but all down the centre there was a kind of pit which went down to the very keel and this was filled with all kinds of things – sacks of flour, casks of water and beer, barrels of pork, jars of honey, skin bottles of wine, apples, nuts, cheeses, biscuits, turnips, sides of bacon. From the roof – that is, from the under side of the deck – hung hams and strings of onions, and also the men of the watch off-duty in their hammocks. Caspian led them aft, stepping from bench to bench; at least, it was stepping for him, and something between a step and a jump for Lucy, and a real long jump for Reepicheep. In this way they came to a partition with a door in it. Caspian opened the door and led them into a cabin which filled the stern underneath the deck cabins in the poop. It was of course not so nice. It was very low and the sides sloped together as they went down so that there was hardly any floor; and though it had windows of thick glass, they were not made to open because they were under water. In fact at this very moment, as the ship pitched they were alternately golden with sunlight and dim green with the sea.

"You and I must lodge here, Edmund," said Caspian. "We'll leave your kinsman the bunk and sling hammocks for ourselves."

"I beseech your Majesty –" said Drinian.

"No, no shipmate," said Caspian, "we have argued all that out already. You and Rhince" (Rhince was the mate) "are sailing the ship and will have cares and labours many a night when we are singing catches or telling stories, so

you and he must have the port cabin above. King Edmund and I can lie very snug here below. But how is the stranger?"

Eustace, very green in the face, scowled and asked whether there was any sign of the storm getting less. But Caspian said, "What storm?" and Drinian burst out laughing.

"Storm, young master!" he roared. "This is as fair weather as a man could ask for."

"Who's that?" said Eustace irritably. "Send him away. His voice goes through my head."

"I've brought you something that will make you feel better, Eustace," said Lucy.

"Oh, go away and leave me alone," growled Eustace. But he took a drop from her flask, and though he said it was beastly stuff (the smell in the cabin when she opened it was delicious) it is certain that his face came the right colour a few moments after he had swallowed it, and he must have felt better because, instead of wailing about the storm and his head, he began demanding to be put ashore and said that at the first port he would "lodge a disposition" against them all with the British Consul. But when Reepicheep asked what a disposition was and how you lodged it (Reepicheep thought it was some new way of arranging a single combat) Eustace could only reply, "Fancy not knowing that." In the end they succeeded in convincing Eustace that they were already sailing as fast as they could towards the nearest land they knew, and that they had no more power of sending him back to Cambridge – which was where Uncle Harold lived – than of sending him to the moon. After that he sulkily agreed to put on the fresh clothes which had been put out for him and come on deck.

Caspian now showed them over the ship, though indeed they had seen most it already. They went up on the forecastle and saw the look-out man standing on a little shelf inside the gilded dragon's neck and peering through its open mouth. Inside the forecastle was the galley (or ship's kitchen) and quarters for such people as the boatswain, the carpenter, the cook and the master-archer. If you think it odd to have the galley in the bows and imagine the smoke from its chimney streaming back over the ship, that is because you are thinking of steamships where there is

always a headwind. On a sailing ship the wind is coming
from behind, and anything smelly is put as far forward as
possible. They were taken up to the fighting top, and at
first it was rather alarming to rock to and fro there and see
the deck looking small and far away beneath. You realized
that if you fell there was no particular reason why you
should fall on board rather than in the sea. Then they were
taken to the poop, where Rhince was on duty with another

man at the great tiller, and behind that the dragon's tail
rose up, covered with gilding, and round inside it ran a
little bench. The name of the ship was *Dawn Treader*. She
was only a little bit of a thing compared with one of our
ships, or even with the cogs, dromonds, carracks and
galleons which Narnia had owned when Lucy and Edmund
had reigned there under Peter as the High King, for nearly
all navigation had died out in the reigns of Caspian's an-
cestors. When his uncle, Miraz the usurper, had sent the
seven lords to sea, they had had to buy a Galmian ship and
man it with hired Galmian sailors. But now Caspian had
begun to teach the Narnians to be sea-faring folk once
more, and the *Dawn Treader* was the finest ship he had
built yet. She was so small that, forward of the mast, there
was hardly any deck room between the central hatch and
the ship's boat on one side and the hen-coop (Lucy fed the
hens) on the other. But she was a beauty of her kind, a

"lady" as sailors say, her lines perfect, her colours pure, and every spar and rope and pin lovingly made. Eustace of course would be pleased with nothing, and kept on boasting about liners and motor-boats and aeroplanes and submarines ("As if *he* knew anything about them," muttered Edmund), but the other two were delighted with the *Dawn Treader*, and when they returned aft to the cabin and supper, and saw the whole western sky lit up with an immense crimson sunset, and felt the quiver of the ship, and tasted the salt on their lips, and thought of unknown lands on the Eastern rim of the world, Lucy felt that she was almost too happy to speak.

What Eustace thought had best be told in his own words, for when they all got their clothes back, dried, next morning, he at once got out a little black notebook and a pencil and started to keep a diary. He always had this notebook with him and kept a record of his marks in it, for though he didn't care much about any subject for its own sake, he cared a great deal about marks and would even go to people and say, "I got so much. What did you get?" But as he didn't seem likely to get many marks on the *Dawn Treader* he now started a diary. This was the first entry.

"7 *August.* Have now been twenty-four hours on this ghastly boat if it isn't a dream. All the time a frightful storm has been raging (it's a good thing I'm not seasick). Huge waves keep coming in over the front and I have seen the boat nearly go under any number of times. All the others pretend to take no notice of this, either from swank or because Harold says one of the most cowardly things ordinary people do is to shut their eyes to Facts. It's madness to come out into the sea in a rotten little thing like this. Not much bigger than a lifeboat. And, of course, absolutely primitive indoors. No proper saloon, no radio, no bathrooms, no deck-chairs. I was dragged all over it yesterday evening and it would make anyone sick to hear Caspian showing off his funny little toy boat as if it was the *Queen Mary*. I tried to tell him what real ships are like, but he's too dense. E. and L., *of course*, didn't back me up. I suppose a kid like L. doesn't realize the danger and E. is buttering up C. as everyone does here. They call him a King. I said I was a Republican but he had to ask me what that meant! He doesn't seem to know anything at all. *Needless to say* I've been put in the worst cabin of the boat, a perfect dungeon, and Lucy has been given a whole room on deck to herself, almost a nice room compared with the rest of this place. C. says that's because she's a girl. I tried to make him see what Alberta says, that all that sort of thing is really lowering girls but he was too dense. Still, he might see that I shall be ill if I'm kept in that *hole* any longer. E. says we mustn't grumble because C. is sharing it with us himself to make room for L. As if that didn't make it more crowded and far worse. Nearly forgot to say that there is also a kind of Mouse thing that gives everyone the most frightful cheek. The others can put up with it if they like but I shall twist his tail pretty soon if he tries it on me. The food is frightful too."

The trouble between Eustace and Reepicheep arrived even sooner than might have been expected. Before dinner next day, when the others were sitting round the table waiting (being at sea gives one a magnificent appetite), Eustace came rushing in, wringing his hand and shouting out:

"That little brute has half killed me. I insist on it being kept under control. I could bring an action against you, Caspian. I could order you to have it destroyed."

At the same moment Reepicheep appeared. His sword

was drawn and his whiskers looked very fierce but he was as polite as ever.

"I ask your pardons all," he said, "and especially her Majesty's. If I had known that he would take refuge here I would have awaited a more reasonable time for his correction."

"What on earth's up?" asked Edmund.

What had really happened was this. Reepicheep, who never felt that the ship was getting on fast enough, loved to sit on the bulwarks far forward just beside the dragon's head, gazing out at the eastern horizon and singing softly

in his little chirruping voice the song the Dryad had made for him. He never held on to anything, however the ship pitched, and kept his balance with perfect ease; perhaps his long tail, hanging down to the deck inside the bulwarks, made this easier. Everyone on board was familiar with this habit, and the sailors liked it because when one was on look-out duty it gave one somebody to talk to. Why exactly Eustace had slipped and reeled and stumbled all the way forward to the forecastle (he had not yet got his sea-legs) I never heard. Perhaps he hoped he would see land, or perhaps he wanted to hang about the galley and scrounge something. Anyway, as soon as he saw that long tail hanging down – and perhaps it was rather tempting – he thought it would be delightful to catch hold of it, swing Reepicheep round by it once or twice upside-down, then run away and laugh. At first the plan seemed to work beautifully. The Mouse was not much heavier than a very large cat. Eustace had him off the rail in a trice and very

silly he looked (thought Eustace) with his little limbs all splayed out and his mouth open. But unfortunately Reepicheep, who had fought for his life many a time, never lost his head even for a moment. Nor his skill. It is not very easy to draw one's sword when one is swinging round in the air by one's tail, but he did. And the next thing Eustace knew was two agonizing jabs in his hand which made him let go of the tail; and the next thing after that was that the Mouse had picked itself up again as if it were a ball bouncing off the deck, and there it was facing him, and a horrid long, bright, sharp thing like a skewer was waving to and fro within an inch of his stomach. (This doesn't count as below the belt for mice in Narnia because they can hardly be expected to reach higher.)

"Stop it," spluttered Eustace, "go away. Put that thing away. It's not safe. Stop it, I say. I'll tell Caspian.

I'll have you muzzled and tied up."

"Why do you not draw your own sword, poltroon!" cheeped the Mouse. "Draw and fight or I'll beat you black and blue with the flat."

"I haven't got one," said Eustace. "I'm a pacifist. I don't believe in fighting."

"Do I understand," said Reepicheep, withdrawing his sword for a moment and speaking very sternly, "that you do not intend to give me satisfaction?"

"I don't know what you mean," said Eustace, nursing his hand. "If you don't know how to take a joke I shan't bother my head about you."

"Then take that," said Reepicheep, "and that – to teach you manners – and the respect due to a knight – and a Mouse – and a Mouse's tail –" and at each word he gave Eustace a blow with the side of his rapier, which was thin, fine dwarf-tempered steel and as supple and effective as a birch rod. Eustace (of course) was at a school where they didn't have corporal punishment, so the sensation was quite new to him. That was why, in spite of having no sea-legs, it took him less than a minute to get off that forecastle and cover the whole length of the deck and burst in at the cabin door – still hotly pursued by Reepicheep. Indeed it seemed to Eustace that the rapier as well as the pursuit was hot. It might have been red-hot by the feel.

There was not much difficulty in settling the matter once Eustace realized that everyone took the idea of a duel seriously and heard Caspian offering to lend him a sword, and Drinian and Edmund discussing whether he ought to be handicapped in some way to make up for his being so much bigger than Reepicheep. He apologized sulkily and went off with Lucy to have his hand bathed and bandaged and then went to his bunk. He was careful to lie on his side.

CHAPTER THREE

THE LONE ISLANDS

"LAND in sight," shouted the man in the bows.

Lucy, who had been talking to Rhince on the poop, came pattering down the ladder and raced forward. As she went she was joined by Edmund, and they found Caspian, Drinian and Reepicheep already on the forecastle. It was a coldish morning, the sky very pale and the sea very dark blue with little white caps of foam, and there, a little way off on the starboard bow, was the nearest of the Lone Islands, Felimath, like a low green hill in the sea, and behind it, further off, the grey slopes of its sister Doorn.

"Same old Felimath! Same old Doorn," said Lucy, clapping her hands. "Oh – Edmund, how long it is since you and I saw them last!"

"I've never understood why they belong to Narnia," said Caspian. "Did Peter the High King conquer them?"

"Oh no," said Edmund. "They were Narnian before our time – in the days of the White Witch."

(By the way, I have never yet heard how these remote islands became attached to the crown of Narnia; if I ever do, and if the story is at all interesting, I may put it in some other book.)

"Are we to put in here, Sire?" asked Drinian.

"I shouldn't think it would be much good landing on Felimath," said Edmund. "It was almost uninhabited in our days and it looks as if it was the same still. The people lived mostly on Doorn and a little on Avra – that's the third one; you can't see it yet. They only kept sheep on Felimath."

"Then we'll have to double that cape, I suppose," said Drinian, "and land on Doorn. That'll mean rowing."

"I'm sorry we're not landing on Felimath," said Lucy. "I'd like to walk there again. It was so lonely – a nice kind of loneliness, and all grass and clover and soft sea air."

"I'd love to stretch my legs now too," said Caspian. "I tell you what. Why shouldn't we go ashore in the boat and send it back, and then we could walk across Felimath and let the *Dawn Treader* pick us up on the other side?"

If Caspian had been as experienced then as he became later on in this voyage he would not have made this suggestion; but at the moment it seemed an excellent one. "Oh do let's," said Lucy.

"You'll come, will you?" said Caspian to Eustace, who had come on deck with his hand bandaged.

"Anything to get off this blasted boat," said Eustace.

"Blasted?" said Drinian. "How do you mean?"

"In a civilized country like where I come from," said Eustace, "the ships are so big that when you're inside you wouldn't know you were at sea at all."

"In that case you might just as well stay ashore," said Caspian. "Will you tell them to lower the boat, Drinian."

The King, the Mouse, the two Pevensies, and Eustace all got into the boat and were pulled to the beach of Felimath. When the boat had left them and was being rowed back they all turned and looked round. They were surprised at how small the *Dawn Treader* looked.

Lucy was of course barefoot, having kicked off her shoes while swimming, but that is no hardship if one is going to walk on downy turf. It was delightful to be ashore again and to smell the earth and grass, even if at first the ground seemed to be pitching up and down like a ship, as it usually does for a while if one has been at sea. It was much warmer here than it had been on board and Lucy found the sand pleasant to her feet as they crossed it. There was a lark singing.

They struck inland and up a fairly steep, though low, hill. At the top of course they looked back, and there was the *Dawn Treader* shining like a great bright insect and crawling slowly north-westward with her oars. Then they went over the ridge and could see her no longer.

Doorn now lay before them, divided from Felimath by a channel about a mile wide; behind it and to the left lay Avra. The little white town of Narrowhaven on Doorn was easily seen.

"Hullo! What's this?" said Edmund suddenly.

In the green valley to which they were descending six or seven rough-looking men, all armed, were sitting by a tree.

"Don't tell them who we are," said Caspian.

"And pray, your Majesty, why not?" said Reepicheep who had consented to ride on Lucy's shoulder.

"It just occurred to me," replied Caspian, "that no one here can have heard from Narnia for a long time. It's just possible they may not still acknowledge our over-lordship. In which case it might not be quite safe to be known as the King."

"We have our swords, Sire," said Reepicheep.

"Yes, Reep, I know we have," said Caspian. "But if it is a question of re-conquering the three islands, I'd prefer to come back with a rather larger army."

By this time they were quite close to the strangers, one of whom – a big black-haired fellow – shouted out, "A good morning to you."

"And a good morning to you," said Caspian. "Is there still a Governor of the Lone Islands?"

"To be sure there is," said the man, "Governor Gumpas. His Sufficiency is at Narrowhaven. But you'll stay and drink with us."

Caspian thanked him, though neither he nor the others much liked the look of their new acquaintance, and all of them sat down. But hardly had they raised their cups to their lips when the black-haired man nodded to his companions and, as quick as lightning, all the five visitors found themselves wrapped in strong arms. There was a moment's struggle but all the advantages were on one side, and soon everyone was disarmed and had their hands tied behind their backs – except Reepicheep, writhing in his captor's grip and biting furiously.

"Careful with that beast, Tacks," said the Leader. "Don't damage him. He'll fetch the best price of the lot, I shouldn't wonder."

"Coward! Poltroon!" squeaked Reepicheep. "Give me my sword and free my paws if you dare."

"Whew!" whistled the slave merchant (for that is what he was). "It can talk! Well I never did. Blowed if I take less than two hundred crescents for him." The Calormen crescent, which is the chief coin in those parts, is worth about a third of a pound.

"So that's what you are," said Caspian. "A kidnapper and slaver. I hope you're proud of it."

"Now, now, now, now," said the slaver. "Don't you start any jaw. The easier you take it, the pleasanter all round, see? I don't do this for fun. I've got my living to make same as anyone else."

"Where will you take us?" asked Lucy, getting the words out with some difficulty.

"Over to Narrowhaven," said the slaver. "For market day tomorrow."

"Is there a British Consul there?" asked Eustace.

"Is there a which?" said the man.

But long before Eustace was tired of trying to explain, the slaver simply said, "Well, I've had enough of this jabber. The Mouse is a fair treat but this one would talk the hind leg off a donkey. Off we go, mates."

Then the four human prisoners were roped together, not cruelly but securely, and made to march down to the shore. Reepicheep was carried. He had stopped biting on a threat

of having his mouth tied up, but he had a great deal to say, and Lucy really wondered how any man could bear to have the things said to him which were said to the slave dealer by the Mouse. But the slave dealer, far from objecting, only said "Go on" whenever Reepicheep paused for breath, occasionally adding, "It's as good as a play," or, "Blimey, you can't help almost thinking it knows what it's saying!" or "Was it one of you what trained it?" This so infuriated Reepicheep that in the end the number of things he thought of saying all at once nearly suffocated him and he became silent.

When they got down to the shore that looked towards Doorn they found a little village and a long-boat on the beach and, lying a little further out, a dirty bedraggled looking ship.

"Now, youngsters," said the slave dealer, "let's have no fuss and then you'll have nothing to cry about. All aboard."

At that moment a fine-looking bearded man came out of one of the houses (an inn, I think) and said:

"Well, Pug. More of your usual wares?"

The slaver, whose name seemed to be Pug, bowed very low, and said in a wheedling kind of voice, "Yes, please your Lordship."

"How much do you want for that boy?" asked the other, pointing to Caspian.

"Ah," said Pug, "I knew your Lordship would pick on the best. No deceiving your Lordship with anything second rate. That boy, now, I've taken a fancy to him myself. Got kind of fond of him, I have. I'm that tender-hearted I didn't ever ought to have taken up this job. Still, to a customer like your Lordship –"

"Tell me your price, carrion," said the Lord sternly. "Do you think I want to listen to the rigmarole of your filthy trade?"

"Three hundred crescents, my Lord to your honourable Lordship, but to anyone else —"

"I'll give you a hundred and fifty."

"Oh please, please," broke in Lucy. "Don't separate us, whatever you do. You don't know —" But then she stopped for she saw that Caspian didn't even now want to be known.

"A hundred and fifty, then," said the Lord. "As for you, little maiden, I am sorry I cannot buy you all. Unrope my boy, Pug. And look — treat these others well while they are in your hands or it'll be the worse for you."

"Well!" said Pug. "Now who ever heard of a gentleman in my way of business who treated his stock better than what I do? Well? Why, I treat 'em like my own chidren."

"That's likely enough to be true," said the other grimly.

The dreadful moment had now come. Caspian was untied and his new master said, "This way, lad," and Lucy burst into tears and Edmund looked very blank. But Caspian looked over his shoulder and said, "Cheer up. I'm sure it will come all right in the end. So long."

"Now, missie," said Pug. "Don't you start taking on and spoiling your looks for the market tomorrow. You be a good girl and then you won't have nothing to cry *about*, see?"

Then they were rowed out to the slave-ship and taken below into a long, rather dark place, none too clean, where they found many other unfortunate prisoners; for Pug was of course a pirate and had just returned from cruising among the islands and capturing what he could. The children didn't meet anyone whom they knew; the prisoners were mostly Galmians and Terebinthians. And there they sat in the straw and wondered what was happening to Caspian and tried to stop Eustace talking as if everyone except himself was to blame.

Meanwhile Caspian was having a much more interesting time. The man who had bought him led him down a little lane between two of the village houses and so out into an open place behind the village. Then he turned and faced him.

"You needn't be afraid of me, boy," he said. "I'll treat you well. I bought you for your face. You reminded me of someone."

"May I ask of whom, my Lord?" said Caspian.

"You remind me of my master, King Caspian of Narnia."

Then Caspian decided to risk everything on one stroke.

"My Lord," he said, "I *am* your master. I am Caspian King of Narnia."

"You make very free," said the other. "How shall I know this is true?"

"Firstly by my face," said Caspian. "Secondly because I know within six guesses who you are. You are one of those seven lords of Narnia whom my Uncle Miraz sent to sea and whom I have come out to look for – Argoz, Bern, Octesian, Restimar, Mavramorn, or – or – I have forgotten the others. And finally, if your Lordship will give me a sword I will prove on any man's body in clean battle that I am Caspian the son of Caspian, lawful King of Narnia, Lord of Cair Paravel, and Emperor of the Lone Islands."

"By heaven," exclaimed the man, "it is his father's very voice and trick of speech. My liege – your Majesty –" And there in the field he knelt and kissed the King's hand.

"The moneys your Lordship disbursed for our person will be made good from our own treasury," said Caspian.

"They're not in Pug's purse yet, Sire," said the Lord Bern, for he it was. "And never will be, I trust. I have moved his Sufficiency the Governor a hundred times to crush this vile traffic in man's flesh."

"My Lord Bern," said Caspian, "we must talk of the state of these Islands. But first what is your Lordship's own story?"

"Short enough, Sire," said Bern. "I came thus far with my six fellows, loved a girl of the islands, and felt I had had enough of the sea. And there was no purpose in returning to Narnia while your Majesty's uncle held the reins. So I married and have lived here ever since."

"And what is this governor, this Gumpas, like? Does he still acknowledge the King of Narnia for his lord?"

"In words, yes. All is done in the King's name. But he would not be best pleased to find a real, live King of Narnia coming in upon him. And if your Majesty came before him alone and unarmed – well he would not deny his allegiance, but he would pretend to disbelieve you. Your Grace's life would be in danger. What following has your Majesty in these waters?"

"There is my ship just rounding the point," said Caspian. "We are about thirty swords if it came to fighting. Shall we not have my ship in and fall upon Pug and free my friends whom he holds captive?"

"Not by my counsel," said Bern. "As soon as there was a fight two or three ships would put out from Narrowhaven to rescue Pug. Your Majesty must work by a show of more power than you really have, and by the terror of the King's name. It must not come to plain battle. Gumpas is a chicken-hearted man and can be over-awed."

After a little more conversation Caspian and Bern walked down to the coast a little west of the village and there Caspian winded his horn. (This was not the great magic horn of Narnia, Queen Susan's Horn: he had left that at home for his regent Trumpkin to use if any great need fell upon the land in the King's absence.) Drinian, who was on the look-out for a signal, recognized the royal horn at once and the *Dawn Treader* began standing in to shore. Then the boat put off again and in a few moments Caspian and the Lord Bern were on deck explaining the situation to Drinian. He, just like Caspian, wanted to lay the *Dawn Treader* alongside the slave-ship at once and board her, but Bern made the same objection.

"Steer straight down this channel, captain," said Bern, "and then round to Avra where my own estates are. But first run up the King's banner, hang out all the shields, and send as many men to the fighting top as you can. And about five bowshots hence, when you get open sea on your port bow, run up a few signals."

"Signals? To whom?" said Drinian.

"Why, to all the other ships we haven't got but which it might be well that Gumpas thinks we have."

"Oh, I see," said Drinian rubbing his hands. "And they'll read our signals. What shall I say? *Whole fleet round the South of Avra and assemble at –?*"

"Bernstead," said the Lord Bern. "That'll do excellently. Their whole journey – if there *were* any ships –

would be out of sight from Narrowhaven."

Caspian was sorry for the others languishing in the hold of Pug's slave-ship, but he could not help finding the rest of that day enjoyable. Late in the afternoon (for they had to do all by oar), having turned to starboard round the northeast end of Doorn and port again round the point of Avra, they entered into a good harbour on Avra's southern shore where Bern's pleasant lands sloped down to the water's edge. Bern's people, many of whom they saw working in the fields, were all freemen and it was a happy and prosperous fief. Here they all went ashore and were royally feasted in a low, pillared house overlooking the bay. Bern and his gracious wife and merry daughters made them good cheer. But after dark Bern sent a messenger over by boat to Doorn to order some preparations (he did not say exactly what) for the following day.

CHAPTER FOUR

WHAT CASPIAN DID THERE

NEXT morning the Lord Bern called his guests early, and after breakfast he asked Caspian to order every man he had into full armour. "And above all," he added, "let everything be as trim and scoured as if it were the morning of the first battle in a great war between noble kings with all the world looking on." This was done; and then in three boatloads Caspian and his people, and Bern with a few of his, put out for Narrowhaven. The king's flag flew in the stern of his boat and his trumpeter was with him.

When they reached the jetty at Narrowhaven, Caspian found a considerable crowd assembled to meet them. "This is what I sent word about last night," said Bern. "They are all friends of mine and honest people." And as soon as Caspian stepped ashore the crowd broke out into hurrahs and shouts of, "Narnia! Narnia! Long live the King." At the same moment – and this was also due to Bern's messengers – bells began ringing from many parts of the town. Then Caspian caused his banner to be advanced and his trumpet to be blown and every man drew his sword and set his face into a joyful sternness, and they marched up the street so that the street shook, and their armour shone (for it was a sunny morning) so that one could hardly look at it steadily.

At first the only people who cheered were those who had been warned by Bern's messenger and knew what was happening and wanted it to happen. But then all the children joined in because they liked a procession and had seen very few. And then all the schoolboys joined in because they also liked processions and felt that the more noise and disturbance there was the less likely they would be to have any school that morning. And then all the old women put their heads out of doors and windows and began chattering and cheering because it was a king, and what is a governor compared with that? And all the young women joined in for the same reason and also because Caspian and Drinian and the rest were so handsome. And then all the young men came to see what the young women were looking at, so that by the time Caspian reached the castle gates, nearly the whole town was shouting; and where Gumpas sat in the castle, muddling and messing about with accounts and forms and rules and regulations, he heard the noise.

At the castle gate Caspian's trumpeter blew a blast and cried, "Open for the King of Narnia, come to visit his trusty and well-beloved servant the governor of the Lone

Islands." In those days everything in the islands was done in a slovenly, slouching manner. Only the little postern opened, and out came a tousled fellow with a dirty old hat on his head instead of a helmet, and a rusty old pike in his hand. He blinked at the flashing figures before him. "Carn – seez – fishansy," he mumbled which was his way of saying, "You can't see his Sufficiency"). "No interviews without 'pointments 'cept 'tween nine 'n' ten p.m. second Saturday every month."

"Uncover before Narnia, you dog," thundered the Lord Bern, and dealt him a rap with his gauntleted hand which sent his hat flying from his head.

"'Ere? Wot's it all about?" began the doorkeeper, but no one took any notice of him. Two of Caspian's men stepped through the postern and after some struggling with bars and bolts (for everything was rusty) flung both wings of the gate wide open. Then the King and his followers strode into the courtyard. Here a number of the governor's guards were lounging about and several more (they were mostly wiping their mouths) came tumbling out of various doorways. Though their armour was in a disgraceful condition, these were fellows who might have fought if they had been led or had known what was happening; so this was the dangerous moment. Caspian gave them no time to think.

"Where is the captain?" he asked.

"I am, more or less, if you know what I mean," said a languid and rather dandified young person without any armour at all.

"It is our wish," said Caspian, "that our royal visitation to our realm of the Lone Islands should, if possible, be an occasion of joy and not of terror to our loyal subjects. If it were not for that, I should have something to say about the state of your men's armour and weapons. As it is, you are pardoned. Command a cask of wine to be opened that your men may drink our health. But at noon tomorrow I wish to see them here in this courtyard looking like men-at-arms and not like vagabonds. See to it on pain of our extreme displeasure."

The captain gaped but Bern immediately cried, "Three cheers for the King," and the soldiers, who had understood about the cask of wine even if they understood nothing else, joined in. Caspian then ordered most of his own men to remain in the courtyard. He, with Bern and Drinian and four others, went into the hall.

Behind a table at the far end with various secretaries about him sat his Sufficiency, the Governor of the Lone Islands. Gumpas was a bilious-looking man with hair that had once been red and was now mostly grey. He glanced up as the strangers entered and then looked down at his papers saying automatically, "No interviews without appointments except between nine and ten p.m. on second Saturdays."

Caspian nodded to Bern and then stood aside. Bern and Drinian took a step forward and each seized one end of the table. They lifted it, and flung it on one side of the hall where it rolled over, scattering a cascade of letters, dossiers, ink-pots, pens, sealing-wax and documents. Then, not roughly but as firmly as if their hands were pincers of steel, they plucked Gumpas out of his chair and deposited him, facing it, about four feet away. Caspian at once sat down in the chair and laid his naked sword across his knees.

"My Lord," said he, fixing his eyes on Gumpas, "you have not given us quite the welcome we expected. I am the King of Narnia."

"Nothing about it in the correspondence," said the governor. "Nothing in the minutes. We have not been notified of any such thing. All irregular. Happy to consider any applications –"

"And we are come to enquire into your Sufficiency's conduct of your office," continued Caspian. "There are two points especially on which I require an explanation. Firstly I find no record that the tribute due from these Islands to the crown of Narnia has been received for about a hundred and fifty years."

"That would be a question to raise at the Council next month," said Gumpas. "If anyone moves that a commission of enquiry be set up to report on the financial history of the islands at the first meeting next year, why then . . ."

"I also find it very clearly written in our laws," Caspian went on, "that if the tribute is not delivered the whole debt has to be paid by the Governor of the Lone Islands out of his private purse."

At this Gumpas began to pay real attention. "Oh, that's quite out of the question," he said. "It is an economic impossibility – er – your Majesty must be joking."

Inside, he was wondering if there were any way of getting rid of these unwelcome visitors. Had he known that Caspian had only one ship and one ship's company with him, he would have spoken soft words for the moment, and hoped to have them all surrounded and killed during the night. But he had seen a ship of war sail down the straits yesterday and seen it signalling, as he supposed, to its consorts. He had not then known it was the King's ship for there was not wind enough to spread the flag out and make the golden lion visible, so he had waited further developments. Now he imagined that Caspian had a whole fleet at Bernstead. It would never have occurred to Gumpas that anyone would walk into Narrowhaven to take the islands with less than fifty men; it was certainly not at all the kind of thing he could imagine doing himself.

"Secondly," said Caspian, "I want to know why you have permitted this abominable and unnatural traffic in slaves to grow up here, contrary to the ancient custom and usage of our dominions."

"Necessary, unavoidable," said his Sufficiency. "An essential part of the economic development of the islands, I assure you. Our present burst of prosperity depends on it."

"What need have you of slaves?"

"For export, your Majesty. Sell 'em to Calormen mostly; and we have other markets. We are a great centre of the trade."

"In other words," said Caspian, "you don't need them. Tell me what purpose they serve except to put money into the pockets of such as Pug?"

"Your Majesty's tender years," said Gumpas, with what was meant to be a fatherly smile, "hardly make it possible that you should understand the economic problem involved. I have statistics, I have graphs, I have –"

"Tender as my years be," said Caspian, "I believe I understand the slave trade from within quite as well as your Sufficiency. And I do not see that it brings into the islands meat or bread or beer or wine or timber or cabbages or books or instruments of music or horses or armour or anything else worth having. But whether it does or not, it must be stopped."

"But that would be putting the clock back," gasped the governor. "Have you no idea of progress, of development?"

"I have seen them both in an egg," said Caspian. "We call it 'Going Bad' in Narnia. This trade must stop."

"I can take no responsibility for any such measure," said Gumpas.

"Very well, then," answered Caspian, "we relieve you of your office. My Lord Bern, come here." And before Gumpas quite realized what was happening, Bern was kneeling with his hands between the King's hands and taking the oath to govern the Lone Islands in accordance with the old customs, rights, usages and laws of Narnia. And Caspian said, "I think we have had enough of governors," and made Bern a Duke, the Duke of the Lone Islands.

"As for you, my Lord," he said to Gumpas, "I forgive you your debt for the tribute. But before noon tomorrow you and yours must be out of the castle, which is now the Duke's residence."

"Look here, this is all very well," said one of Gumpas's secretaries, "but suppose all you gentlemen stop play-acting and we do a little business. The question before us really is—"

"The question is," said the Duke, "whether you and the rest of the rabble will leave without a flogging or with one. You may choose which you prefer."

When all this had been pleasantly settled, Caspian ordered horses, of which there were a few in the castle, though very ill-groomed and he, with Bern and Drinian and a few others, rode out into the town and made for the slave market. It was a long low building near the harbour and the scene which they found going on inside was very much like any other auction; that is to say, there was a great crowd and Pug, on a platform, was roaring out in a raucous voice:

"Now, gentlemen, lot twenty-three. Fine Terebinthian agricultural labourer, suitable for the mines or the galleys. Under twenty-five years of age. Not a bad tooth in his head. Good, brawny fellow. Take off his shirt, Tacks, and let the gentlemen see. There's muscle for you! Look at the chest on him. Ten crescents from the gentleman in the corner. You must be joking, sir. Fifteen! Eighteen! Eighteen is bidden for lot twenty-three. Any advance on eighteen? Twenty-one. Thank you, sir. Twenty-one is bidden –"

But Pug stopped and gaped when he saw the mail-clad figures who had clanked up to the platform.

"On your knees, every man of you, to the King of Narnia," said the Duke. Everyone heard the horses jingling and stamping outside and many had heard some rumour of the landing and the events at the castle. Most obeyed. Those who did not were pulled down by their neighbours. Some cheered.

"Your life is forfeit, Pug, for laying hands on our royal person yesterday," said Caspian. "But your ignorance is pardoned. The slave trade was forbidden in all our dominions quarter of an hour ago. I declare every slave in this market free."

He held up his hand to check the cheering of the slaves and went on, "Where are my friends?"

"That dear little gel and the nice young gentleman?" said Pug with an ingratiating smile. "Why, they were snapped up at once –"

"We're here, we're here, Caspian," cried Lucy and Edmund together and, "At your service, Sire," piped Reepicheep from another corner. They had all been sold but the men who had bought them were staying to bid for other slaves and so they had not yet been taken away. The crowd parted to let the three of them out and there was great hand-clasping and greeting between them and Caspian. Two merchants of Calormen at once approached. The Calormen have dark faces and long beards. They wear flowing robes and orange-coloured turbans, and they are a wise, wealthy, courteous, cruel and ancient people. They bowed most politely to Caspian and paid him long compliments, all about the fountains of prosperity irrigating the gardens of prudence and virtue – and things like that – but of course what they wanted was the money they had paid.

"That is only fair, sirs," said Caspian. "Every man who has bought a slave today must have his money back. Pug, bring out your takings to the last minim." (A minim is the fortieth part of a crescent.)

"Does your good Majesty mean to beggar me?" whined Pug.

"You have lived on broken hearts all your life," said Caspian, "and if you *are* beggared, it is better to be a beggar than a slave. But where is my other friend?"

"Oh *him*?" said Pug. "Oh take *him* and welcome. Glad to have him off my hands. I've never seen such a drug in the market in all my born days. Priced him at five crescents in the end and even so nobody'd have him. Threw him in free with other lots and still no one would have him. Wouldn't touch him. Wouldn't look at him. Tacks, bring out Sulky."

Thus Eustace was produced, and sulky he certainly looked; for though no one would want to be sold as a slave, it is perhaps even more galling to be a sort of utility slave whom no one will buy. He walked up to Caspian and said, "I see. As usual. Been enjoying yourself somewhere while the rest of us were prisoners. I suppose you haven't even found out about the British Consul. Of course not."

That night they had a great feast in the castle of Narrowhaven and then, "Tomorrow for the beginning of our real adventures!" said Reepicheep when he had made his bows to everyone and went to bed. But it could not really be tomorrow or anything like it. For now they were preparing to leave all known lands and seas behind them and the fullest preparations had to be made. The *Dawn Treader* was emptied and drawn on land by eight horses over rollers and every bit of her was gone over by the most skilled shipwrights. Then she was launched again and victualled and watered as full as she could hold – that is to say for twenty-eight days. Even this, as Edmund noticed with disappointment, only gave them a fortnight's eastward sailing before they had to abandon their quest.

While all this was being done Caspian missed no chance of questioning all the oldest sea captains whom he could find in Narrowhaven to learn if they had any knowledge or

even any rumours of land further to the east. He poured out many a flagon of the castle ale to weather-beaten men with short grey beards and clear blue eyes, and many a tall yarn he heard in return. But those who seemed the most truthful could tell of no lands beyond the Lone Islands, and many thought that if you sailed too far east you would come into the surges of a sea without lands that swirled perpetually round the rim of the world – "And that, I reckon, is where your Majesty's friends went to the bottom." The rest had only wild stories of islands inhabited by headless men, floating islands, waterspouts, and a fire that burned along the water. Only one, to Reepicheep's delight, said, "And beyond that, Aslan country. But that's beyond the end of the world and you can't get there." But when they questioned him he could only say that he'd heard it from his father.

Bern could only tell them that he had seen his six companions sail away eastward and that nothing had ever been heard of them again. He said this when he and Caspian were standing on the highest point of Avra looking down on the eastern ocean. "I've often been up here of a morning," said the Duke, "and seen the sun come up out of the sea, and sometimes it looked as if it were only a couple of miles away. And I've wondered about my friends and wondered what there really is behind that horizon. Nothing, most likely, yet I am always half ashamed that I stayed behind. But I wish your Majesty wouldn't go. We may need your help here. This closing the slave market might make a new world; war with Calormen is what I foresee. My liege, think again."

"I have an oath, my lord Duke," said Caspian. "And anyway, what *could* I say to Reepicheep?"

CHAPTER FIVE

THE STORM AND WHAT CAME OF IT

IT was nearly three weeks after their landing that the *Dawn Treader* was towed out of Narrowhaven harbour. Very solemn farewells had been spoken and a great crowd had assembled to see her departure. There had been cheers, and tears too, when Caspian made his last speech to the Lone Islanders and parted from the Duke and his family, but as the ship, her purple sail still flapping idly, drew further from the shore, and the sound of Caspian's trumpet from the poop came fainter across the water, everyone became silent. Then she came into the wind. The sail swelled out, the tug cast off and began rowing back, the first real wave ran up under the *Dawn Treader*'s prow, and she was a live ship again. The men off duty went below, Drinian took the first watch on the poop, and she turned her head eastward round the south of Avra.

The next few days were delightful. Lucy thought she was the most fortunate girl in the world, as she woke each morning to see the reflections of the sunlit water dancing on the ceiling of her cabin and looked round on all the nice new things she had got in the Lone Islands — seaboots and buskins and cloaks and jerkins and scarves. And then she would go on deck and take a look from the forecastle at a sea which was a brighter blue each morning and drink in an air that was a little warmer day by day. After that came breakfast and such an appetite as one only has at sea.

She spent a good deal of time sitting on the little bench in the stern playing chess with Reepicheep. It was amusing to see him lifting the pieces, which were far too big for him, with both paws and standing on tiptoes if he made a move near the centre of the board. He was a good player and when he remembered what he was doing he usually won. But every now and then Lucy won because the Mouse did something quite ridiculous like sending a knight into the danger of a queen and castle combined. This happened because he had momentarily forgotten it was a game of chess and was thinking of a real battle and making the knight do what he would certainly have done in its place. For his mind was full of forlorn hopes, death-or-glory charges, and last stands.

But this pleasant time did not last. There came an evening when Lucy, gazing idly astern at the long furrow or wake they were leaving behind them, saw a great rack of clouds building itself up in the west with amazing speed.

Then a gap was torn in it and a yellow sunset poured through the gap. All the waves behind them seemed to take on unusual shapes and the sea was a drab or yellowish colour like dirty canvas. The air grew cold. The ship seemed to move uneasily as if she felt danger behind her. The sail would be flat and limp one minute and wildly full the next. While she was noting these things and wondering at a sinister change which had come over the very noise of the wind, Drinian cried, "All hands on deck." In a moment everyone became frantically busy. The hatches were battened down, the galley fire was put out, men went aloft to reef the sail. Before they had finished the storm struck them. It seemed to Lucy that a great valley in the sea opened just before their bows, and they rushed down into it, deeper down than she would have believed possible. A great grey hill of water, far higher than the mast, rushed to meet them; it looked certain death but they were tossed to the top of it. Then the ship seemed to spin round. A cataract of water poured over the deck; the poop and forecastle were like two islands with a fierce sea between them. Up aloft the sailors were lying out along the yard desperately trying to get control of the sail. A broken rope stood out sideways in the wind as straight and stiff as if it was a poker.

"Get below, Ma'am," bawled Drinian. And Lucy, knowing that landsmen – and landswomen – are a nuisance to the crew, began to obey. It was not easy. The *Dawn Treader* was listing terribly to starboard and the deck sloped like the roof of a house. She had to clamber round to the top of the ladder, holding on to the rail, and then stand by while two men climbed up it, and then get down it as best she could. It was well she was already holding on tight for at the foot of the ladder another wave roared across the deck, up to her shoulders. She was already almost wet through with spray and rain but this was colder. Then she made a dash for the cabin door and got in and shut out for a moment the appalling sight of the speed with which they were rushing into the dark, but not of course the horrible confusion of creakings, groanings, snappings, clatterings, roarings and boomings which only sounded more alarming below than they had done on the poop.

And all next day and all the next it went on. It went on till one could hardly even remember a time before it had begun. And there always had to be three men at the tiller and it was as much as three could do to keep any kind of a course. And there always had to be men at the pump. And there was hardly any rest for anyone, and nothing could be cooked and nothing could be dried, and one man was lost overboard, and they never saw the sun.

When it was over Eustace made the following entry in his diary.

"*3 September*. The first day for ages when I have been able to write. We had been driven before a hurricane for thirteen days and nights. I know that because I kept a careful count, though the others all say it was only twelve. *Pleasant* to be embarked on a dangerous voyage with people who can't even count right! I have had a ghastly time, up and down enormous waves hour after hour, usually wet to the skin, and not even an *attempt* at giving us proper meals. Needless to say there's no wireless or even a rocket, so no chance of signalling anyone for help. It all proves what I keep on telling them, the madness of setting out in a rotten little tub like this. It would be bad enough even if one was with decent people instead of fiends in human form. Caspian and Edmund are simply brutal to me. The night we lost our mast (there's only a stump left now), though I was *not at all* well, they forced me to come on deck and work like a slave. Lucy shoved her oar in by saying that Reepicheep was longing to go only he was too small. I wonder she doesn't see that everything that little beast does is all for the sake of *showing off*. Even at her age

she ought to have that amount of sense. Today the beastly boat is level at last and the sun's out and we have all been jawing about what to do. We have food enough, pretty beastly stuff most of it, to last for sixteen days. (The poultry were all washed overboard. Even if they hadn't been, the storm would have stopped them laying.) The real trouble is water. Two casks seem to have got a leak knocked in them and are empty. (Narnian efficiency again.) On short rations, half a pint a day each, we've got enough for twelve days. (There's still lots of rum and wine but even *they* realize that would only make them thirstier.)

"If we could, of course, the sensible thing would be to turn west at once and make for the Lone Islands. But it took us eighteen days to get where we are, running like mad

with a gale behind us. Even if we got an east wind it might
take us far longer to get back. And at present there's no sign
of an east wind – in fact there's no wind at all. As for rowing
back, it would take far too long and Caspian says the men
couldn't row on half a pint of water a day. I'm pretty sure
this is wrong. I tried to explain that perspiration really
cools people down, so the men would need less water if
they were working. He didn't take any notice of this, which
is always his way when he can't think of an answer. The
others all voted for going *on* in the hope of finding land. I
felt it my duty to point out that we didn't know there *was*
any land ahead and tried to get them to see the dangers of
wishful thinking. Instead of producing a better plan they
had the cheek to ask me what I proposed. So I just
explained coolly and quietly that I had been kidnapped and
brought away on this *idiotic* voyage without my consent,
and it was hardly *my* business to get *them* out of their
scrape.

"4 September. Still becalmed. Very short rations for
dinner and I got less than anyone. Caspian is very clever at
helping and thinks I don't see! Lucy for some reason tried
to make up to me by offering me some of hers but that
interfering prig Edmund wouldn't let her. Pretty hot sun.
Terribly thirsty all evening.

"5 September. Still becalmed and very hot. Feeling
rotten all day and am sure I've got a temperature. Of
course they haven't the sense to keep a thermometer on
board.

"6 September. A horrible day. Woke up in the night
knowing I was feverish and *must* have a drink of water.
Any doctor would have said so. Heaven knows I'm the last
person to try to get any unfair advantage but I never
dreamed that this water-rationing would be meant to apply
to a sick man. In fact I would have woken the others up

and asked for some only I thought it would be selfish to wake them. So I got up and took my cup and tiptoed out of the Black Hole we slept in, taking great care not to disturb Caspian and Edmund, for they've been sleeping badly since the heat and the short water began. I always try to consider others whether they are nice to me or not. I got out all right into the big room, if you can call it a room, where the rowing benches and the luggage are. The thing of water is at this end. All was going beautifully, but before I'd drawn a cupful who should catch me but that *little spy* Reep. I tried to explain that I was going on deck for a breath of air (the business about the water had nothing to do with him) and he asked me why I had a cup. He made such a noise that the whole ship was roused. They treated me scandalously. I asked, as I think anyone would have, why Reepicheep was sneaking about the water cask in the middle of the night. He said that as he was too small to be any use on deck, he did sentry over the water every night so that one more man could go to sleep. Now comes their rotten unfairness: they all believed *him*. Can you beat it?

"I had to apologize or the dangerous little brute would have been at me with his sword. And then Caspian showed up in his true colours as a brutal tyrant and said out loud for everyone to hear that anyone found "stealing" water in future would "get two dozen". I didn't know what this meant till Edmund explained to me. It comes in the sort of books those Pevensie kids read.

"After this cowardly threat Caspian changed his tune and started being *patronizing*. Said he was sorry for me and that everyone felt just as feverish as I did and we must all make the best of it, etc., etc. Odious stuck-up prig. Stayed in bed all day today.

"*7 September.* A little wind today but still from the west.

Made a few miles eastward with part of the sail, set on what Drinian calls the jury-mast – that means the bowsprit set upright and tied (they call it "lashed") to the stump of the real mast. Still terribly thirsty.

"*8 September*. Still sailing east. I stay in my bunk all day now and see no one except Lucy till the two *fiends* come to bed. Lucy gives me a little of her water ration. She says girls don't get as thirsty as boys. I had often thought this but it ought to be more generally known at sea.

"*9 September*. Land in sight; a very high mountain a long way off to the south-east.

"*10 September*. The mountain is bigger and clearer but still a long way off. Gulls again today for the first time since I don't know how long.

"*11 September*. Caught some fish and had them for dinner. Dropped anchor at about 7 p.m. in three fathoms of water in a bay of this mountainous island. That idiot Caspian wouldn't let us go ashore because it was getting dark and he was afraid of savages and wild beasts. Extra water ration tonight."

What awaited them on this island was going to concern Eustace more than anyone else, but it cannot be told in his words because after September 11 he forgot about keeping his diary for a long time.

When morning came, with a low, grey sky but very hot, the adventurers found they were in a bay encircled by such cliffs and crags that it was like a Norwegian fjord. In front of them, at the head of the bay, there was some level land heavily overgrown with trees that appeared to be cedars, through which a rapid stream came out. Beyond that was a steep ascent ending in a jagged ridge and behind that a vague darkness of mountains which ran into dull-coloured clouds so that you could not see their tops. The nearer cliffs, at each side of the bay, were streaked here and there with lines of white which everyone knew to be waterfalls, though at that distance they did not show any movement or make any noise. Indeed the whole place was very silent and the water of the bay as smooth as glass. It reflected every detail of the cliffs. The scene would have been pretty in a picture but was rather oppressive in real life. It was not a country that welcomed visitors.

The whole ship's company went ashore in two boat-loads and everyone drank and washed deliciously in the river and had a meal and a rest before Caspian sent four men back to keep the ship, and the day's work began. There was everything to be done. The casks must be brought ashore and the faulty ones mended if possible and all refilled; a tree – a pine if they could get it – must be felled and made into a new mast; sails must be repaired; a hunting party organized to shoot any game the land might yield; clothes to be washed and mended; and countless small breakages on board to be set right. For the *Dawn Treader* herself – and this was more obvious now that they saw her at a distance – could hardly be recognized as the same gallant ship which had left Narrowhaven. She looked a crippled, discoloured hulk which anyone might have taken for a wreck. And her officers and crew were no better – lean, pale, red-eyed from lack of sleep, and dressed in rags.

As Eustace lay under a tree and heard all these plans being discussed his heart sank. Was there going to be no rest? It looked as if their first day on the longed-for land was going to be quite as hard work as a day at sea. Then a delightful idea occurred to him. Nobody was looking – they were all chattering about their ship as if they actually liked the beastly thing. Why shouldn't he simply slip away? He would take a stroll inland, find a cool, airy place up in

the mountains, have a good long sleep, and not rejoin
the others till the day's work was over. He felt it would
do him good. But he would take great care to keep the bay
and the ship in sight so as to be sure of his way back.

He wouldn't like to be left behind in this country.

He at once put his plan into action. He rose quietly from his place and walked away among the trees, taking care to go slowly and in an aimless manner so that anyone who saw him would think he was merely stretching his legs. He was surprised to find how quickly the noise of conversation died away behind him and how very silent and warm and dark green the wood became. Soon he felt he could venture on a quicker and more determined stride.

This soon brought him out of the wood. The ground began sloping steeply up in front of him. The grass was dry and slippery but manageable if he used his hands as well as his feet, and though he panted and mopped his forehead a good deal, he plugged away steadily. This showed, by the way, that his new life, little as he suspected it, had already done him some good; the old Eustace, Harold and Alberta's Eustace, would have given up the climb after about ten minutes.

Slowly, and with several rests, he reached the ridge. Here he had expected to have a view into the heart of the island, but the clouds had now come lower and nearer and a sea of fog was rolling to meet him. He sat down and looked back. He was now so high that the bay looked small beneath him and miles of sea were visible. Then the fog from the mountains closed in all round him, thick but not cold, and he lay down and turned this way and that to find the most comfortable position to enjoy himself.

But he didn't enjoy himself, or not for very long. He began, almost for the first time in his life, to feel lonely. At first this feeling grew very gradually. And then he began to worry about the time. There was not the slightest sound. Suddenly it occurred to him that he might have been lying there for hours. Perhaps the others had gone! Perhaps they had let him wander away on purpose simply in order to leave him behind! He leaped up in a panic and began the descent.

At first he tried to do it too quickly, slipped on the steep grass, and slid for several feet. Then he thought this had carried him too far to the left – and as he came up he had seen precipices on that side. So he clambered up again, as near as he could guess to the place he had started from, and began the descent afresh, bearing to his right. After that things seemed to be going better. He went very cautiously, for he could not see more than a yard ahead, and there was still perfect silence all around him. It is very unpleasant to have to go cautiously when there is a voice inside you saying all the time, "Hurry, hurry, hurry." For every moment the terrible idea of being left behind grew stronger. If he had understood Caspian and the Pevensies at all he would have known, of course, that there was not

the least chance of their doing any such thing. But he had persuaded himself that they were all fiends in human form.

"At last!" said Eustace as he came slithering down a slide of loose stones (*scree*, they call it) and found himself on the level. "And now, where are those trees? There *is* something dark ahead. Why, I do believe the fog is clearing."

It was. The light increased every moment and made him blink. The fog lifted. He was in an utterly unknown valley and the sea was nowhere in sight.

CHAPTER SIX

THE ADVENTURES OF EUSTACE

At that very moment the others were washing hands and faces in the river and generally getting ready for dinner and a rest. The three best archers had gone up into the hills north of the bay and returned laden with a pair of wild goats which were now roasting over a fire. Caspian had ordered a cask of wine ashore, strong wine of Archenland which had to be mixed with water before you drank it, so there would be plenty for all. The work had gone well so far and it was a merry meal. Only after the seond helping of goat did Edmund say, "Where's that blighter Eustace?"

Meanwhile Eustace stared round the unknown valley. It was so narrow and deep, and the precipices which surrounded it so sheer, that it was like a huge pit or trench. The floor was grassy though strewn with rocks, and here and there Eustace saw black burnt patches like those you see on the sides of a railway embankment in a dry summer.

About fifteen yards away from him was a pool of clear, smooth water. There was, at first, nothing else at all in the valley; not an animal, not a bird, not an insect. The sun beat down and grim peaks and horns of mountains peered over the valley's edge.

Eustace realized of course that in the fog he had come down the wrong side of the ridge, so he turned at once to see about getting back. But as soon as he had looked he shuddered. Apparently he had by amazing luck found the only possible way down – a long green spit of land, horribly steep and narrow, with precipices on either side. There was no other possible way of getting back. But could he do it, now that he saw what it was really like? His head swam at the very thought of it.

He turned round again, thinking that at any rate he'd better have a good drink from the pool first. But as soon as he had turned and before he had taken a step forward into the valley he heard a noise behind him. It was only a small noise but it sounded loud in that immense silence. It froze him dead-still where he stood for a second. Then he slewed round his neck and looked.

At the bottom of the cliff a little on his left hand was a low, dark hole – the entrance to a cave perhaps. And out of this two thin wisps of smoke were coming. And the loose stones just beneath the dark hollow were moving (that was the noise he had heard) just as if something were crawling in the dark behind them.

Something *was* crawling. Worse still, something was coming out. Edmund or Lucy or you would have recognized it at once, but Eustace had read none of the right books. The thing that came out of the cave was something he had never even imagined – a long lead-coloured snout, dull red eyes, no feathers or fur, a long lithe body that trailed on the ground, legs whose elbows went up

higher than its back like a spider's, cruel claws, bat's wings that made a rasping noise on the stones, yards of tail. And the lines of smoke were coming from its two nostrils. He never said the word *Dragon* to himself. Nor would it have made things any better if he had.

But perhaps if he had known something about dragons he would have been a little surprised at this dragon's behaviour. It did not sit up and clap its wings, nor did it shoot out a stream of flame from its mouth. The smoke from its nostrils was like the smoke of a fire that will not last much longer. Nor did it seem to have noticed Eustace. It moved very slowly towards the pool – slowly and with many pauses. Even in his fear Eustace felt that it was an old, sad creature. He wondered if he dared make a dash for the ascent. But it might look round if he made any noise. It might come more to life. Perhaps it was only shamming. Anyway, what was the use of trying to escape by climbing from a creature that could fly?

It reached the pool and slid its horrible scaly chin down over the gravel to drink: but before it had drunk there came from it a great croaking or clanging cry and after a

few twitches and convulsions it rolled round on its side and
lay perfectly still with one claw in the air. A little dark
blood gushed from its wide-opened mouth. The smoke
from its nostrils turned black for a moment and then
floated away. No more came.

For a long time Eustace did not dare to move. Perhaps

this was the brute's trick, the way it lured travellers to their
doom. But one couldn't wait for ever. He took a step
nearer, then two steps, and halted again. The dragon
remained motionless; he noticed too that the red fire had
gone out of its eyes. At last he came up to it. He was quite
sure now that it was dead. With a shudder he touched it;
nothing happened.

The relief was so great that Eustace almost laughed out
loud. He began to feel as if he had fought and killed the
dragon instead of merely seeing it die. He stepped over it
and went to the pool for his drink, for the heat was getting

unbearable. He was not surprised when he heard a peal of thunder. Almost immediately afterwards the sun disappeared and before he had finished his drink big drops of rain were falling.

The climate of this island was a very unpleasant one. In less than a minute Eustace was wet to the skin and half blinded with such rain as one never sees in Europe. There was no use trying to climb out of the valley as long as this lasted. He bolted for the only shelter in sight – the dragon's cave. There he lay down and tried to get his breath.

Most of us know what we should expect to find in a dragon's lair, but, as I said before, Eustace had read only the wrong books. They had a lot to say about exports and imports and governments and drains, but they were weak on dragons. That is why he was so puzzled at the surface on which he was lying. Parts of it were too prickly to be stones and too hard to be thorns, and there seemed to be a great many round, flat things, and it all clinked when he moved. There was light enough at the cave's mouth to examine it by. And of course Eustace found it to be what any of us could have told him in advance – treasure. There were crowns (those were the prickly things), coins, rings, bracelets, ingots, cups, plates and gems.

Eustace (unlike most boys) had never thought much of treasure but he saw at once the use it would be in this new world which he had so foolishly stumbled into through the picture in Lucy's bedroom at home. "They don't have any tax here," he said, "And you don't have to give treasure to the government. With some of this stuff I could have quite a decent time here – perhaps in Calormen. It sounds the least phoney of these countries. I wonder how much I can carry? That bracelet now – those things in it are probably diamonds – I'll slip that on my own wrist. Too big, but not if I push it right up here above my elbow. Then fill my pockets with diamonds – that's easier than gold. I wonder when this infernal rain's going to let up?" He got into a less uncomfortable part of the pile, where it was mostly coins, and settled down to wait. But a bad fright, when once it is over, and especially a bad fright following a mountain walk, leaves you very tired. Eustace fell asleep.

By the time he was sound asleep and snoring the others had finished dinner and became seriously alarmed about him. They shouted, "Eustace! Eustace! Coo-ee!" till they were hoarse and Caspian blew his horn.

"He's nowhere near or he'd have heard that," said Lucy with a white face.

"Confound the fellow," said Edmund. "What on earth did he want to slink away like this for?"

"But we must do something," said Lucy. "He may have got lost, or fallen into a hole, or been captured by savages."

"Or killed by wild beasts," said Drinian.

"And a good riddance if he has, *I* say," muttered Rhince.

"Master Rhince," said Reepicheep, "you never spoke a word that became you less. The creature is no friend of mine but he is of the Queen's blood, and while he is one of our fellowship it concerns our honour to find him and to avenge him if he is dead."

"Of course we've got to find him (if we *can*)," said Caspian wearily. "That's the nuisance of it. It means a search party and endless trouble. Bother Eustace."

Meanwhile Eustace slept and slept – and slept. What woke him was a pain in his arm. The moon was shining in at the mouth of the cave, and the bed of treasures seemed to have grown much more comfortable: in fact he could hardly feel it at all. He was puzzled by the pain in his arm at first, but presently it occurred to him that the bracelet which he had shoved up above his elbow had become strangely tight. His arm must have swollen while he was asleep (it was his left arm).

He moved his right arm in order to feel his left, but stopped before he had moved it an inch and bit his lip in terror. For just in front of him, and a little on his right, where the moonlight fell clear on the floor of the cave, he saw a hideous shape moving. He knew that shape: it was a dragon's claw. It had moved as he moved his hand and became still when he stopped moving his hand.

"Oh, what a fool I've been," thought Eustace. "Of course, the brute had a mate and it's lying beside me."

For several minutes he did not dare to move a muscle. He saw two thin columns of smoke going up before his eyes, black against the moonlight; just as there had been smoke coming from the other dragon's nose before it died. This was so alarming that he held his breath. The two columns of smoke vanished. When he could hold his breath no longer he let it out stealthily; instantly two jets of smoke appeared again. But even yet he had no idea of the truth.

Presently he decided that he would edge very cautiously to his left and try to creep out of the cave. Perhaps the creature was asleep – and anyway it was his only chance. But of course before he edged to the left he looked to the left. Oh horror! there was a dragon's claw on that side too.

No one will blame Eustace if at this moment he shed tears. He was surprised at the size of his own tears as he saw them splashing on to the treasure in front of him. They also seemed strangely hot; steam went up from them.

But there was no good crying. He must try to crawl out from between the two dragons. He began extending his right arm. The dragon's fore-leg and claw on his right went through exactly the same motion. Then he thought he would try his left. The dragon limb on that side moved too.

Two dragons, one on each side, mimicking whatever he did! His nerve broke and he simply made a bolt for it.

There was such a clatter and rasping, and clinking of gold, and grinding of stones, as he rushed out of the cave that he thought they were both following him. He daren't look back. He rushed to the pool. The twisted shape of the dead dragon lying in the moonlight would have been enough to frighten anyone but now he hardly noticed it. His idea was to get into the water.

But just as he reached the edge of the pool two things happened. First of all it came over him like a thunder-clap that he had been running on all fours – and why on earth had he been doing that? And secondly, as he bent towards the water, he thought for a second that yet another dragon was staring up at him out of the pool. But in an instant he realized the truth. The dragon face in the pool was his own reflection. There was no doubt of it. It moved as he moved: it opened and shut its mouth as he opened and shut his.

He had turned into a dragon while he was asleep. Sleeping on a dragon's hoard with greedy, dragonish thoughts in his heart, he had become a dragon himself.

That explained everything. There had been no two dragons beside him in the cave. The claws to right and left had been his own right and left claw. The two columns of smoke had been coming from his own nostrils. As for the pain in his left arm (or what had been his left arm) he could now see what had happened by squinting with his left eye. The bracelet which had fitted very nicely on the upper arm of a boy was far too small for the thick, stumpy foreleg of a dragon. It had sunk deeply into his scaly flesh and there was a throbbing bulge on each side of it. He tore at the place with his dragon's teeth but could not get it off.

In spite of the pain, his first feeling was one of relief. There was nothing to be afraid of any more. He was a terror himself and nothing in the world but a knight (and not all of those) would dare to attack him. He could get even with Caspian and Edmund now –

But the moment he thought this he realized that he didn't want to. He wanted to be friends. He wanted to get back among humans and talk and laugh and share things. He realized that he was a monster cut off from the whole human race. An appalling loneliness came over him. He began to see that the others had not really been fiends at all. He began to wonder if he himself had been such a nice person as he had always supposed. He longed for their voices. He would have been grateful for a kind word even from Reepicheep.

When he thought of this the poor dragon that had been Eustace lifted up its voice and wept. A powerful dragon crying its eyes out under the moon in a deserted valley is a sight and a sound hardly to be imagined.

At last he decided he would try to find his way back to the shore. He realized now that Caspian would never have sailed away and left him. And he felt sure that somehow or other he would be able to make people understand who he was.

He took a long drink and then (I know this sounds shocking, but it isn't if you think it over) he ate nearly all the dead dragon. He was half-way through it before he realized what he was doing; for, you see, though his mind was the mind of Eustace, his tastes and his digestion were dragonish. And there is nothing a dragon likes so well as fresh dragon. That is why you so seldom find more than one dragon in the same county.

Then he turned to climb out of the valley. He began the climb with a jump and as soon as he jumped he found that he was flying. He had quite forgotten about his wings and it was a great surprise to him – the first pleasant surprise he

had had for a long time. He rose high into the air and
saw innumerable mountain-tops spread out beneath him in
the moonlight. He could see the bay like a silver slab and
the *Dawn Treader* lying at anchor and camp fires
twinkling in the woods beside the beach. From a great

height he launched himself down towards them in a single
glide.

Lucy was sleeping very soundly for she had sat up till the
return of the search party in hope of good news about
Eustace. It had been led by Caspian and had come back
late and weary. Their news was disquieting. They had
found no trace of Eustace but had seen a dead dragon in a
valley. They tried to make the best of it and everyone
assured everyone else that there were not likely to be more

dragons about, and that one which was dead at about three o'clock that afternoon (which was when they had seen it) would hardly have been killing people a very few hours before.

"Unless it ate the little brat and died of him: he'd poison anything," said Rhince. But he said this under his breath and no one heard it.

But later in the night Lucy was wakened, very softly, and found the whole company gathered close together and talking in whispers.

"What is it?" said Lucy.

"We must all show great constancy," Caspian was saying. "A dragon has just flown over the tree-tops and lighted on the beach. Yes, I am afraid it is between us and the ship. And arrows are no use against dragons. And they're not at all afraid of fire."

"With your Majesty's leave –" began Reepicheep.

"No, Reepicheep," said the King very firmly, "you are *not* to attempt a single combat with it. And unless you promise to obey me in this matter I'll have you tied up. We must just keep close watch and, as soon as it is light, go down to the beach and give it battle. I will lead. King Edmund will be on my right and the Lord Drinian on my left. There are no other arrangements to be made. It will be light in a couple of hours. In an hour's time let a meal be served out and what is left of the wine. And let everything be done silently."

"Perhaps it will go away," said Lucy.

"It'll be worse if it does," said Edmund, "because then we shan't know where it is. If there's a wasp in the room I like to be able to see it."

The rest of the night was dreadful, and when the meal came, though they knew they ought to eat, many found that they had very poor appetites. And endless hours seemed to pass before the darkness thinned and birds began chirping here and there and the world got colder and wetter than it had been all night and Caspian said, "Now for it, friends."

They got up, all with swords drawn, and formed themselves into a solid mass with Lucy in the middle and Reepicheep on her shoulder. It was nicer than the waiting about and everyone felt fonder of everyone else than at ordinary times. A moment later they were marching. It grew lighter as they came to the edge of the wood. And there on the sand, like a giant lizard, or a flexible crocodile, or a serpent with legs, huge and horrible and humpy, lay the dragon.

But when it saw them, instead of rising up and blowing fire and smoke, the dragon retreated – you could almost say it waddled – back into the shallows of the bay.

"What's it wagging its head like that for?" said Edmund.

"And now it's nodding," said Caspian.

"And there's something coming from its eyes," said Drinian.

"Oh, can't you see," said Lucy. "It's crying. Those are tears."

"I shouldn't trust to that, Ma'am," said Drinian. "That's what crocodiles do, to put you off your guard."

"It wagged its head when you said that," remarked Edmund. "Just as if it meant No. Look, there it goes again."

"Do you think it understands what we're saying?" asked Lucy.

The dragon nodded its head violently.

Reepicheep slipped off Lucy's shoulder and stepped to the front.

"Dragon," came his shrill voice, "can you understand speech?"

The dragon nodded.

"Can you speak?"

It shook its head.

"Then," said Reepicheep, "it is idle to ask you your business. But if you will swear friendship with us raise your left foreleg above your head."

It did so, but clumsily because that leg was sore and swollen with the golden bracelet.

"Oh look," said Lucy, "there's something wrong with its leg. The poor thing – that's probably what it was crying about. Perhaps it came to us to be cured like in Androcles and the lion."

"Be careful, Lucy," said Caspian. "It's a very clever dragon but it may be a liar."

Lucy had, however, already run forward, followed by Reepicheep, as fast as his short legs could carry him, and then of course the boys and Drinian came, too.

"Show me your poor paw," said Lucy, "I might be able to cure it."

The dragon-that-had-been-Eustace held out its sore leg gladly enough, remembering how Lucy's cordial had cured him of sea-sickness before he became a dragon. But he was disappointed. The magic fluid reduced the swelling and eased the pain a little but it could not dissolve the gold.

Everyone had now crowded round to watch the treatment, and Caspian suddenly exclaimed, "Look!" He was staring at the bracelet.

CHAPTER SEVEN

HOW THE ADVENTURE ENDED

"Look at what?" said Edmund.

"Look at the device on the gold," said Caspian.

"A little hammer with a diamond above it like a star," said Drinian. "Why, I've seen that before."

"Seen it!" said Caspian. "Why, of course you have. It is the sign of a great Narnian house. This is the Lord Octesian's arm-ring."

"Villain," said Reepicheep to the dragon, "have you devoured a Narnian lord?" But the dragon shook his head violently.

"Or perhaps," said Lucy, "this *is* the Lord Octesian, turned into a dragon – under an enchantment, you know."

"It needn't be either," said Edmund. "All dragons collect gold. But I think it's a safe guess that Octesian got no further than this island."

"Are you the Lord Octesian?" said Lucy to the dragon, and then, when it sadly shook its head, "Are you someone enchanted – someone human, I mean?"

It nodded violently.

And then someone said – people disputed afterwards whether Lucy or Edmund said it first – "You're not – not Eustace by any chance?"

And Eustace nodded his terrible dragon head and thumped his tail in the sea and everyone skipped back (some of the sailors with ejaculations I will not put down in writing) to avoid the enormous and boiling tears which flowed from his eyes.

Lucy tried hard to console him and even screwed up her courage to kiss the scaly face, and nearly everyone said

"Hard luck" and several assured Eustace that they would all stand by him and many said there was sure to be some way of disenchanting him and they'd have him as right as rain in a day or two. And of course they were all very anxious to hear his story, but he couldn't speak. More than once in the days that followed he attempted to write it for them on the sand. But this never succeeded. In the first place Eustace (never having read the right books) had no idea how to tell a story straight. And for another thing, the muscles and nerves of the dragon-claws that he had to use had never learned to write and were not built for writing anyway. As a result he never got nearly to the end before the tide came in and washed away all the writing except the bits he had already trodden on or accidentaly swished out with his tail. And all that anyone had seen would be something like this – the dots are for the bits he had smudged out–

I WNET TO SLEE . . . RGOS AGRONS I MEAN DRANGONS CAVE CAUSE ITWAS DEAD AND AINING SO HAR . . . WOKE UP AND COU . . . GET OFFF MI ARM OH BOTHER . . .

It was, however, clear to everyone that Eustace's character had been rather improved by becoming a dragon. He was anxious to help. He flew over the whole island and found it was all mountainous and inhabited only by wild goats and droves of wild swine. Of these he brought back many carcasses as provisions for the ship. He was a very humane killer too, for he could dispatch a beast with one blow of his tail so that it didn't know (and presumably still doesn't know) it had been killed. He ate a few himself, of course, but always alone, for now that he was a dragon he liked his food raw but he could never bear to let others see him at his messy meals. And one day, flying slowly and wearily but in great triumph, he bore back to camp a great tall pine tree which he had torn up by the roots in a distant valley and which could be made into a capital mast. And in the evening if it turned chilly, as it sometimes did after the heavy rains, he was a comfort to everyone, for the whole party would come and sit with their backs against his hot sides and get well warmed and dried; and one puff of his fiery breath would light the most obstinate fire. Sometimes he would take a select party for a fly on his back, so that they could see wheeling below them the green slopes, the rocky heights, the narrow pit-like valleys and far out over the sea to the eastward a spot of darker blue on the blue horizon which might be land.

The pleasure (quite new to him) of being liked and, still more, of liking other people, was what kept Eustace from despair. For it was very dreary being a dragon. He shuddered whenever he caught sight of his own reflection as he flew over a mountain lake. He hated the huge batlike wings, the saw-edged ridge on his back, and the cruel, curved claws. He was almost afraid to be alone with himself and yet he was ashamed to be with the others. On the evenings when he was not being used as a hot-water bottle he would slink away from the camp and lie curled up like a snake between the wood and the water. On such occasions, greatly to his surprise, Reepicheep was his most constant comforter. The noble Mouse would creep away from the merry circle at the camp fire and sit down by the dragon's head, well to the windward to be out of the way of his smoky breath. There he would explain that what had happened to Eustace was a striking illustration of the turn of Fortune's wheel, and that if he had Eustace at his own house in Narnia (it was really a hole not a house and the dragon's head, let alone his body, would not have fitted in) he could show him more than a hundred examples of

emperors, kings, dukes, knights, poets, lovers, astronomers, philosophers, and magicians, who had fallen from prosperity into the most distressing circumstances, and of whom many had recovered and lived happily ever afterwards. It did not, perhaps, seem so very comforting at the time, but it was kindly meant and Eustace never forgot it.

But of course what hung over everyone like a cloud was the problem of what to do with their dragon when they were ready to sail. They tried not to talk of it when he was there, but he couldn't help overhearing things like, "Would he fit all along one side of the deck? And we'd have to shift all the stores to the other side down below so as to balance," or, "Would towing him be any good?" or "Would he be able to keep up by flying?" and (most often of all), "But how are we to feed him?" And poor Eustace realized more and more that since the first day he came on board he had been an unmitigated nuisance and that he was now a greater nuisance still. And this ate into his mind, just as that bracelet ate into his foreleg. He knew that it only made it worse to tear at it with his great teeth, but he couldn't help tearing now and then, especially on hot nights.

*

About six days after they had landed on Dragon Island, Edmund happened to wake up very early one morning. It was just getting grey so that you could see the tree-trunks if they were between you and the bay but not in the other direction. As he woke he thought he heard something moving, so he raised himself on one elbow and looked about him: and presently he thought he saw a dark figure moving on the seaward side of the wood. The idea that at once occurred to his mind was, "Are we so sure there are no natives on this island after all?" Then he thought it was Caspian – it was about the right size – but he knew that Caspian had been sleeping next to him and could see that he hadn't moved. Edmund made sure that his sword was in its place and then rose to investigate.

He came down softly to the edge of the wood and the dark figure was still there. He saw now that it was too small for Caspian and too big for Lucy. It did not run away. Edmund drew his sword and was about to challenge the stranger when the stranger said in a low voice, "Is that you, Edmund?"

"Yes. Who are you?" said he.

"Don't you know me?" said the other. "It's me – Eustace."

"By jove," said Edmund, "so it is. My dear chap –"

"Hush," said Eustace and lurched as if he were going to fall.

"Hello!" said Edmund, steadying him. "What's up? Are you ill?"

Eustace was silent for so long that Edmund thought he was fainting; but at last he said, "It's been ghastly. You don't know . . . but it's all right now. Could we go and talk somewhere? I don't want to meet the others just yet."

"Yes, rather, anywhere you like," said Edmund. "We can go and sit on the rocks over there. I say, I *am* glad to see you – er – looking yourself again. You must have had a pretty beastly time."

They went to the rocks and sat down looking out across the bay while the sky got paler and paler and the stars disappeared except for one very bright one low down and near the horizon.

"I won't tell you how I became a – a dragon till I can tell the others and get it all over," said Eustace. "By the way, I didn't even know it *was* a dragon till I heard you all using the word when I turned up here the other morning. I want to tell you how I stopped being one."

"Fire ahead," said Edmund.

"Well, last night I was more miserable than ever. And that beastly arm-ring was hurting like anything –"

"Is that all right now?"

Eustace laughed – a different laugh from any Edmund had heard him give before – and slipped the bracelet easily off his arm. "There it is," he said, "and anyone who likes can have it as far as I'm concerned. Well, as I say, I was lying awake and wondering what on earth would become of me. And then – but, mind you, it may have been all a dream. I don't know."

"Go on," said Edmund, with considerable patience.

"Well, anyway, I looked up and saw the very last thing I expected: a huge lion coming slowly towards me. And one queer thing was that there was no moon last night, but there was moonlight where the lion was. So it came nearer and nearer. I was terribly afraid of it. You may think that, being a dragon, I could have knocked any lion out easily enough. But it wasn't that kind of fear. I wasn't afraid of it eating me, I was just afraid of *it* – if you can understand. Well, it came close up to me and looked straight into my eyes. And I shut my eyes tight. But that wasn't any good because it told me to follow it."

"You mean it spoke?"

"I don't know. Now that you mention it, I don't think it did. But it told me all the same. And I knew I'd have to do what it told me, so I got up and followed it. And it led me a long way into the mountains. And there was always this moonlight over and round the lion wherever we went. So at last we came to the top of a mountain I'd never seen before and on the top of this mountain there was a garden – trees and fruit and everything. In the middle of it there was a well.

"I knew it was a well because you could see the water bubbling up from the bottom of it: but it was a lot bigger than most wells – like a very big, round bath with marble steps going down into it. The water was as clear as anything and I thought if I could get in there and bathe it would ease the pain in my leg. But the lion told me I must undress first. Mind you, I don't know if he said any words out loud or not.

"I was just going to say that I couldn't undress because I hadn't any clothes on when I suddenly thought that dragons are snaky sort of things and snakes can cast their skins. Oh, of course, thought I, that's what the lion means. So I started scratching myself and my scales began coming off all over the place. And then I scratched a little deeper and, instead of just scales coming off here and there, my whole skin started peeling off beautifully, like it does after an illness, or as if I was a banana. In a minute or two I just stepped out of it. I could see it lying there beside me, looking rather nasty. It was a most lovely feeling. So I started to go down into the well for my bathe.

"But just as I was going to put my feet into the water I looked down and saw that they were all hard and rough and wrinkled and scaly just as they had been before. Oh, that's all right, said I, it only means I had another smaller suit on underneath the first one, and I'll have to get out of it too. So I scratched and tore again and this underskin peeled off beautifully and out I stepped and left it lying beside the other one and went down to the well for my bathe.

"Well, exactly the same thing happened again. And I thought to myself, oh dear, how ever many skins have I got to take off? For I was longing to bathe my leg. So I scratched away for the third time and got off a third skin, just like the two others, and stepped out of it. But as soon as I looked at myself in the water I knew it had been no good.

"Then the lion said – but I don't know if it spoke – "You will have to let me undress you." I was afraid of his claws, I can tell you, but I was pretty nearly desperate now. So I just lay flat down on my back to let him do it.

"The very first tear he made was so deep that I thought it had gone right into my heart. And when he began pulling the skin off, it hurt worse than anything I've ever felt. The only thing that made me able to bear it was just the pleasure of feeling the stuff peel off. You know – if you've ever picked the scab off a sore place. It hurts like billy-oh but it *is* such fun to see it coming away."

"I know exactly what you mean," said Edmund.

"Well, he peeled the beastly stuff right off – just as I thought I'd done it myself the other three times, only they hadn't hurt – and there it was lying on the grass: only ever so much thicker, and darker, and more knobbly-looking than the others had been. And there was I as smooth and soft as a peeled switch and smaller than I had been. Then he caught hold of me – I didn't like that much for I was very tender underneath now that I'd no skin on – and threw me into the water. It smarted like anything but only for a moment. After that it became perfectly delicious and as soon as I started swimming and splashing I found that all the pain had gone from my arm. And then I saw why. I'd turned into a boy again. You'd think me simply phoney if I told you how I felt about my own arms. I know they've no muscle and are pretty mouldy compared with Caspian's, but I was so glad to see them.

"After a bit the lion took me out and dressed me –"

"Dressed you. With his paws?"

"Well, I don't exactly remember that bit. But he did somehow or other: in new clothes – the same I've got on now, as a matter of fact. And then suddenly I was back here. Which is what makes me think it must have been a dream."

"No. It wasn't a dream," said Edmund.

"Why not?"

"Well, there are the clothes, for one thing. And you have been – well, un-dragoned, for another."

"What do you think it was, then?" asked Eustace.

"I think you've seen Aslan," said Edmund.

"Aslan!" said Eustace. "I've heard that name mentioned several times since we joined the *Dawn Treader*. And I felt – I don't know what – I hated it. But I was hating everything then. And by the way, I'd like to apologize. I'm afraid I've been pretty beastly."

"That's all right," said Edmund. "Between ourselves, you haven't been as bad as I was on my first trip to Narnia. You were only an ass, but I was a traitor."

"Well, don't tell me about it, then," said Eustace. "But who is Aslan? Do you know him?"

"Well – he knows me," said Edmund. "He is the great Lion, the son of the Emperor-beyond-the-Sea, who saved me and saved Narnia. We've all seen him. Lucy sees him most often. And it may be Aslan's country we are sailing to."

Neither said anything for a while. The last bright star had vanished and though they could not see the sunrise because of the mountains on their right, they knew it was going on because the sky above them and the bay before them turned the colour of roses. Then some bird of the parrot kind screamed in the wood behind them, they heard movements among the trees, and finally a blast on Caspian's horn. The camp was astir.

ƎN
CTESIAN
ʼATH

Great was the rejoicing when Edmund and the restored Eustace walked into the breakfast circle round the camp fire. And now of course everyone heard the earlier part of his story. People wondered whether the other dragon had killed the Lord Octesian several years ago or whether Octesian himself had been the old dragon. The jewels with which Eustace had crammed his pockets in the cave had disappeared along with the clothes he had then been wearing: but no one, least of all Eustace himself, felt any desire to go back to that valley for more treasure.

In a few days now the *Dawn Treader*, remasted, re-painted, and well stored, was ready to sail. Before they embarked Caspian caused to be cut on a smooth cliff facing the bay the words:

DRAGON ISLAND
DISCOVERED BY CASPIAN X, KING OF NARNIA, ETC.
IN THE FOURTH
YEAR OF HIS REIGN.
HERE, AS WE SUPPOSE, THE LORD OCTESIAN
HAD HIS DEATH

It would be nice, and fairly true, to say that "from that time forth Eustace was a different boy". To be strictly accurate, he began to be a different boy. He had relapses. There were still many days when he could be very tiresome. But most of those I shall not notice. The cure had begun.

The Lord Octesian's arm ring had a curious fate. Eustace did not want it and offered it to Caspian and Caspian offered it to Lucy. She did not care about having it. "Very well, then, catch as catch can," said Caspian and flung it up in the air. This was when they were all standing looking at the inscription. Up went the ring, flashing in the sunlight, and caught, and hung, as neatly as a well-thrown quoit, on a little projection on the rock. No one could climb up to get it from below and no one could climb down to get it from above. And there, for all I know, it is hanging still and may hang till that world ends.

CHAPTER EIGHT

TWO NARROW ESCAPES

EVERYONE was cheerful as the *Dawn Treader* sailed from Dragon Island. They had fair winds as soon as they were out of the bay and came early next morning to the unknown land which some of them had seen when flying over the mountains while Eustace was still a dragon. It was a low green island inhabited by nothing but rabbits and a few goats, but from the ruins of stone huts, and from blackened places where fires had been, they judged that it had been peopled not long before. There were also some bones and broken weapons.

"Pirates' work," said Caspian.

"Or the dragon's," said Edmund.

The only other thing they found there was a little skin boat, or coracle, on the sands. It was made of hide stretched over a wicker framework. It was a tiny boat, barely four feet long, and the paddle which still lay in it was in proportion. They thought that either it had been made for a child or else that the people of that country had been Dwarfs. Reepicheep decided to keep it, as it was just the right size for him; so it was taken on board. They called that land Burnt Island, and sailed away before noon.

For some five days they ran before a south-south-east wind, out of sight of all lands and seeing neither fish nor gull. Then they had a day when it rained hard till the afternoon. Eustace lost two games of chess to Reepicheep and began to get like his old and disagreeable self again, and Edmund said he wished they could have gone to America with Susan. Then Lucy looked out of the stern windows and said:

"Hello! I do believe it's stopping. And what's *that*?"

They all tumbled up to the poop at this and found that the rain had stopped and that Drinian, who was on watch, was also staring hard at something astern. Or rather, at several things. They looked a little like smooth rounded rocks, a whole line of them with intervals of about forty feet in between.

"But they can't be rocks," Drinian was saying, "because they weren't there five minutes ago."

"And one's just disappeared," said Lucy.

"Yes, and there's another one coming up," said Edmund.

"And nearer," said Eustace.

"Hang it!" said Caspian. "The whole thing is moving this way."

"And moving a great deal quicker than we can sail, Sire," said Drinian. "It'll be up with us in a minute."

They all held their breath, for it is not at all nice to be pursued by an unknown something either on land or sea. But what it turned out to be was far worse than anyone had suspected. Suddenly, only about the length of a cricket pitch from their port side, an appalling head reared itself out of the sea. It was all greens and vermilions with purple blotches – except where shell fish clung to it – and shaped rather like a horse's, though without ears. It had enormous eyes, eyes made for staring through the dark depths of the ocean, and a gaping mouth filled with double rows of sharp fish-like teeth. It came up on what they first took to be a huge neck, but as more and more of it emerged everyone knew that this was not its neck but its body and that at last they were seeing what so many people have foolishly wanted to see – the great Sea Serpent. The folds of its gigantic tail could be seen far away, rising at intervals from the surface. And now its head was towering up higher than the mast.

Every man rushed to his weapon, but there was nothing to be done, the monster was out of reach. "Shoot! Shoot!" cried the Master Bowman, and several obeyed, but the arrows glanced off the Sea Serpent's hide as if it was iron-plated. Then, for a dreadful minute, everyone was still, staring up at its eyes and mouth and wondering where it would pounce.

But it didn't pounce. It shot its head forward across the

ship on a level with the yard of the mast. Now its head was just beside the fighting top. Still it stretched and stretched till its head was over the starboard bulwark. Then down it began to come – not on to the crowded deck but into the water, so that the whole ship was under an arch of serpent. And almost at once that arch began to get smaller: indeed on the starboard the Sea Serpent was now almost touching the *Dawn Treader*'s side.

Eustace (who had really been trying very hard to behave well, till the rain and the chess put him back) now did the first brave thing he had ever done. He was wearing a sword that Caspian had lent him. As soon as the serpent's body was near enough on the starboard side he jumped on to the bulwark and began hacking at it with all his might. It is true that he accomplished nothing beyond breaking Caspian's second-best sword into bits, but it was a fine thing for a beginner to have done.

Others would have joined him if at that moment Reepicheep had not called out, "Don't fight! Push!" It was so unusual for the Mouse to advise anyone not to fight that, even in that terrible moment, every eye turned to him. And when he jumped up on to the bulwark, forward of the snake, and set his little furry back against its huge scaly, slimy back, and began pushing as hard as he could, quite a number of people saw what he meant and rushed to both sides of the ship to do the same. And when, a moment later, the Sea Serpent's head appeared again, this time on the port side, and this time with its back to them, then everyone understood.

The brute had made a loop of itself round the *Dawn Treader* and was beginning to draw the loop tight. When it got quite tight – snap! – there would be floating matchwood where the ship had been and it could pick them out of the water one by one. Their only chance was to push the loop backward till it slid over the stern; or else (to put the same thing another way) to push the ship forward out of the loop.

Reepicheep alone had, of course, no more chance of doing this than of lifting up a cathedral, but he had nearly killed himself with trying before others shoved him aside. Very soon the whole ship's company except Lucy and the Mouse (which was fainting) was in two long lines along the two bulwarks, each man's chest to the back of the man in front, so that the weight of the whole line was in the last man, pushing for their lives. For a few sickening seconds (which seemed like hours) nothing appeared to happen. Joints cracked, sweat dropped, breath came in grunts and gasps. Then they felt that the ship was moving. They saw that the snake-loop was further from the mast than it had been. But they also saw that it was smaller. And now the real danger was at hand. Could they get it over the poop, or was it already too tight? Yes. It would just fit. It was resting on the poop rails. A dozen or more sprang up on the poop. This was far better. The Sea Serpent's body was so low now that they could make a line across the poop and push side by side. Hope rose high till everyone remembered the high carved stern, the dragon tail, of the *Dawn Treader*. It would be quite impossible to get the brute over that.

"An axe," cried Caspian hoarsely, "and still shove." Lucy, who knew where everything was, heard him where she was standing on the main deck staring up at the poop. In a few seconds she had been below, got the axe, and was rushing up the ladder to the poop. But just as she reached the top there came a great crashing noise like a tree coming down and the ship rocked and darted forward. For at that very moment, whether because the Sea Serpent was being pushed so hard, or because it foolishly decided to draw the noose tight, the whole of the carved stern broke off and the ship was free.

The others were too exhausted to see what Lucy saw. There, a few yards behind them, the loop of Sea Serpent's body got rapidly smaller and disappeared into a splash. Lucy always said (but of course she was very excited at the moment, and it may have been only imagination) that she saw a look of idiotic satisfaction on the creature's face. What is certain is that it was a very stupid animal, for instead of pursuing the ship it turned its head round and began nosing all along its own body as if it expected to find the wreckage of the *Dawn Treader* there. But the *Dawn Treader* was already well away, running before a fresh breeze, and the men lay and sat panting and groaning all about the deck, till presently they were able to talk about it, and then to laugh about it. And when some rum had been served out they even raised a cheer; and everyone praised the valour of Eustace (though it hadn't done any good) and of Reepicheep.

After this they sailed for three days more and saw nothing but sea and sky. On the fourth day the wind changed to the north and the seas began to rise; by the afternoon it had nearly become a gale. But at the same time they sighted land on their port bow.

"By your leave, Sire," said Drinian, "we will try to get under the lee of that country by rowing and lie in harbour, maybe till this is over." Caspian agreed, but a long row against the gale did not bring them to the land before evening. By the last light of that day they steered into a natural harbour and anchored, but no one went ashore that night. In the morning they found themselves in the green bay of a rugged, lonely-looking country which sloped up to a rocky summit. From the windy north beyond that summit clouds came streaming rapidly. They lowered the boat and loaded her with any of the water casks which were now empty.

"Which stream shall we water at, Drinian?" said Caspian as he took his seat in the stern-sheets of the boat. "There seem to be two coming down into the bay."

"It makes little odds, Sire," said Drinian. "But I think it's a shorter pull to that on the starboard – the eastern one."

"Here comes the rain," said Lucy.

"I should think it does!" said Edmund, for it was already pelting hard. "I say, let's go to the other stream. There are trees there and we'll have some shelter."

"Yes, let's," said Eustace. "No point in getting wetter than we need."

But all the time Drinian was steadily steering to the starboard, like tiresome people in cars who continue at forty miles an hour while you are explaining to them that they are on the wrong road.

"They're right, Drinian," said Caspian. "Why don't you bring her head round and make for the western stream?"

"As your Majesty pleases," said Drinian a little shortly. He had had an anxious day with the weather yesterday, and he didn't like advice from landsmen. But he altered course; and it turned out afterwards that it was a good thing he did.

By the time they had finished watering, the rain was over and Caspian, with Eustace, the Pevensies, and Reepicheep, decided to walk up to the top of the hill and see what could be seen. It was a stiffish climb through coarse grass and heather and they saw neither man nor beast, except seagulls. When they reached the top they saw that it was a very small island, not more than twenty acres; and from this height the sea looked larger and more desolate than it did from the deck, or even the fighting top, of the *Dawn Treader*.

"Crazy, you know," said Eustace to Lucy in a low voice,

looking at the eastern horizon. "Sailing on and on into *that* with no idea what we may get to." But he only said it out of habit, not really nastily as he would have done at one time.

It was too cold to stay long on the ridge for the wind still blew freshly from the north.

"Don't let's go back the same way," said Lucy as they turned; "let's go along a bit and come down by the other stream, the one Drinian wanted to go to."

Everyone agreed to this and after about fifteen minutes they were at the source of the second river. It was a more interesting place than they had expected; a deep little mountain lake, surrounded by cliffs except for a narrow channel on the seaward side out of which the water flowed. Here at last they were out of the wind, and all sat down in the heather above the cliff for a rest.

All sat down, but one (it was Edmund) jumped up again very quickly.

"They go in for sharp stones on this island," he said, groping about in the heather. "Where is the wretched thing? . . . Ah, now I've got it . . . Hullo! It wasn't a stone at all, it's a sword-hilt. No, by jove, it's a whole sword; what the rust has left of it. It must have lain here for ages."

"Narnian, too, by the look of it," said Caspian, as they all crowded round.

"I'm sitting on something too," said Lucy. "Something hard." It turned out to be the remains of a mail-shirt. By this time everyone was on hands and knees, feeling in the thick heather in every direction. Their search revealed, one by one, a helmet, a dagger, and a few coins; not Calormen crescents but genuine Narnian "Lions" and "Trees" such as you might see any day in the market-place of Beaversdam or Beruna.

"Looks as if this might be all that's left of one of our seven lords," said Edmund.

"Just what I was thinking," said Caspian. "I wonder which it was. There's nothing on the dagger to show. And I wonder how he died."

"And how we are to avenge him," added Reepicheep.

Edmund, the only one of the party who had read several detective stories, had meanwhile been thinking.

"Look here," he said, "there's something very fishy about this. He can't have been killed in a fight."

"Why not?" asked Caspian.

"No bones," said Edmund. "An enemy might take the armour and leave the body. But who ever heard of a chap who'd won a fight carrying away the body and leaving the armour?"

"Perhaps he was killed by a wild animal," Lucy suggested.

"It'd be a clever animal," said Edmund, "that would take a man's mail shirt off."

"Perhaps a dragon?" said Caspian.

"Nothing doing," said Eustace. "A dragon couldn't do it. I ought to know."

"Well, let's get away from the place, anyway," said Lucy. She had not felt like sitting down again since Edmund had raised the question of bones.

"If you like," said Caspian, getting up. "I don't think any of this stuff is worth taking away."

They came down and round to the little opening where the stream came out of the lake, and stood looking at the deep water within the circle of cliffs. If it had been a hot day, no doubt some would have been tempted to bathe and everyone would have had a drink. Indeed, even as it was, Eustace was on the very point of stooping down and scooping up some water in his hands when Reepicheep and Lucy both at the same moment cried, "Look," so he forgot about his drink and looked.

The bottom of the pool was made of large greyish-blue stones and the water was perfectly clear, and on the bottom lay a life-size figure of a man, made apparently of gold. It lay face downwards with its arms stretched out above its head. And it so happened that as they looked at it, the clouds parted and the sun shone out. The golden shape was lit up from end to end. Lucy thought it was the most beautiful statue she had ever seen.

"Well!" whistled Caspian. "That was worth coming to see! I wonder, can we get it out?"

"We can dive for it, Sire," said Reepicheep.

"No good at all," said Edmund. "At least, if it's really gold – solid gold – it'll be far too heavy to bring up. And that pool's twelve or fifteen feet deep if it's an inch. Half a moment, though. It's a good thing I've brought a hunting spear with me. Let's see what the depth *is* like. Hold on to

my hand, Caspian, while I lean out over the water a bit." Caspian took his hand and Edmund, leaning forward, began to lower his spear into the water.

Before it was half-way in Lucy said, "I don't believe the statue is gold at all. It's only the light. Your spear looks just the same colour."

"What's wrong?" asked several voices at once; for Edmund had suddenly let go of the spear.

"I couldn't hold it," gasped Edmund, "it seemed so *heavy*."

"And there it is on the bottom now," said Caspian, "and Lucy is right. It looks just the same colour as the statue."

But Edmund, who appeared to be having some trouble with his boots – at least he was bending down and looking at them – straightened himself all at once and shouted out in the sharp voice which people hardly ever disobey:

"Get back! Back from the water. All of you. At once!!"

They all did and stared at him.

"Look," said Edmund, "look at the toes of my boots."

"They look a bit yellow," began Eustace.

"They're gold, solid gold," interrupted Edmund. "Look at them. Feel them. The leather's pulled away from it already. And they're as heavy as lead."

"By Aslan!" said Caspian. "You don't mean to say –?"

"Yes, I do," said Edmund. "That water turns things into gold. It turned the spear into gold, that's why it got so heavy. And it was just lapping against my feet (it's a good thing I wasn't barefoot) and it turned the toe-caps into gold. And that poor fellow on the bottom – well, you see."

"So it isn't a statue at all," said Lucy in a low voice.

"No. The whole thing is plain now. He was here on a hot day. He undressed on top of the cliff – where we were sitting. The clothes have rotted away or been taken by birds to line nests with; the armour's still there. Then he dived and –"

"Don't," said Lucy. "What a horrible thing."

"And what a narrow shave *we've* had," said Edmund.

"Narrow indeed," said Reepicheep. "Anyone's finger, anyone's foot, anyone's whisker, or anyone's tail, might have slipped into the water at any moment."

"All the same," said Caspian, "we may as well test it." He stooped down and wrenched up a spray of heather. Then, very cautiously, he knelt beside the pool and dipped it in. It was heather that he dipped; what he drew out was a perfect model of heather made of the purest gold, heavy and soft as lead.

"The King who owned this island," said Caspian slowly, and his face flushed as he spoke, "would soon be the richest of all the Kings of the world. I claim this land for ever as a Narnian possession. It shall be called Goldwater Island. And I bind all of you to secrecy. No one must know of this. Not even Drinian – on pain of death, do you hear?"

"Who are talking to?" said Edmund. "I'm no subject of yours. If anything it's the other way round. I am one of the four ancient sovereigns of Narnia and you are under allegiance to the High King my brother."

"So it has come to that, King Edmund, has it?" said Caspian, laying his hand on his sword-hilt.

"Oh, stop it, both of you," said Lucy. "That's the worst of doing anything with boys. You're all such swaggering, bullying idiots – oooh! –" Her voice died away into a gasp. And everyone else saw what she had seen.

Across the grey hillside above them – grey, for the heather was not yet in bloom – without noise, and without looking at them, and shining as if he were in bright sunlight though the sun had in fact gone in, passed with slow pace the hugest lion that human eyes have ever seen. In describing the scene Lucy said afterwards, "He was the size of an elephant," though at another time she only said, "The size of a cart-horse." But it was not the size that mattered. Nobody dared to ask what it was. They knew it was Aslan.

And nobody ever saw how or where he went. They looked at one another like people waking from sleep.

"What were we talking about?" said Caspian. "Have

I been making rather an ass of myself?"

"Sire," said Reepicheep, "this is a place with a curse on it. Let us get back on board at once. And if I might have the honour of naming this island, I should call it Deathwater."

"That strikes me as a very good name, Reep," said Caspian, "though now that I come to think of it, I don't know why. But the weather seems to be settling and I dare say Drinian would like to be off. What a lot we shall have to tell him."

But in fact they had not much to tell for the memory of the last hour had all become confused.

"Their Majesties all seemed a bit bewitched when they came aboard," said Drinian to Rhince some hours later when the *Dawn Treader* was once more under sail and Deathwater Island already below the horizon. "Something happened to them in that place. The only thing I could get clear was that they think they've found the body of one of these lords we're looking for."

"You don't say so, Captain," answered Rhince. "Well, that's three. Only four more. At this rate we might be home soon after the New Year. And a good thing too. My baccy's running a bit low. Good night, Sir."

CHAPTER NINE

THE ISLAND OF THE VOICES

AND now the winds which had so long been from the north-west began to blow from the west itself and every morning when the sun rose out of the sea the curved prow of the *Dawn Treader* stood up right across the middle of the sun. Some thought that the sun looked larger than it looked from Narnia, but others disagreed. And they sailed and sailed before a gentle yet steady breeze and saw neither fish nor gull nor ship nor shore. And stores began to get low again, and it crept into their hearts that perhaps they might have come to a sea which went on for ever. But when the very last day on which they thought they could risk continuing their eastward voyage dawned, it showed, right ahead between them and the sunrise, a low land lying like a cloud.

They made harbour in a wide bay about the middle of the afternoon and landed. It was a very different country from any they had yet seen. For when they had crossed the sandy beach they found all silent and empty as if it were an uninhabited land, but before them there were level lawns in which the grass was as smooth and short as it used to be in the grounds of a great English house where ten gardeners were kept. The trees, of which there were many, all stood well apart from one another, and there were no broken branches and no leaves lying on the ground. Pigeons sometimes cooed but there was no other noise.

Presently they came to a long, straight, sanded path with not a weed growing on it and trees on either hand. Far off at the other end of this avenue they now caught sight of a house – very long and grey and quiet-looking in the afternoon sun.

Almost as soon as they entered this path Lucy noticed that she had a little stone in her shoe. In that unknown place it might have been wiser for her to ask the others to wait while she took it out. But she didn't; she just dropped quietly behind and sat down to take off her shoe. Her lace had got into a knot.

Before she had undone the knot the others were a fair distance ahead. By the time she had got the stone out and was putting the shoe on again she could no longer hear

them. But almost at once she heard something else. It was not coming from the direction of the house.

What she heard was a thumping. It sounded as if dozens of strong workmen were hitting the ground as hard as they could with great wooden mallets. And it was very quickly coming nearer. She was already sitting with her back to a tree, and as the tree was not one she could climb, there was really nothing to do but to sit dead still and press herself against the tree and hope she wouldn't be seen.

Thump, thump, thump . . . and whatever it was must be very close now for she could feel the ground shaking. But she could see nothing. She thought the thing – or things – must be just behind her. But then there came a thump on the path right in front of her. She knew it was on the path not only by the sound but because she saw the sand scatter as if it had been struck a heavy blow. But she could see nothing that had struck it. Then all the thumping noises drew together about twenty feet away from her and suddenly ceased. Then came the Voice.

It was really very dreadful because she could still see nobody at all. The whole of that park-like country still looked as quiet and empty as it had looked when they first landed. Nevertheless, only a few feet away from her, a voice spoke. And what it said was:

"Mates, now's our chance."

Instantly a whole chorus of other voices replied, "Hear him. Hear him. 'Now's our chance', he said. Well done, Chief. You never said a truer word."

"What I say," continued the first voice, "is, get down to the shore between them and their boat, and let every mother's son look to his weapons. Catch 'em when they try to put to sea."

"Eh, that's the way," shouted all the other voices. "You never made a better plan, Chief. Keep it up, Chief. You couldn't have a better plan than that."

"Lively, then, mates, lively," said the first voice. "Off we go."

"Right again, Chief," said the others. "Couldn't have a better order. Just what we were going to say ourselves. Off we go."

Immediately the thumping began again – very loud at first but soon fainter and fainter, till it died out in the direction of the sea.

Lucy knew there was no time to sit puzzling as to what these invisible creatures might be. As soon as the thumping noise had died away she got up and ran along the path after the others as quickly as her legs would carry her. They must at all costs be warned.

While this had been happening the others had reached the house. It was a low building – only two stories high – made of a beautiful mellow stone, many-windowed, and partially covered with ivy. Everything was so still that

Eustace said, "I think it's empty," but Caspian silently pointed to the column of smoke which rose from one chimney.

They found a wide gateway open and passed through it into a paved courtyard. And it was here that they had their first indication that there was something odd about this island. In the middle of the courtyard stood a pump, and

beneath the pump a bucket. There was nothing odd about that. But the pump handle was moving up and down, though there seemed to be no one moving it.

"There's some magic at work here," said Caspian.

"Machinery!" said Eustace. "I do believe we've come to a civilized country at last."

At that moment Lucy, hot and breathless, rushed into the courtyard behind them. In a low voice she tried to make them understand what she had overheard. And when they had partly understood it even the bravest of them did not look very happy.

"Invisible enemies," muttered Caspian. "And cutting us

off from the boat. This is an ugly furrow to plough."

"You've no idea what *sort* of creatures they are, Lu?" asked Edmund.

"How can I, Ed, when I couldn't see them?"

"Did they sound like humans from their footsteps?"

"I didn't hear any noise of feet – only voices and this frightful thudding and thumping – like a mallet."

"I wonder," said Reepicheep, "do they become visible when you drive a sword into them?"

"It looks as if we shall find out," said Caspian. "But let's get out of this gateway. There's one of these gentry at that pump listening to all we say."

They came out and went back on to the path where the trees might possibly make them less conspicuous. "Not that it's any good *really*," said Eustace, "trying to hide from people you can't see. They may be all round us."

"Now, Drinian," said Caspian. "How would it be if we gave up the boat for lost, went down to another part of the bay, and signalled to the *Dawn Treader* to stand in and take us aboard?"

"Not depth for her, Sire," said Drinian.

"We could swim," said Lucy.

"Your Majesties all," said Reepicheep, "hear me. It is folly to think of avoiding an invisible enemy by any amount of creeping and skulking. If these creatures mean to bring us to battle, be sure they will succeed. And whatever comes of it I'd sooner meet them face to face than be caught by the tail."

"I really think Reep is in the right this time," said Edmund.

"Surely," said Lucy, "if Rhince and the others on the *Dawn Treader* see us fighting on the shore they'll be able to do *something*."

"But they won't see us fighting if they can't see any

enemy," said Eustace miserably. "They'll think we're just swinging our swords in the air for fun."

There was an uncomfortable pause.

"Well," said Caspian at last, "let's get on with it. We must go and face them. Shake hands all round – arrow on the string, Lucy – swords out, everyone else – and now for it. Perhaps they'll parley."

It was strange to see the lawns and the great trees looking so peaceful as they marched back to the beach. And when they arrived there, and saw the boat lying where they had left her, and the smooth sand with no one to be seen on it, more than one doubted whether Lucy had not merely imagined all she had told them. But before they reached the sand, a voice spoke out of the air.

"No further, masters, no further now," it said. "We've got to talk with you first. There's fifty of us and more here with weapons in our fists."

"Hear him, hear him," came the chorus. "That's our Chief. You can depend on what he says. He's telling you the truth, he is."

"I do not see these fifty warriors," observed Reepicheep.

"That's right, that's right," said the Chief Voice. "You don't see us. And why not? Because we're invisible."

"Keep it up, Chief, keep it up," said the Other Voices. "You're talking like a book. They couldn't ask for a better answer than that."

"Be quiet, Reep," said Caspian, and then added in a louder voice, "You invisible people, what do you want with us? And what have we done to earn your enmity?"

"We want something that little girl can do for us," said the Chief Voice. (The others explained that this was just what they would have said themselves.)

"Little girl!" said Reepicheep. "The lady is a queen."

"We don't know about queens," said the Chief Voice.

("No more we do, no more we do," chimed in the others.) "But we want something she can do."

"What is it?" said Lucy.

"And if it is anything against her Majesty's honour or safety," added Reepicheep, "you will wonder to see how many we can kill before we die."

"Well," said the Chief Voice. "It's a long story. Suppose we all sit down?"

The proposal was warmly approved by the other voices but the Narnians remained standing.

"Well," said the Chief Voice. "It's like this. This island has been the property of a great magician time out of mind. And we all are – or perhaps in a manner of speaking, I might say, we were – his servants. Well, to cut a long story short, this magician that I was speaking about, he told us to do something we didn't like. And why not? Because we didn't want to. Well, then, this same magician he fell into a great rage; for I ought to tell you he owned the island and he wasn't used to being crossed. He was terribly downright, you know. But let me see, where am I? Oh yes, this magician then, he goes upstairs (for you must know he kept all his magic things up there and we all lived down below), I say he goes upstairs and puts a spell on us. An uglifying spell. If you saw us now, which in my opinion you may thank your stars you can't, you wouldn't believe what we looked like before we were uglified. You wouldn't really. So there we all were so ugly we couldn't bear to look at one another. So then what did we do? Well, I'll tell you what we did. We waited till we thought this same magician would be asleep in the afternoon and we creep upstairs and go to his magic book, as bold as brass, to see if we can do anything about this uglification. But we were all of a sweat and a tremble, so I won't deceive you. But, believe me or believe me not, I do assure you that we couldn't find anything in the way of a spell for taking off the ugliness. And what with time getting on and being afraid that the old gentleman might wake up any minute – I was all of a muck sweat, so I won't deceive you – well, to cut a long story short, whether we did right or whether we did wrong, in the end we see a spell for making people invisible. And we thought we'd rather be invisible than go on being as ugly as all that. And why? Because we'd like it better. So my little girl, who's just about your little girl's age, and a sweet child she was before she was uglified, though now – but least said soonest mended – I say, my little girl she says the spell, for it's got to be a little girl or else the magician himself, if you see my meaning, for otherwise it won't work. And why not? Because nothing happens. So my Clipsie says the spell, for I ought to have told you she reads beautifully, and there we all were as invisible as you could wish to see. And I do assure you it was a relief not to see one another's faces. At first, anyway. But the long and the short of it is we're mortal tired of being invisible. And there's another thing. We never reckoned on this magician (the one I was telling you about before) going invisible too. But we haven't ever seen him since. So we don't know if he's dead, or gone away, or whether he's just sitting upstairs being invisible, and perhaps coming down and being invisible there. And, believe me, it's no manner of use listening because he always did go about with his bare feet on, making no more noise than a great big cat. And I'll tell all you gentlemen straight, it's getting more than what our nerves can stand."

Such was the Chief Voice's story, but very much shortened, because I have left out what the Other Voices said. Actually he never got out more than six or seven words without being interrupted by their agreements and encouragements, which drove the Narnians nearly out of their minds with impatience. When it was over there was a very long silence.

"But," said Lucy at last, "what's all this got to do with us? I don't understand."

"Why, bless me, if I haven't gone and left out the whole point," said the Chief Voice.

"That you have, that you have," roared the Other Voices with great enthusiasm. "No one couldn't have left it out cleaner and better. Keep it up, Chief, keep it up."

"Well, I needn't go over the whole story again," began the Chief Voice.

"No. Certainly not," said Caspian and Edmund.

"Well, then, to put it in a nutshell," said the Chief Voice, "we've been waiting for ever so long for a nice little girl from foreign parts, like it might be you, Missie – that would go upstairs and go to the magic book and find the spell that takes off the invisibleness, and say it. And we all swore that the first strangers as landed on this island (having a nice little girl with them, I mean, for if they hadn't it'd be another matter) we wouldn't let them go away alive unless they'd done the needful for us. And that's why, gentlemen, if your little girl doesn't come up to scratch, it will be our painful duty to cut all your throats. Merely in the way of business, as you might say, and no offence, I hope."

"I don't see all your weapons," said Reepicheep. "Are they invisible too?" The words were scarcely out of his mouth before they heard a whizzing sound and next moment a spear had stuck, quivering, in one of the trees behind them.

"That's a spear, that is," said the Chief Voice.

"That it is, Chief, that it is," said the others. "You couldn't have put it better."

"And it came from my hand," the Chief Voice continued. "They get visible when they leave us."

"But why do you want *me* to do this?" asked Lucy.

"Why can't one of your own people? Haven't you got any girls?"

"We dursen't, we dursen't," said all the Voices. "We're not going upstairs again."

"In other words," said Caspian, "you are asking this lady to face some danger which you daren't ask your own sisters and daughters to face!"

"That's right, that's right," said all the Voices cheerfully. "You couldn't have said it better. Eh, you've had some education, you have. Anyone can see that."

"Well, of all the outrageous – " began Edmund, but Lucy interrupted.

"Would I have to go upstairs at night, or would it do in daylight?"

"Oh, daylight, daylight, to be sure," said the Chief Voice. "Not at night. No one's asking you to do that. Go upstairs in the dark? Ugh."

"All right, then, I'll do it," said Lucy. "No," she said, turning to the others, "don't try to stop me. Can't you see it's no use? There are dozens of them there. We can't fight them. And the other way there *is* a chance."

"But a magician!" said Caspian.

"I know," said Lucy. "But he mayn't be as bad as they make out. Don't you get the idea that these people are not very brave?"

"They're certainly not very clever," said Eustace.

"Look here, Lu," said Edmund. "We really can't let you do a thing like this. Ask Reep, I'm sure he'll say just the same."

"But it's to save my own life as well as yours," said Lucy. "I don't want to be cut to bits with invisible swords any more than anyone else."

"Her Majesty is in the right," said Reepicheep. "If we had any assurance of saving *her* by battle, our duty would be very plain. It appears to me that we have none. And the service they ask of her is in no way contrary to her Majesty's honour, but a noble and heroical act. If the Queen's heart moves her to risk the magician, I will not speak against it."

As no one had ever known Reepicheep to be afraid of anything, he could say this without feeling at all awkward. But the boys, who had all been afraid quite often, grew very red. None the less, it was such obvious sense that they had to give in. Loud cheers broke from the invisible people when their decision was announced, and the Chief Voice (warmly supported by all the others) invited the Narnians to come to supper and spend the night. Eustace didn't want to accept, but Lucy said, "I'm sure they're not treacherous. They're not like that at all," and the others agreed. And so, accompanied by an enormous noise of thumpings (which became louder when they reached the flagged and echoing courtyard) they all went back to the house.

CHAPTER TEN

THE MAGICIAN'S BOOK

THE invisible people feasted their guests royally. It was very funny to see the plates and dishes coming to the table and not to see anyone carrying them. It would have been funny even if they had moved along level with the floor, as you would expect things to do in invisible hands. But they didn't. They progressed up the long dining-hall in a series of bounds or jumps. At the highest point of each jump a dish would be about fifteen feet up in the air; then it would come down and stop quite suddenly about three feet from the floor. When the dish contained anything like soup or stew the result was rather disastrous.

"I'm beginning to feel very inquisitive about these people," whispered Eustace to Edmund. "Do you think they're human at all? More like huge grasshoppers or giant frogs, I should say."

"It does look like it," said Edmund. "But don't put the idea of the grasshoppers into Lucy's head. She's not too keen on insects; especially big ones."

The meal would have been pleasanter if it had not been so exceedingly messy, and also if the conversation had not consisted entirely of agreements. The invisible people agreed about everything. Indeed most of their remarks were the sort it would not be easy to disagree with: "What I always say is, when a chap's hungry, he likes some victuals," or "Getting dark now; always does at night," or even "Ah, you've come over the water. Powerful wet stuff, ain't it?" And Lucy could not help looking at the dark yawning entrance to the foot of the staircase – she could see it from where she sat – and wondering what she would find when she went up those stairs next morning. But it was a good meal otherwise, with mushroom soup and boiled chickens and hot boiled ham and gooseberries, redcurrants, curds, cream, milk, and mead. The others liked the mead but Eustace was sorry afterwards that he had drunk any.

When Lucy woke up next morning it was like waking up on the day of an examination or a day when you are going to the dentist. It was a lovely morning with bees buzzing in and out of her open window and the lawn outside looking very like somewhere in England. She got up and dressed and tried to talk and eat ordinarily at breakfast. Then, after being instructed by the Chief Voice about what she was to do upstairs, she bid goodbye to the others, said nothing, walked to the bottom of the stairs, and began going up them without once looking back.

It was quite light, that was one good thing. There was, indeed, a window straight ahead of her at the top of the first flight. As long as she was on that flight she could hear the *tick-tock-tick-tock* of a grandfather clock in the hall below. Then she came to the landing and had to turn to her left up the next flight; after that she couldn't hear the clock any more.

Now she had come to the top of the stairs. Lucy looked and saw a long, wide passage with a large window at the far end. Apparently the passage ran the whole length of the house. It was carved and panelled and carpeted and very many doors opened off it on each side. She stood still and couldn't hear the squeak of a mouse, or the buzzing of a fly, or the swaying of a curtain, or anything – except the beating of her own heart.

"The last doorway on the left," she said to herself. It did seem a bit hard that it should be the last. To reach it she would have to walk past room after room. And in any room there might be the magician – asleep, or awake, or invisible, or even dead. But it wouldn't do to think about that. She set out on her journey. The carpet was so thick that her feet made no noise.

"There's nothing whatever to be afraid of yet," Lucy told herself. And certainly it was a quiet, sunlit passage; perhaps a bit too quiet. It would have been nicer if there had not been strange signs painted in scarlet on the doors – twisty, complicated things which obviously had a meaning and it mightn't be a very nice meaning either. It would have been nicer still if there weren't those masks hanging on the wall. Not that they were exactly ugly – or not so very ugly – but the empty eye-holes did look queer, and if you let yourself you would soon start imagining that the masks were

doing things as soon as your back was turned to them.

After about the sixth door she got her first real fright. For one second she felt almost certain that a wicked little bearded face had popped out of the wall and made a grimace at her. She forced herself to stop and look at it. And it was not a face at all. It was a little mirror just the size and shape of her own face, with hair on the top of it and a beard hanging down from it, so that when you looked in the mirror your own face fitted into the hair and beard and it looked as if they belonged to you. "I just caught my own reflection with the tail of my eye as I went past," said Lucy to herself. "That was all it was. It's quite harmless." But she didn't like the look of her own face with that hair and beard, and went on. (I don't know what the Bearded Glass was for because I am not a magician.)

Before she reached the last door on the left, Lucy was beginning to wonder whether the corridor had grown longer since she began her journey and whether this was part of the magic of the house. But she got to it at last. And the door was open.

It was a large room with three big windows and it was lined from floor to ceiling with books; more books than Lucy had ever seen before, tiny little books, fat and dumpy books, and books bigger than any church Bible you have ever seen, all bound in leather and smelling old and learned and magical. But she knew from her instructions that she need not bother about any of these. For *the* Book, the Magic Book, was lying on a reading-desk in the very middle of the room. She saw she would have to read it standing (and anyway there were no chairs) and also that she would have to stand with her back to the door while she read it. So at once she turned to shut the door.

It wouldn't shut.

Some people may disagree with Lucy about this, but I

think she was quite right. She said she wouldn't have minded if she could have shut the door, but that it was unpleasant to have to stand in a place like that with an open doorway right behind your back. I should have felt just the same. But there was nothing else to be done.

One thing that worried her a good deal was the size of the Book. The Chief Voice had not been able to give her any idea whereabouts in the Book the spell for making things visible came. He even seemed rather surprised at her asking. He expected her to begin at the beginning and go on till she came to it; obviously he had never thought that there was any other way of finding a place in a book. "But it might take me days and weeks!" said Lucy, looking at the huge volume, "and I feel already as if I'd been in this place for hours."

She went up to the desk and laid her hand on the book; her fingers tingled when she touched it as if it were full of electricity. She tried to open it but couldn't at first; this, however, was only because it was fastened by two leaden clasps, and when she had undone these it opened easily enough. And what a book it was!

It was written, not printed; written in a clear, even hand, with thick downstrokes and thin upstrokes, very large, easier than print, and so beautiful that Lucy stared at it for a whole minute and forgot about reading it. The paper was crisp and smooth and a nice smell came from it; and in the margins, and round the big coloured capital letters at the beginning of each spell, there were pictures.

There was no title page or title; the spells began straight away, and at first there was nothing very important in them. They were cures for warts (by washing your hands in moonlight in a silver basin) and toothache and cramp, and a spell for taking a swarm of bees. The picture of the man with toothache was so lifelike that it would have set your

Cure for warts: wash in a silver basin by moonlight.

own teeth aching if you looked at it too long, and the golden bees which were dotted all round the fourth spell looked for a moment as if they were really flying.

Lucy could hardly tear herself away from that first page, but when she turned over, the next was just as interesting. "But I must get on," she told herself. And on she went for about thirty pages which, if she could have remembered them, would have taught her how to find buried treasure, how to remember things forgotten, how to forget things you wanted to forget, how to tell whether anyone was speaking the truth, how to call up (or prevent) wind, fog, snow, sleet or rain, how to produce enchanted sleeps and how to give a man an ass's head (as they did to poor Bottom). And the longer she read the more wonderful and more real the pictures became.

Then she came to a page which was such a blaze of pictures that one hardly noticed the writing. Hardly – but she *did* notice the first words. They were, *An infallible spell to make beautiful her that uttereth it beyond the lot of mortals.* Lucy peered at the pictures with her face close to the page, and though they had seemed crowded and muddlesome before, she found she could now see them quite clearly. The first was a picture of a girl standing at a reading-desk reading in a huge book. And the girl was dressed exactly like Lucy. In the next picture Lucy (for the girl in the picture was Lucy herself) was standing up with her mouth open and a rather terrible expression on her face, chanting or reciting something. In the third picture the beauty beyond the lot of mortals had come to her. It was strange, considering how small the pictures had looked at first, that the Lucy in the picture now seemed quite as big as the real Lucy; and they looked into each other's eyes and the real Lucy looked away after a few minutes because she was dazzled by the beauty of the other Lucy; though she could still see a sort of likeness to herself in that beautiful face. And now the pictures came crowding on her thick and fast. She saw herself throned on high at a great tournament in Calormen and all the Kings of the world fought because of her beauty. After that it turned from tournaments to real wars, and all Narnia and Archenland, Telmar and Calormen, Galma and Terebinthia, were laid waste with the fury of the kings and dukes and great lords who fought for her favour. Then it changed and Lucy, still beautiful beyond the lot of mortals, was back in England. And Susan (who had always been the beauty of the family) came home from America. The Susan in the picture looked exactly like the real Susan only plainer and with a nasty expression. And Susan was jealous of the dazzling beauty of Lucy, but that didn't matter a bit because no one cared anything about Susan now.

"I *will* say the spell," said Lucy. "I don't care. I will."

She said *I don't care* because she had a strong feeling that she mustn't.

But when she looked back at the opening words of the spell, there in the middle of the writing, where she felt quite sure there had been no picture before, she found the great face of a lion, of The Lion, Aslan himself, staring into hers. It was painted such a bright gold that it seemed to be coming towards her out of the page; and indeed she never was quite sure afterwards that it hadn't really moved a little. At any rate she knew the expression on his face quite well. He was growling and you could see most of his teeth. She became horribly afraid and turned over the page at once.

A little later she came to a spell which would let you know what your friends thought about you. Now Lucy had wanted very badly to try the other spell, the one that made you beautiful beyond the lot of mortals. So she felt that to make up for not having said it, she really would say this one. And all in a hurry, for fear her mind would change, she said the words (nothing will induce me to tell you what they were). Then she waited for something to happen.

As nothing happened she began looking at the pictures. And all at once she saw the very last thing she expected – a picture of a third-class carriage in a train, with two schoolgirls sitting in it. She knew them at once. They were Marjorie Preston and Anne Featherstone. Only now it was much more than a picture. It was alive. She could see the telegraph posts flicking past outside the window. Then gradually (like when the radio is "coming on") she could hear what they were saying.

"Shall I see anything of you this term?" said Anne, "or are you still going to be all taken up with Lucy Pevensie."

"Don't know what you mean by *taken up*," said Marjorie.

"Oh yes, you do," said Anne. "You were crazy about her last term."

"No, I wasn't," said Marjorie. "I've got more sense than that. Not a bad little kid in her way. But I was getting pretty tired of her before the end of term."

"Well, you jolly well won't have the chance any other term!" shouted Lucy. "Two-faced little beast." But the sound of her own voice at once reminded her that she was talking to a picture and that the real Marjorie was far away in another world.

"Well," said Lucy to herself, "I did think better of her than that. And I did all sorts of things for her last term, and I stuck to her when not many other girls would. And she knows it too. And to Anne Featherstone of all people! I wonder are all my friends the same? There are lots of other pictures. No. I won't look at any more. I won't, I won't' — and with a great effort she turned over the page, but not before a large, angry tear had splashed on it.

On the next page she came to a spell "for the refreshment of the spirit'. The pictures were fewer here but very beautiful. And what Lucy found herself reading was more like a story than a spell. It went on for three pages and before she had read to the bottom of the page she had forgotten that she was reading at all. She was living in the story as if it were real, and all the pictures were real too. When she had got to the third page and come to the end, she said, "That is the loveliest story I've ever read or ever shall read in my whole life. Oh, I wish I could have gone on reading it for ten years. At least I'll read it over again."

But here part of the magic of the Book came into play. You couldn't turn back. The right-hand pages, the ones ahead, could be turned; the left-hand pages could not.

"Oh, what a shame!" said Lucy. "I did so want to read it again. Well, at least I must remember it. Let's see . . . it was about ... about ... oh dear, it's all fading away again. And even this last page is going blank. This is a very queer book. How can I have forgotten? It was about a cup and a sword and a tree and a green hill, I know that much. But I can't remember and what *shall* I do?"

And she never could remember; and ever since that day what Lucy means by a good story is a story which reminds her of the forgotten story in the Magician's Book.

She turned on and found to her surprise a page with no pictures at all; but the first words were *A Spell to make hidden things visible*. She read it through to make sure of all the hard words and then said it out loud. And she knew at once that it was working because as she spoke the colours came into the capital letters at the top of the page and the pictures began appearing in the margins. It was like when you hold to the fire something written in Invisible Ink and the writing gradually shows up; only instead of the dingy colour of lemon juice (which is the easiest Invisible Ink) this was all gold and blue and scarlet. They were odd pictures and contained many figures that Lucy did not much like the look of. And then she thought, "I suppose I've made everything visible, and not only the Thumpers. There might be lots of other invisible things hanging about a place like this. I'm not sure that I want to see them all."

At that moment she heard soft, heavy footfalls coming along the corridor behind her; and of course she remembered what she had been told about the Magician walking in his bare feet and making no more noise than a cat. It is always better to turn round than to have anything creeping up behind your back. Lucy did so.

Then her face lit up till, for a moment (but of course she didn't know it), she looked almost as beautiful as that other Lucy in the picture, and she ran forward with a little cry of delight and with her arms stretched out. For what stood in the doorway was Aslan himself, The Lion, the highest of all High Kings. And he was solid and real and warm and he let her kiss him and bury herself in his shining mane. And from the low, earthquake-like sound that came from inside him, Lucy even dared to think that he was purring.

"Oh, Aslan," said she, "it was kind of you to come."

"I have been here all the time," said he, "but you have just made me visible."

"Aslan!" said Lucy almost a little reproachfully. "Don't make fun of me. As if anything *I* could do would make *you* visible!"

"It did," said Aslan. "Do you think I wouldn't obey my own rules?"

After a little pause he spoke again.

"Child," he said, "I think you have been eaves-dropping."

"Eavesdropping?"

"You listened to what your two schoolfellows were saying about you."

"Oh that? I never thought that was eavesdropping, Aslan. Wasn't it magic?"

"Spying on people by magic is the same as spying on them in any other way. And you have misjudged your friend. She is weak, but she loves you. She was afraid of the older girl and said what she does not mean."

"I don't think I'd ever be able to forget what I heard her say."

"No, you won't."

"Oh dear," said Lucy. "Have I spoiled everything? Do you mean we would have gone on being friends if it hadn't been for this – and been really great friends – all our lives perhaps – and now we never shall."

"Child," said Aslan, "did I not explain to you once

before that no one is ever told what *would have happened?*"

"Yes, Aslan, you did," said Lucy. "I'm sorry. But please —"

"Speak on, dear heart."

"Shall I ever be able to read that story again; the one I couldn't remember? Will you tell it to me, Aslan? Oh do, do, do."

"Indeed, yes, I will tell it to you for years and years. But now, come. We must meet the master of this house."

CHAPTER ELEVEN

THE DUFFLEPUDS MADE HAPPY

LUCY followed the great Lion out into the passage and at once she saw coming towards them an old man, barefoot, dressed in a red robe. His white hair was crowned with a chaplet of oak leaves, his beard fell to his girdle, and he supported himself with a curiously carved staff. When he saw Aslan he bowed low and said,

"Welcome, Sir, to the least of your houses."

"Do you grow weary, Coriakin, of ruling such foolish subjects as I have given you here?"

"No," said the Magician, "they are very stupid but there is no real harm in them. I begin to grow rather fond of the creatures. Sometimes, perhaps, I am a little impatient, waiting for the day when they can be governed by wisdom instead of this rough magic."

"All in good time, Coriakin," said Aslan.

"Yes, all in very good time, Sir," was the answer. "Do you intend to show yourself to them?"

"Nay," said the Lion, with a little half-growl that meant (Lucy thought) the same as a laugh. "I should frighten them out of their senses. Many stars will grow old and come to take their rest in islands before your people are ripe for that. And today before sunset I must visit Trumpkin the Dwarf where he sits in the castle of Cair Paravel counting the days till his master Caspian comes home. I will tell him all your story, Lucy. Do not look so sad. We shall meet soon again."

"Please, Aslan," said Lucy, "what do you call *soon*?"

"I call all times soon," said Aslan; and instantly he was vanished away and Lucy was alone with the Magician.

"Gone!" said he, "and you and I quite crestfallen. It's always like that, you can't keep him; it's not as if he were a *tame* lion. And how did you enjoy my book?"

"Parts of it very much indeed," said Lucy. "Did you know I was there all the time?"

"Well, of course I knew when I let the Duffers make themselves invisible that you would be coming along presently to take the spell off. I wasn't quite sure of the exact day. And I wasn't especially on the watch this morning. You see they had made me invisible too and being invisible always makes me so sleepy. Heigh-ho – there I'm yawning again. Are you hungry?"

"Well, perhaps I am a little," said Lucy. "I've no idea what the time is."

"Come," said the Magician. "All times may be soon to Aslan; but in my home all hungry times are one o'clock."

He led her a little way down the passage and opened a door. Passing in, Lucy found herself in a pleasant room full of sunlight and flowers. The table was bare when they entered, but it was of course a magic table, and at a word from the old man the tablecloth, silver, plates, glasses and food appeared.

"I hope that is what you would like," said he. "I have tried to give you food more like the food of your own land than perhaps you have had lately."

"It's lovely," said Lucy, and so it was; an omelette, piping hot, cold lamb and green peas, a strawberry ice, lemon-squash to drink with the meal and a cup of chocolate to follow. But the magician himself drank only wine and ate only bread. There was nothing alarming about him, and Lucy and he were soon chatting away like old friends.

"When will the spell work?" asked Lucy. "Will the Duffers be visible again at once?"

"Oh yes, they're visible now. But they're probably all asleep still; they always take a rest in the middle of the day."

"And now that they're visible, are you going to let them off being ugly? Will you make them as they were before?"

"Well, that's rather a delicate question," said the Magician. "You see, it's only *they* who think they were so nice to look at before. They say they've been uglified, but that isn't what I called it. Many people might say the change was for the better."

"Are they awfully conceited?"

"They are. Or at least the Chief Duffer is, and he's taught all the rest to be. They always believe every word he says."

"We'd noticed that," said Lucy.

"Yes — we'd get on better without him, in a way. Of course I could turn him into something else, or even put a spell on him which would make them not believe a word he said. But I don't like to do that. It's better for them to admire him than to admire nobody."

"Don't they admire *you*?" asked Lucy.

"Oh, not *me*," said the Magician. "They wouldn't admire *me*."

"What was it you uglified them for – I mean, what they call *uglified*?"

"Well, they wouldn't do what they were told. Their work is to mind the garden and raise food – not for me, as they imagine, but for themselves. They wouldn't do it at all if I didn't make them. And of course for a garden you want water. There is a beautiful spring about half a mile away up the hill. And from that spring there flows a stream which comes right past the garden. All I asked them to do was to take their water from the stream instead of trudging up to the spring with their buckets two or three times a day and tiring themselves out besides spilling half of it on the way back. But they wouldn't see it. In the end they refused point blank."

"Are they as stupid as all that?" asked Lucy.

The Magician sighed. "You wouldn't believe the troubles I've had with them. A few months ago they were all for washing up the plates and knives before dinner: they said it saved time afterwards. I've caught them planting boiled potatoes to save cooking them when they were dug up. One day the cat got into the dairy and twenty of them were at work moving all the milk out; no one thought of moving the cat. But I see you've finished. Let's go and look at the Duffers now they can be looked at."

They went into another room which was full of polished instruments hard to understand – such as Astrolabes, Orreries, Chronoscopes, Poesimeters, Choriambuses and Theodolinds – and here, when they had come to the window, the Magician said, "There. There are your Duffers."

"I don't see anybody," said Lucy. "And what are those mushroom things?"

The things she pointed at were dotted all over the level grass. They were certainly very like mushrooms, but far too big – the stalks about three feet high and the umbrellas about the same length from edge to edge. When she looked carefully she noticed too that the stalks joined the umbrellas not in the middle but at one side which gave an unbalanced look to them. And there was something – a sort of little bundle – lying on the grass at the foot of each stalk. In fact the longer she gazed at them the less like mushrooms they appeared. The umbrella part was not

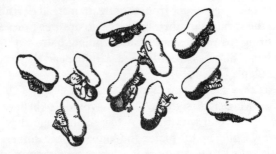

really round as she had thought at first. It was longer than it was broad, and it widened at one end. There were a great many of them, fifty or more.

The clock struck three.

Instantly a most extraordinary thing happened. Each of the "mushrooms" suddenly turned upside-down. The little bundles which had lain at the bottom of the stalks were heads and bodies. The stalks themselves were legs. But not two legs to each body. Each body had a single thick leg right under it (not to one side like the leg of a one-legged man) and at the end of it, a single enormous foot – a broad-toed foot with the toes curling up a little so that it looked rather like a small canoe. She saw in a moment why they had looked like mushrooms. They had been lying flat on their backs each with its single leg straight up in the air and

its enormous foot spread out above it. She learned afterwards that this was their ordinary way of resting; for the
foot kept off both rain and sun and for a Monopod to lie
under its own foot is almost as good as being in a tent.

"Oh, the funnies, the funnies," cried Lucy, bursting into
laughter. "Did *you* make them like that?"

"Yes, yes. I made the Duffers into Monopods," said the

Magician. He too was laughing till the tears ran down his
cheeks. "But watch," he added.

It was worth watching. Of course these little one-footed
men couldn't walk or run as we do. They got about by
jumping, like fleas or frogs. And what jumps they made! —
as if each big foot were a mass of springs. And with what a
bounce they came down; that was what made the thumping noise which had so puzzled Lucy yesterday. For now
they were jumping in all directions and calling out to one
another, "Hey, lads! We're visible again."

"Visible we are," said one in a tasselled red cap who was

obviously the Chief Monopod. "And what I say is, when chaps are visible, why, they can see one another."

"Ah, there it is, there it is, Chief," cried all the others. "There's the point. No one's got a clearer head than you. You couldn't have made it plainer."

"She caught the old man napping, that little girl did," said the Chief Monopod. "We've beaten him this time."

"Just what we were going to say ourselves," chimed the chorus. "You're going stronger than ever today, Chief. Keep it up, keep it up."

"But do they dare to talk about you like that?" said Lucy. "They seemed to be so afraid of you yesterday. Don't they know you might be listening?"

"That's one of the funny things about the Duffers," said the Magician. "One minute they talk as if I ran everything and overheard everything and was extremely dangerous. The next moment they think they can take me in by tricks that a baby would see through – bless them!"

"Will they have to be turned back into their proper shapes?" asked Lucy. "Oh, I do hope it wouldn't be unkind to leave them as they are. Do they really mind very much? They seem pretty happy. I say – look at that jump. What were they like before?"

"Common little dwarfs," said he. "Nothing like so nice as the sort you have in Narnia."

"It *would* be a pity to change them back," said Lucy. "They're so funny: and they're rather nice. Do you think it would make any difference if I told them that?"

"I'm sure it would – if you could get it into their heads."

"Will you come with me and try?"

"No, no. You'll get on far better without me."

"Thanks awfully for the lunch," said Lucy and turned quickly away. She ran down the stairs which she had come up so nervously that morning and cannoned into Edmund at the bottom. All the others were there with him waiting, and Lucy's conscience smote her when she saw their anxious faces and realized how long she had forgotten them.

"It's all right," she shouted. "Everything's all right. The Magician's a brick – and I've seen *Him* – Aslan."

After that she went from them like the wind and out into the garden. Here the earth was shaking with the jumps and the air ringing with the shouts of the Monopods. Both were redoubled when they caught sight of her.

"Here she comes, here she comes," they cried. "Three cheers for the little girl. Ah! She put it across the old gentleman properly, she did."

"And we're extremely regrettable," said the Chief Monopod, "that we can't give you the pleasure of seeing us as we were before we were uglified, for you wouldn't believe the difference, and that's the truth, for there's no denying we're mortal ugly now, so we won't deceive you."

"Eh, that we are, Chief, that we are," echoed the others, bouncing like so many toy balloons. "You've said it, you've said it."

"But I don't think you are at all," said Lucy, shouting to make herself heard. "I think you look very nice."

"Hear her, hear her," said the Monopods. "True for you, Missie. Very nice we look. You couldn't find a handsomer lot." They said this without any surprise and did not seem to notice that they had changed their minds.

"She's a-saying," remarked the Chief Monopod, "as how we looked very nice before we were uglified."

"True for you, Chief, true for you," chanted the others. "That's what she says. We heard her ourselves."

"I did *not*," bawled Lucy. "I said you're very nice *now*."

"So she did, so she did," said the Chief Monopod, "said we were very nice then."

"Hear 'em both, hear 'em both," said the Monopods. "There's a pair for you. Always right. They couldn't have put it better."

"But we're saying just the opposite," said Lucy, stamping her foot with impatience.

"So you are, to be sure, so you are," said the Monopods. "Nothing like an opposite. Keep it up, both of you."

"You're enough to drive anyone mad," said Lucy, and gave it up. But the Monopods seemed perfectly contented, and she decided that on the whole the conversation had been a success.

And before everyone went to bed that evening something else happened which made them even more satisfied with their one-legged condition. Caspian and all the Narnians went back as soon as possible to the shore to give their news to Rhince and the others on board the *Dawn Treader*, who were by now very anxious. And, of course, the Monopods went with them, bouncing like footballs and agreeing with one another in loud voices till Eustace said, "I wish the Magician would make them inaudible instead of invisible." (He was soon sorry he had spoken because then he had to explain that an inaudible thing is something you can't hear, and though he took a lot of trouble he never felt sure that the Monopods had really understood, and what especially annoyed him was that they said in the end, "Eh, he can't put things the way our Chief does. But you'll learn, young man. Hark to *him*. He'll show you how to say things. There's a speaker for you!") When they reached the bay, Reepicheep had a brilliant idea. He had his little coracle lowered and paddled himself about in it till the Monopods were thoroughly interested. He then stood up in it and said, "Worthy and intelligent Monopods, you do not need boats. Each of you has a foot that will do instead. Just jump as lightly as you can on the water and see what happens."

The Chief Monopod hung back and warned the others that they'd find the water powerful wet, but one or two of the younger ones tried it almost at once; and then a few others followed their example, and at last the whole lot did the same. It worked perfectly. The huge single foot of a Monopod acted as a natural raft or boat, and when Reepicheep had taught them how to cut rude paddles for themselves, they all paddled about the bay and round the *Dawn Treader*, looking for all the world like a fleet of little canoes with a fat dwarf standing up in the extreme stern of each. And they had races, and bottles of wine were lowered down to them from the ship as prizes, and the sailors stood leaning over the ship's sides and laughed till their own sides ached.

The Duffers were also very pleased with their new name of Monopods, which seemed to them a magnificent name though they never got it right. "That's what we are," they bellowed, "Moneypuds, Pomonods, Poddymons. Just what it was on the tips of our tongues to call ourselves." But they soon got it mixed up with their old name of Duffers and finally settled down to calling themselves the Dufflepuds; and that is what they will probably be called for centuries.

That evening all the Narnians dined upstairs with the Magician, and Lucy noticed how different the whole top floor looked now that she was no longer afraid of it. The mysterious signs on the doors were still mysterious but now looked as if they had kind and cheerful meanings, and even the bearded mirror now seemed funny rather than frightening. At dinner everyone had by magic what everyone liked best to eat and drink, and after dinner the Magician did a very useful and beautiful piece of magic. He laid two blank sheets of parchment on the table and asked Drinian to give him an exact account of their voyage up to date: and as Drinian spoke, everything he described came out on the parchment in fine clear lines till at last each sheet was a splendid map of the Eastern Ocean, showing Galma, Terebinthia, the Seven Isles, the Lone Islands, Dragon Island, Burnt Island, Deathwater, and the land of the Duffers itself, all exactly the right sizes and in the right positions. They were the first maps ever made of those seas and better than any that have been made since without magic. For on these, though the towns and mountains looked at first just as they would on an ordinary map, when the Magician lent them a magnifying glass you saw that they were perfect little pictures of the real things, so that you could see the very castle and slave market and streets in Narrowhaven, all very clear though very distant, like things seen through the wrong end of a telescope. The only drawback was that the coastline of most of the islands was incomplete, for the map showed only what Drinian had seen with his own eyes. When they were finished the Magician kept one himself and presented the other to Caspian: it still hangs in his Chamber of Instruments at Cair Paravel. But the Magician could tell them nothing about seas or lands further east. He did, however, tell them that about seven years before a Narnian ship had put in at his waters and that she had on board the lords Revilian, Argoz, Mavramorn and Rhoop: so they judged that the golden man they had seen lying in Deathwater must be the Lord Restimar.

Next day, the Magician magically mended the stern of the *Dawn Treader* where it had been damaged by the Sea Serpent and loaded her with useful gifts. There was a most friendly parting, and when she sailed, two hours after noon, all the Dufflepuds paddled out with her to the harbour mouth, and cheered until she was out of sound of their cheering.

CHAPTER TWELVE

THE DARK ISLAND

AFTER this adventure they sailed on south and a little east for twelve days with a gentle wind, the skies being mostly clear and the air warm, and saw no bird or fish, except that once there were whales spouting a long way to starboard. Lucy and Reepicheep played a good deal of chess at this time. Then on the thirteenth day, Edmund, from the fighting top, sighted what looked like a great dark mountain rising out of the sea on their port bow.

They altered course and made for this land, mostly by oar, for the wind would not serve them to sail north-east. When evening fell they were still a long way from it and rowed all night. Next morning the weather was fair but a flat calm. The dark mass lay ahead, much nearer and larger, but still very dim, so that some thought it was still a long way off and others thought they were running into a mist.

About nine that morning, very suddenly, it was so close that they could see that it was not land at all, nor even, in an ordinary sense, a mist. It was a Darkness. It is rather hard to describe, but you will see what it was like if you imagine yourself looking into the mouth of a railway tunnel – a tunnel either so long or so twisty that you cannot see the light at the far end. And you know what it would be like. For a few feet you would see the rails and sleepers and gravel in broad daylight; then there would

come a place where they were in twilight; and then, pretty suddenly, but of course without a sharp dividing line, they would vanish altogether into smooth, solid blackness. It was just so here. For a few feet in front of their bows they

could see the swell of the bright greenish-blue water.
Beyond that, they could see the water looking pale and
grey as it would look late in the evening. But beyond that
again, utter blackness as if they had come to the edge of
moonless and starless night.

Caspian shouted to the boatswain to keep her back, and
all except the rowers rushed forward and gazed from the
bows. But there was nothing to be seen by gazing. Behind
them was the sea and the sun, before them the Darkness.

"Do we go into this?" asked Caspian at length.

"Not by my advice," said Drinian.

"The Captain's right," said several sailors.

"I almost think he is," said Edmund.

Lucy and Eustace didn't speak but they felt very glad
inside at the turn things seemed to be taking. But all at once
the clear voice of Reepicheep broke in upon the silence.

"And why not?" he said. "Will someone explain to me
why not."

No one was anxious to explain, so Reepicheep continued:

"If I were addressing peasants or slaves," he said, "I
might suppose that this suggestion proceeded from
cowardice. But I hope it will never be told in Narnia that a
company of noble and royal persons in the flower of their
age turned tail because they were afraid of the dark."

"But what manner of use would it be ploughing through
that blackness?" asked Drinian.

"Use?" replied Reepicheep. "Use, Captain? If by use you
mean filling our bellies or our purses, I confess it will be no
use at all. So far as I know we did not set sail to look for
things useful but to seek honour and adventure. And here
is as great an adventure as ever I heard of, and here, if we
turn back, no little impeachment of all our honours."

Several of the sailors said things under their breath

that sounded like "Honour be blowed", but Caspian said:

"Oh, *bother* you, Reepicheep. I almost wish we'd left you at home. All right! If you put it that way, I suppose we shall have to go on. Unless Lucy would rather not?"

Lucy felt that she would very much rather not, but what she said out loud was, "I'm game."

"Your Majesty will at least order lights?" said Drinian.

"By all means," said Caspian. "See to it, Captain."

So the three lanterns, at the stern, and the prow and the masthead, were all lit, and Drinian ordered two torches amidships. Pale and feeble they looked in the sunshine. Then all the men except some who were left below at the oars were ordered on deck and fully armed and posted in their battle stations with swords drawn. Lucy and two archers were posted on the fighting top with bows bent and arrows on the string. Rynelf was in the bows with his line ready to take soundings. Reepicheep, Edmund, Eustace and Caspian, glittering in mail, were with him. Drinian took the tiller.

"And now, in Aslan's name, forward!" cried Caspian. "A slow, steady stroke. And let every man be silent and keep his ears open for orders."

With a creak and a groan the *Dawn Treader* started to creep forward as the men began to row. Lucy, up in the fighting top, had a wonderful view of the exact moment at which they entered the darkness. The bows had already disappeared before the sunlight had left the stern. She saw it go. At one minute the gilded stern, the blue sea, and the sky, were all in broad daylight: next minute the sea and sky had vanished, the stern lantern – which had been hardly noticeable before – was the only thing to show where the ship ended. In front of the lantern she could see the black shape of Drinian crouching at the tiller. Down below her the two torches made visible two small patches of deck and gleamed on swords and helmets, and forward there was another island of light on the forecastle. Apart from that, the fighting top, lit by the masthead light which was only just above her, seemed to be a little lighted world of its own floating in lonely darkness. And the lights themselves, as always happens with lights when you have to have them at the wrong time of day, looked lurid and unnatural. She also noticed that she was very cold.

How long this voyage into the darkness lasted, nobody knew. Except for the creak of the rowlocks and the splash of the oars there was nothing to show that they were moving at all. Edmund, peering from the bows, could see nothing except the reflection of the lantern in the water before him. It looked a greasy sort of reflection, and the ripple made by their advancing prow appeared to be heavy, small, and lifeless. As time went on everyone except the rowers began to shiver with cold.

Suddenly, from somewhere – no one's sense of direction was very clear by now – there came a cry, either of some inhuman voice or else a voice of one in such extremity of terror that he had almost lost his humanity.

Caspian was still trying to speak – his mouth was too dry – when the shrill voice of Reepicheep, which sounded louder than usual in that silence, was heard.

"Who calls?" it piped. "If you are a foe we do not fear you, and if you are a friend your enemies shall be taught the fear of us."

"Mercy!" cried the voice. "Mercy! Even if you are only one more dream, have mercy. Take me on board. Take me, even if you strike me dead. But in the name of all mercies do not fade away and leave me in this horrible land."

"Where are you?" shouted Caspian. "Come aboard and welcome."

There came another cry, whether of joy or terror, and

then they knew that someone was swimming towards them.

"Stand by to heave him up, men," said Caspian.

"Aye, aye, your Majesty," said the sailors. Several crowded to the port bulwark with ropes and one, leaning far out over the side, held the torch. A wild, white face appeared in the blackness of the water, and then, after some scrambling and pulling, a dozen friendly hands had heaved the stranger on board.

Edmund thought he had never seen a wilder-looking man. Though he did not otherwise look very old, his hair was an untidy mop of white, his face was thin and drawn, and, for clothing, only a few wet rags hung about him. But what one mainly noticed were his eyes, which were so widely opened that he seemed to have no eyelids at all, and stared as if in an agony of pure fear. The moment his feet reached the deck he said:

"Fly! Fly! About with your ship and fly! Row, row, row for your lives away from this accursed shore."

"Compose yourself," said Reepicheep, "and tell us what the danger is. We are not used to flying."

The stranger started horribly at the voice of the Mouse, which he had not noticed before.

"Nevertheless you will fly from here," he gasped. "This is the Island where Dreams come true."

"That's the island I've been looking for this long time," said one of the sailors. "I reckoned I'd find I was married to Nancy if we landed here."

"And I'd find Tom alive again," said another.

"Fools!" said the man, stamping his foot with rage. "That is the sort of talk that brought me here, and I'd better have been drowned or never born. Do you hear what I say? This is where dreams – dreams, do you understand – come to life, come real. Not daydreams: dreams."

There was about half a minute's silence and then, with a great clatter of armour, the whole crew were tumbling down the main hatch as quick as they could and flinging themselves on the oars to row as they had never rowed before; and Drinian was swinging round the tiller, and the boatswain was giving out the quickest stroke that had ever been heard at sea. For it had taken everyone just that half-minute to remember certain dreams they had had – dreams that make you afraid of going to sleep again – and to realize what it would mean to land on a country where dreams come true.

Only Reepicheep remained unmoved.

"Your Majesty, your Majesty," he said, "are you going to tolerate this mutiny, this poltroonery? This is a panic, this is a rout."

"Row, row," bellowed Caspian. "Pull for all our lives. Is her head right, Drinian? You can say what you like, Reepicheep. There are some things no man can face."

"It is, then, my good fortune not to be a man," replied Reepicheep with a very stiff bow.

Lucy from up aloft had heard it all. In an instant that one of her own dreams which she had tried hardest to forget came back to her as vividly as if she had only just woken from it. So *that* was what was behind them, on the island, in the darkness! For a second she wanted to go down to the deck and be with Edmund and Caspian. But what was the use? If dreams began coming true, Edmund and Caspian themselves might turn into something horrible just as she reached them. She gripped the rail of the fighting top and tried to steady herself. They were rowing back to the light as hard as they could: it would be all right in a few seconds. But oh, if only it could be all right now!

Though the rowing made a good deal of noise it did not quite conceal the total silence which surrounded the ship.

Everyone knew it would be better not to listen, not to strain his ears for any sound from the darkness. But no one could help listening. And soon everyone was hearing things. Each one heard something different.

"Do you hear a noise like . . . like a huge pair of scissors opening and shutting . . . over there?" Eustace asked Rynelf.

"Hush!" said Rynelf. "I can hear *them* crawling up the sides of the ship."

"*It's* just going to settle on the mast," said Caspian.

"Ugh!" said a sailor. "There are the gongs beginning. I knew they would."

Caspian, trying not to look at anything (especially not to keep looking behind him), went aft to Drinian.

"Drinian," he said in a very low voice. "How long did we take rowing in? — I mean rowing to where we picked up the stranger."

"Five minutes, perhaps," whispered Drinian. "Why?"

"Because we've been more than that already trying to get out."

Drinian's hand shook on the tiller and a line of cold sweat ran down his face. The same idea was occurring to everyone on board. "We shall never get out, never get out," moaned the rowers. "He's steering us wrong. We're going round and round in circles. We shall never get out." The stranger, who had been lying in a huddled heap on the deck, sat up and burst out into a horrible screaming laugh.

"Never get out!" he yelled. "That's it. Of course. We shall never get out. What a fool I was to have thought they would let me go as easily as that. No, no, we shall never get out."

Lucy leant her head on the edge of the fighting top and whispered, "Aslan, Aslan, if ever you loved us at all, send us help now." The darkness did not grow any less, but she began to feel a little – a very, very little – better. "After all, nothing has really happened to us yet," she thought.

"Look!" cried Rynelf's voice hoarsely from the bows. There was a tiny speck of light ahead, and while they watched a broad beam of light fell from it upon the ship. It did not alter the surrounding darkness, but the whole ship was lit up as if by searchlight. Caspian blinked, stared round, saw the faces of his companions all with wild, fixed expressions. Everyone was staring in the same direction: behind everyone lay his black, sharply-edged shadow.

Lucy looked along the beam and presently saw something in it. At first it looked like a cross, then it looked like an aeroplane, then it looked like a kite, and at last with a whirring of wings it was right overhead and was an albatross. It circled three times round the mast and then perched for an instant on the crest of the gilded dragon at the prow. It called out in a strong sweet voice what seemed to be words though no one understood them. After that it spread its wings, rose, and began to fly slowly ahead, bearing a little to starboard. Drinian steered after it not doubting that it offered good guidance. But no one except Lucy knew that as it circled the mast it had whispered to her, "Courage, dear heart," and the voice, she felt sure, was Alsan's, and with the voice a delicious smell breathed in her face.

In a few moments the darkness turned into a greyness ahead, and then, almost before they dared to begin hoping, they had shot out into the sunlight and were in the warm, blue world again. And all at once everybody realized that there was nothing to be afraid of and never had been. They blinked their eyes and looked about them. The brightness of the ship herself astonished them: they had half expected to find that the darkness would cling to the white and the green and the gold in the form of some grime or scum. And then first one, and then another, began laughing.

"I reckon we've made pretty good fools of ourselves," said Rynelf.

Lucy lost no time in coming down to the deck, where she found the others all gathered round the newcomer. For a long time he was too happy to speak, and could only gaze at the sea and the sun and feel the bulwarks and the ropes, as if to make sure he was really awake, while tears rolled down his cheeks.

"Thank you," he said at last. "You have saved me from . . . but I won't talk of that. And now let me know who you are. I am a Telmarine of Narnia, and when I was worth anything men called me the Lord Rhoop."

"And I," said Caspian, "am Caspian, King of Narnia, and I sail to find you and your companions who were my father's friends."

Lord Rhoop fell on his knees and kissed the King's hand. "Sire," he said, "you are the man in all the world I most wished to see. Grant me a boon."

"What is it?" asked Caspian.

"Never to bring me back there," he said. He pointed astern. They all looked. But they saw only bright blue sea and bright blue sky. The Dark Island and the darkness had vanished for ever.

"Why!" cried Lord Rhoop. "You have destroyed it!"

"I don't think it was us," said Lucy.

"Sire," said Drinian, "this wind is fair for the southeast. Shall I have our poor fellows up and set sail? And after that, every man who can be spared, to his hammock."

"Yes," said Caspian, "and let there be grog all round. Heigh-ho, I feel I could sleep the clock round myself."

So all afternoon with great joy they sailed south-east with a fair wind. But nobody noticed when the albatross had disappeared.

CHAPTER THIRTEEN

THE THREE SLEEPERS

THE wind never failed but it grew gentler every day till at length the waves were little more than ripples, and the ship glided on hour after hour almost as if they were sailing on a lake. And every night they saw that there rose in the east new constellations which no one had ever seen in Narnia and perhaps, as Lucy thought with a mixture of joy and fear, no living eye had seen at all. Those new stars were big and bright and the nights were warm. Most of them slept on deck and talked far into the night or hung over the ship's side watching the luminous dance of the foam thrown up by their bows.

On an evening of startling beauty, when the sunset behind them was so crimson and purple and widely spread that the very sky itself seemed to have grown larger, they came in sight of land on their starboard bow. It came slowly nearer and the light behind them made it look as if the capes and headlands of this new country were all on fire. But presently they were sailing along its coast and its western cape now rose up astern of them, black against the red sky and sharp as if it was cut out of cardboard, and then they could see better what this country was like. It had no mountains but many gentle hills with slopes like pillows. An attractive smell came from it – what Lucy called "a dim, purple kind of smell", which Edmund said (and Rhince thought) was rot, but Caspian said, "I know what you mean."

They sailed on a good way, past point after point, hoping to find a nice deep harbour, but had to content themselves in the end with a wide and shallow bay. Though it had seemed calm out at sea there was of course surf breaking on the sand and they could not bring the *Dawn Treader* as far in as they would have liked. They dropped anchor a good way from the beach and had a wet and tumbling landing in the boat. The Lord Rhoop remained on board the *Dawn Treader*. He wished to see no more islands. All the time that they remained in this country the sound of the long breakers was in their ears.

Two men were left to guard the boat and Caspian led the others inland, but not far because it was too late for exploring and the light would soon go. But there was no need to go far to find an adventure. The level valley which lay at the head of the bay showed no road or track or other sign of habitation. Underfoot was fine springy turf dotted here and there with a low bushy growth which Edmund and Lucy took for heather. Eustace, who was really rather good at botany, said it wasn't, and he was probably right; but it was something of very much the same kind.

When they had gone less than a bowshot from the shore, Drinian said, "Look! What's that?" and everyone stopped.

"Are they great trees?" said Caspian.

"Towers, I think," said Eustace.

"It might be giants," said Edmund in a lower voice.

"The way to find out is to go right in among them," said Reepicheep, drawing his sword and pattering off ahead of everyone else.

"I think it's a ruin," said Lucy when they had got a good

deal nearer, and her guess was the best so far. What they now saw was a wide oblong space flagged with smooth stones and surrounded by grey pillars but unroofed. And from end to end of it ran a long table laid with a rich crimson cloth that came down nearly to the pavement. At either side of it were many chairs of stone richly carved and with silken cushions upon the seats. But on the table itself there was set out such a banquet as had never been seen, not even when Peter the High King kept his court at Cair Paravel. There were turkeys and geese and peacocks, there were boars' heads and sides of venison, there were pies shaped like ships under full sail or like dragons and elephants, there were ice puddings and bright lobsters and gleaming salmon, there were nuts and grapes, pineapples and peaches, pomegranates and melons and tomatoes. There were flagons of gold and silver and curiously-wrought glass; and the smell of the fruit and the wine blew towards them like a promise of all happiness.

"I *say*!" said Lucy.

They came nearer and nearer, all very quietly.

"But where are the guests?" asked Eustace.

"We can provide that, Sir," said Rhince.

"Look!" said Edmund sharply. They were actually within the pillars now and standing on the pavement. Everyone looked where Edmund had pointed. The chairs were not all empty. At the head of the table and in the two places beside it there was something – or possibly three somethings.

"What are *those*?" asked Lucy in a whisper. "It looks like three beavers sitting on the table."

"Or a huge bird's nest," said Edmund.

"It looks more like a haystack to me," said Caspian.

Reepicheep ran forward, jumped on a chair and thence on to the table, and ran along it, threading his way as nimbly as a dancer between jewelled cups and pyramids of fruit and ivory salt-cellars. He ran right up to the mysterious grey mass at the end: peered, touched, and then called out:

"These will not fight, I think."

Everyone now came close and saw that what sat in those three chairs was three men, though hard to recognize as men till you looked closely. Their hair, which was grey,

had grown over their eyes till it almost concealed their faces, and their beards had grown over the table, climbing round and entwining plates and goblets as brambles entwine a fence, until, all mixed in one great mat of hair, they flowed over the edge and down to the floor. And from their heads the hair hung over the backs of their chairs so that they were wholly hidden. In fact the three men were nearly all hair.

"Dead?" said Caspian.

"I think not, Sire," said Reepicheep, lifting one of their hands out of its tangle of hair in his two paws. "This one is warm and his pulse beats."

"This one, too, and this," said Drinian.

"Why, they're only asleep," said Eustace.

"It's been a long sleep, though," said Edmund, "to let their hair grow like this."

"It must be an enchanted sleep," said Lucy. "I felt the moment we landed on this island that it was full of magic. Oh! do you think we have perhaps come here to break it?"

"We can try," said Caspian, and began shaking the nearest of the three sleepers. For a moment everyone thought he was going to be successful, for the man breathed hard and muttered, "I'll go eastward no more. Out oars for Narnia." But he sank back almost at once into a yet deeper sleep than before: that is, his heavy head sagged a few inches lower towards the table and all efforts to rouse him again were useless. With the second it was much the same. "Weren't born to live like animals. Get to the east while you've a chance – lands behind the sun," and sank down. And the third only said, "Mustard, please," and slept hard.

"*Out oars for Narnia*, eh?" said Drinian.

"Yes," said Caspian, "you are right, Drinian. I think our quest is at an end. Let's look at their rings. Yes, these are their devices. This is the Lord Revilian. This is the Lord Argoz: and this, the Lord Mavramorn."

"But we can't wake them," said Lucy. "What are we to do?"

"Begging your Majesties' pardons all," said Rhince, "but why not fall to while you're discussing it? We don't see a dinner like this every day."

"Not for your life!" said Caspian.

"That's right, that's right," said several of the sailors.

"Too much magic about here. The sooner we're back on board the better."

"Depend upon it," said Reepicheep, "it was from eating this food that these three lords came by a seven years' sleep."

"I wouldn't touch it to save my life," said Drinian.

"The light's going uncommon quick," said Rynelf.

"Back to ship, back to ship," muttered the men.

"I really think," said Edmund, "they're right. We can decide what to do with the three sleepers tomorrow. We daren't eat the food and there's no point in staying here for the night. The whole place smells of magic — and danger."

"I am entirely of King Edmund's opinion," said Reepicheep, "as far as concerns the ship's company in general. But I myself will sit at this table till sunrise."

"Why on earth?" said Eustace.

"Because," said the Mouse, "this is a very great adventure, and no danger seems to me so great as that of knowing when I get back to Narnia that I left a mystery behind me through fear."

"I'll stay with you, Reep," said Edmund.

"And I too," said Caspian.

"And me," said Lucy. And then Eustace volunteered also. This was very brave of him because never having read of such things or even heard of them till he joined the *Dawn Treader* made it worse for him than for the others.

"I beseech your Majesty —" began Drinian.

"No, my Lord," said Caspian. "Your place is with the ship, and you have had a day's work while we five have idled." There was a lot of argument about this but in the end Caspian had his way. As the crew marched off to the shore in the gathering dusk none of the five watchers, except perhaps Reepicheep, could avoid a cold feeling in the stomach.

They took some time choosing their seats at the perilous table. Probably everyone had the same reason but no one said it out loud. For it was really a rather nasty choice. One could hardly bear to sit all night next to those three terrible hairy objects which, if not dead, were certainly not alive in the ordinary sense. On the other hand, to sit at the far end, so that you would see them less and less as the night grew darker, and wouldn't know if they were moving, and perhaps wouldn't see them at all by about two o'clock — no, it was not to be thought of. So they sauntered round and round the table saying, "What about here?" and "Or perhaps a bit further on," or, "Why not on this side?" till at last they settled down somewhere about the middle but nearer to the sleepers than to the other end. It was about ten by now and almost dark. Those strange new constellations burned in the east. Lucy would have liked it better if they had been the Leopard and the Ship and other old friends of the Narnian sky.

They wrapped themselves in their sea cloaks and sat still and waited. At first there was some attempt at talk but it didn't come to much. And they sat and sat. And all the time they heard the waves breaking on the beach.

After hours that seemed like ages there came a moment when they all knew they had been dozing a moment before but were all suddenly wide awake. The stars were all in quite different positions from those they had last noticed. The sky was very black except for the faintest possible greyness in the east. They were cold, though thirsty, and stiff. And none of them spoke because now at last something was happening.

Before them, beyond the pillars, there was the slope of a low hill. And now a door opened in the hillside, and light appeared in the doorway, and a figure came out, and the door shut behind it. The figure carried a light, and this light was really all that they could see distinctly. It came slowly nearer and nearer till at last it stood right at the table opposite to them. Now they could see that it was a tall girl, dressed in a single long garment of clear blue which left her arms bare. She was bareheaded and her yellow hair hung down her back. And when they looked at her they thought they had never before known what beauty meant.

The light which she had been carrying was a tall candle in a silver candlestick which she now set upon the table. If there had been any wind off the sea earlier in the night it must have died down by now, for the flame of the candle burned as straight and still as if it were in a room with the windows shut and the curtains drawn. Gold and silver on the table shone in its light.

Lucy now noticed something lying lengthwise on the table which had escaped her attention before. It was a knife of stone, sharp as steel, a cruel-looking, ancient-looking thing.

No one had yet spoken a word. Then – Reepicheep first, and Caspian next – they all rose to their feet, because they felt that she was a great lady.

"Travellers who have come from far to Aslan's table," said the girl. "Why do you not eat and drink?"

"Madam," said Caspian, "we feared the food because we thought it had cast our friends into an enchanted sleep."

"They have never tasted it," she said.

"Please," said Lucy, "what happened to them?"

"Seven years ago," said the girl, "they came here in a ship whose sails were rags and her timbers ready to fall apart. There were a few others with them, sailors, and when they came to this table one said, 'Here is the good place. Let us set sail and reef sail and row no longer but sit down and end our days in peace!' And the second said, 'No, let us re-embark and sail for Narnia and the west; it may be that Miraz is dead.' But the third, who was a very masterful man, leaped up and said, 'No, by heaven. We are men and Telmarines, not brutes. What should we do but seek adventure after adventure? We have not long to live in any event. Let us spend what is left in seeking the unpeopled world behind the sunrise.' And as they quarrelled he caught up the Knife of Stone which lies there on the table and would have fought with his comrades. But it is a thing not right for him to touch. And as his fingers closed upon the hilt, deep sleep fell upon all the three. And till the enchantment is undone they will never wake."

"What is this Knife of Stone?" asked Eustace.

"Do none of you know it?" said the girl.

"I – I think," said Lucy, "I've seen something like it before. It was a knife like it that the White Witch used when she killed Aslan at the Stone Table long ago."

"It was the same," said the girl, "and it was brought here to be kept in honour while the world lasts."

Edmund, who had been looking more and more uncomfortable for the last few minutes, now spoke.

"Look here," he said, "I hope I'm not a coward – about eating this food, I mean – and I'm sure I don't mean to be rude. But we have had a lot of queer adventures on this voyage of ours and things aren't always what they seem. When I look in your face I can't help believing all you say: but then that's just what might happen with a witch too. How are we to know you're a friend?"

"You can't know," said the girl. "You can only believe – or not."

After a moment's pause Reepicheep's small voice was heard.

"Sire," he said to Caspian, "of your courtesy fill my cup with wine from that flagon: it is too big for me to lift. I will drink to the lady."

Caspian obeyed and the Mouse, standing on the table, held up a golden cup between its tiny paws and said, "Lady, I pledge you." Then it fell to on cold peacock, and in a short while everyone else followed its example. All were very hungry and the meal, if not quite what you wanted for a very early breakfast, was excellent as a very late supper.

"Why is it called Aslan's table?" asked Lucy presently.

"It is set here by his bidding," said the girl, "for those who come so far. Some call this island the World's End, for though you can sail further, this is the beginning of the end."

"But how does the food *keep*?" asked the practical Eustace.

"It is eaten, and renewed every day," said the girl. "This you will see."

"And what are we to do about the Sleepers?" asked Caspian. "In the world from which my friends come" (here he nodded at Eustace and the Pevensies) "they have a story of a prince or a king coming to a castle where all the people lay in an enchanted sleep. In that story he could not dissolve the enchantment until he had kissed the Princess."

"But here," said the girl, "it is different. Here he cannot kiss the Princess till he has dissolved the enchantment."

"Then," said Caspian, "in the name of Aslan, show me how to set about that work at once."

"My father will teach you that," said the girl.

"Your father!" said everyone. "Who is he? And where?"

"Look," said the girl, turning round and pointing at the door in the hillside. They could see it more easily now, for while they had been talking the stars had grown fainter and great gaps of white light were appearing in the greyness of the eastern sky.

CHAPTER FOURTEEN

THE BEGINNING OF THE END
OF THE WORLD

SLOWLY the door opened again and out there came a figure as tall and straight as the girl's but not so slender. It carried no light but light seemed to come from it. As it came nearer, Lucy saw that it was like an old man. His silver beard came down to his bare feet in front and his silver hair hung down to his heels behind and his robe appeared to be made from the fleece of silver sheep. He looked so mild and grave that once more all the travellers rose to their feet and stood in silence.

But the old man came on without speaking to the travellers and stood on the other side of the table opposite to his daughter. Then both of them held up their arms before them and turned to face the east. In that position they began to sing. I wish I could write down the song, but no one who was present could remember it. Lucy said afterwards that it was high, almost shrill, but very beautiful, "A cold kind of song, an early morning kind of song." And as they sang, the grey clouds lifted from the eastern sky and the white patches grew bigger and bigger till it was all white, and the sea began to shine like silver. And long afterwards (but those two sang all the time) the east began to turn red and at last, unclouded, the sun came up out of the sea and its long level ray shot down the length of the table on the gold and silver and on the Stone Knife.

Once or twice before, the Narnians had wondered whether the sun at its rising did not look bigger in these seas than it had looked at home. This time they were certain. There was no mistaking it. And the brightness of its ray on the dew and on the table was far beyond any morning brightness they had ever seen. And as Edmund said afterwards, "Though lots of things happened on that trip which *sound* more exciting, that moment was really the most exciting." For now they knew that they had truly come to the beginning of the End of the World.

Then something seemed to be flying at them out of the very centre of the rising sun: but of course one couldn't look steadily in that direction to make sure. But presently the air became full of voices – voices which took up the same song that the Lady and her Father were singing, but in far wilder tones and in a language which no one knew. And soon after that the owners of these voices could be seen. They were birds, large and white, and they came by hundreds and thousands and alighted on everything; on the grass, and the pavement, on the table, on your shoulders, your hands, and your head, till it looked as if heavy snow had fallen. For, like snow, they not only made everything white but blurred and blunted all shapes. But Lucy, looking out from between the wings of the birds that covered her, saw one bird fly to the Old Man with something in its beak that looked like a little fruit, unless it was a little live coal, which it might have been, for it was too bright to look at. And the bird laid it in the Old Man's mouth.

Then the birds stopped their singing and appeared to be very busy about the table. When they rose from it again everything on the table that could be eaten or drunk had disappeared. These birds rose from their meal in their thousands and hundreds and carried away all the things that could not be eaten or drunk, such as bones, rinds, and shells, and took their flight back to the rising sun. But now, because they were not singing, the whir of their wings seemed to set the whole air a-tremble. And there was the table pecked clean and empty, and the three old Lords of Narnia still fast asleep.

Now at last the Old Man turned to the travellers and bade them welcome.

"Sir," said Caspian, "will you tell us how to undo the enchantment which holds these three Narnian Lords asleep."

"I will gladly tell you that, my son," said the Old Man. "To break this enchantment you must sail to the World's End, or as near as you can come to it, and you must come back having left at least one of your company behind."

"And what must happen to that one?" asked Reepicheep.

"He must go on into the utter east and never return into the world."

"That is my heart's desire," said Reepicheep.

"And are we near the World's End now, Sir?" asked Caspian. "Have you any knowledge of the seas and lands further east than this?"

"I saw them long ago," said the Old Man, "but it was from a great height. I cannot tell you such things as sailors need to know."

"Do you mean you were flying in the air?" Eustace blurted out.

"I was a long way above the air, my son," replied the Old Man. "I am Ramandu. But I see that you stare at one another and have not heard this name. And no wonder, for the days when I was a star had ceased long before any of you knew this world, and all the constellations have changed."

"Golly," said Edmund under his breath. "He's a *retired* star."

"Aren't you a star any longer?" asked Lucy.

"I am a star at rest, my daughter," answered Ramandu.

"When I set for the last time, decrepit and old beyond all that you can reckon, I was carried to this island. I am not so old now as I was then. Every morning a bird brings me a fire-berry from the valleys in the Sun, and each fire-berry takes away a little of my age. And when I have become as young as the child that was born yesterday, then I shall take my rising again (for we are at earth's eastern rim) and once more tread the great dance."

"In our world," said Eustace, "a star is a huge ball of flaming gas."

"Even in your world, my son, that is not what a star is but only what it is made of. And in this world you have already met a star: for I think you have been with Coriakin."

"Is he a retired star, too?" said Lucy.

"Well, not quite the same," said Ramandu. "It was not quite as a rest that he was set to govern the Duffers. You might call it a punishment. He might have shone for thousands of years more in the southern winter sky if all had gone well."

"What did he do, Sir?" asked Caspian.

"My son," said Ramandu, "it is not for you, a son of Adam, to know what faults a star can commit. But come, we waste time in such talk. Are you yet resolved? Will you sail further east and come again, leaving one to return no more, and so break the enchantment? Or will you sail westward?"

"Surely, Sire," said Reepicheep, "there is no question about that? It is very plainly part of our quest to rescue these three lords from enchantment."

"I think the same, Reepicheep," replied Caspian. "And even if it were not so, it would break my heart not to go as near the World's End as the *Dawn Treader* will take us. But I am thinking of the crew. They signed on to seek the seven lords, not to reach the rim of the Earth. If we sail east from here we sail to find the edge, the utter east. And no one knows how far it is. They're brave fellows, but I see signs that some of them are weary of the voyage and long to have our prow pointing to Narnia again. I don't think I should take them further without their knowledge and consent. And then there's the poor Lord Rhoop. He's a broken man."

"My son," said the star, "it would be no use, even though you wished it, to sail for the World's End with men unwilling or men deceived. That is not how great unenchantments are achieved. They must know where they go and why. But who is this broken man you speak of?"

Caspian told Ramandu the story of Rhoop.

"I can give him what he needs most," said Ramandu. "In this island there is sleep without stint or measure, and sleep in which no faintest footfall of a dream was ever heard. Let him sit beside these other three and drink oblivion till your return."

"Oh, do let's do that, Caspian," said Lucy. "I'm sure it's just what he would love."

At that moment they were interrupted by the sound of many feet and voices: Drinian and the rest of the ship's company were approaching. They halted in surprise when they saw Ramandu and his daughter; and then, because these were obviously great people, every man uncovered his head. Some sailors eyed the empty dishes and flagons on the table with regret.

"My lord," said the King to Drinian, "pray send two men back to the *Dawn Treader* with a message to the Lord Rhoop. Tell him that the last of his old shipmates are here asleep – a sleep without dreams – and that he can share it."

When this had been done, Caspian told the rest to sit down and laid the whole situation before them. When he had finished there was a long silence and some whispering until presently the Master Bowman got to his feet, and said:

"What some of us have been wanting to ask for a long time, your Majesty, is how we're ever to get home when we do turn, whether we turn here or somewhere else. It's been west and north-west winds all the way, barring an occasional calm. And if that doesn't change, I'd like to know what hopes we have of seeing Narnia again. There's not much chance of supplies lasting while we *row* all that way."

"That's landsman's talk," said Drinian. "There's always a prevailing west wind in these seas all through the late summer, and it always changes after the New Year. We'll have plenty of wind for sailing westward; more than we shall like from all accounts."

"That's true, Master," said an old sailor who was a Galmian by birth. "You get some ugly weather rolling up from the east in January and February. And by your leave, Sire, if I was in command of this ship I'd say to winter here and begin the voyage home in March."

"What'd you eat while you were wintering here?" asked Eustace.

"This table," said Ramandu, "will be filled with a king's feast every day at sunset."

"Now you're talking!" said several sailors.

"Your Majesties and gentlemen and ladies all," said Rynelf, "there's just one thing I want to say. There's not one of us chaps as was pressed on this journey. We're volunteers. And there's some here that are looking very hard at that table and thnking about king's feasts who were talking very loud about adventures on the day we sailed from Cair Paravel, and swearing they wouldn't come home till we'd found the end of the world. And there were some standing on the quay who would have given all they had to come with us. It was thought a finer thing then to have a cabin-boy's berth on the *Dawn Treader* than to wear a knight's belt. I don't know if you get the hang of what I'm saying. But what I mean is that I think chaps who set out like us will look as silly as – as those Dufflepuds – if we come home and say we got to the beginning of the world's end and hadn't the heart to go further."

Some of the sailors cheered at this but some said that that was all very well.

"This isn't going to be much fun," whispered Edmund to Caspian. "What are we to do if half those fellows hang back?"

"Wait," Caspian whispered back. "I've still a card to play."

"Aren't you going to say anything, Reep?" whispered Lucy.

"No. Why should your Majesty expect it?" answered Reepicheep in a voice that most people heard. "My own plans are made. While I can, I sail east in the *Dawn Treader*. When she fails me, I paddle east in my coracle. When she sinks, I shall swim east with my four paws. And when I can swim no longer, if I have not reached Aslan's country, or shot over the edge of the world in some vast cataract, I shall sink with my nose to the sunrise and Peepiceek will be head of the talking mice in Narnia."

"Hear, hear," said a sailor, "I'll say the same, barring the bit about the coracle, which wouldn't bear me." He added in a lower voice, "I'm not going to be outdone by a mouse."

At this point Caspian jumped to his feet. "Friends," he said, "I think you have not quite understood our purpose. You talk as if we had come to you with our hat in our hand, begging for shipmates. It isn't like that at all. We and our royal brother and sister and their kinsman and Sir Reepicheep, the good knight, and the Lord Drinian have an errand to the world's edge. It is our pleasure to choose from among such of you as are willing those whom we deem worthy of so high an enterprise. We have not said that any can come for the asking. That is why we shall now command the Lord Drinian and Master Rhince to consider carefully what men among you are the hardest in battle, the most skilled seamen, the purest in blood, the most loyal to our person, and the cleanest of life and manners; and to give their names to us in a schedule." He paused and went on in a quicker voice, "Aslan's mane!" he exclaimed. "Do you think that the privilege of seeing the last things is to be bought for a song? Why, every man that comes with us shall bequeath the title of Dawn Treader to all his descendants, and when we land at Cair Paravel on the homeward voyage he shall have either gold or land enough to make him rich all his life. Now – scatter over the island, all of you. In half an hour's time I shall receive the names that Lord Drinian brings me."

There was rather a sheepish silence and then the crew made their bows and moved away, one in this direction and one in that, but mostly in little knots or bunches, talking.

"And now for the Lord Rhoop," said Caspian.

But turning to the head of the table he saw that Rhoop was already there. He had arrived, silent and unnoticed, while the discussion was going on, and was seated beside the Lord Argoz. The daughter of Ramandu stood beside him as if she had just helped him into his chair; Ramandu stood behind him and laid both his hands on Rhoop's grey head. Even in daylight a faint silver light came from the hands of the star. There was a smile on Rhoop's haggard face. He held out one of his hands to Lucy and the other to

Caspian. For a moment it looked as if he were going to say something. Then his smile brightened as if he were feeling some delicious sensation, a long sigh of contentment came from his lips, his head fell forward, and he slept.

"Poor Rhoop," said Lucy. "I *am* glad. He must have had terrible times."

"Don't let's even think of it," said Eustace.

Meanwhile Caspian's speech, helped perhaps by some magic of the island, was having just the effect he intended. A good many who had been anxious enough to *get* out of the voyage felt quite differently about being *left* out of it. And of course whenever any one sailor announced that he had made up his mind to ask for permission to sail, the ones who hadn't said this felt that they were getting fewer and more uncomfortable. So that before the half-hour was nearly over several people were positively "sucking up" to Drinian and Rhince (at least that was what they called it at my school) to get a good report. And soon there were only three left who didn't want to go, and those three were trying very hard to persuade others to stay with them. And very shortly after that there was only one left. And in the end he began to be afraid of being left behind all on his own and changed his mind.

At the end of the half-hour they all came trooping back to Aslan's Table and stood at one end while Drinian and Rhince went and sat down with Caspian and made their report; and Caspian accepted all the men but that one who had changed his mind at the last moment. His name was Pittencream and he stayed on the Island of the Star all the time the others were away looking for the World's End, and he very much wished he had gone with them. He wasn't the sort of man who could enjoy talking to Ramandu and Ramandu's daughter (nor they to him), and it rained a good deal, and though there was a wonderful feast on the Table every night, he didn't very much enjoy it. He said it gave him the creeps sitting there alone (and in the rain as likely as not) with those four Lords asleep at the end of the Table. And when the others returned he felt so out of things that he deserted on the voyage home at the Lone Islands, and went and lived in Calormen, where he told wonderful stories about his adventures at the End of the World, until at last he came to believe them himself. So you may say, in a sense, that he lived happily ever after. But he could never bear mice.

That night they all ate and drank together at the great Table between the pillars where the feast was magically renewed: and next morning the *Dawn Treader* set sail once more just when the great birds had come and gone again.

"Lady," said Caspian, "I hope to speak with you again when I have broken the enchantments." And Ramandu's daughter looked at him and smiled.

CHAPTER FIFTEEN

THE WONDERS OF THE LAST SEA

VERY soon after they had left Ramandu's country they began to feel that they had already sailed beyond the world. All was different. For one thing they all found that they were needing less sleep. One did not want to go to bed nor to eat much, nor even to talk except in low voices. Another thing was the light. There was too much of it. The sun when it came up each morning looked twice, if not three times, its usual size. And every morning (which gave Lucy the strangest feeling of all) the huge white birds, singing their song with human voices in a language no one knew, streamed overhead and vanished astern on their way to their breakfast at Aslan's Table. A little later they came flying back and vanished into the east.

"How beautifully clear the water is!" said Lucy to herself, as she leaned over the port side early in the afternoon of the second day.

And it was. The first thing that she noticed was a little black object, about the size of a shoe, travelling along at the same speed as the ship. For a moment she thought it was something floating on the surface. But then there came floating past a bit of stale bread which the cook had just thrown out of the galley. And the bit of bread looked as if it were going to collide with the black thing, but it didn't. It passed above it, and Lucy now saw that the black thing could not be on the surface. Then the black thing suddenly got very much bigger and flicked back to normal size a moment later.

Now Lucy knew she had seen something just like that happen somewhere else – if only she could remember where. She held her hand to her head and screwed up her face and put out her tongue in the effort to remember. At last she did. Of course! It was like what you saw from a train on a bright sunny day. You saw the black shadow of your own coach running along the fields at the same pace as the train. Then you went into a cutting; and immediately the same shadow flicked close up to you and got big, racing along the grass of the cutting-bank. Then you came out of the cutting and – flick! – once more the black shadow had gone back to its normal size and was running along the fields.

"It's our shadow! – the shadow of the *Dawn Treader*," said Lucy. "Our shadow running along on the bottom of the sea. That time when it got bigger it went over a hill. But in that case the water must be clearer than I thought! Good gracious, I must be seeing the bottom of the sea; fathoms and fathoms down."

As soon as she had said this she realized that the great silvery expanse which she had been seeing (without notic-ing) for some time was really the sand on the sea-bed and that all sorts of darker or brighter patches were not lights and shadows on the surface but real things on the bottom. At present, for instance, they were passing over a mass of soft purply green with a broad, winding strip of pale grey in the middle of it. But now that she knew it was on the bottom she saw it much better. She could see that bits of the dark stuff were much higher than other bits and were waving gently. "Just like trees in a wind," said Lucy. "And I do believe that's what they are. It's a submarine forest."

They passed on above it and presently the pale streak was joined by another pale streak. "If I was down there," thought Lucy, "that streak would be just like a road through the wood. And that place where it joins the other would be a crossroads. Oh, I do wish I was. Hallo! the forest is coming to an end. And I do believe the streak really was a road! I can still see it going on across the open sand. It's a different colour. And it's marked out with something at the edges – dotted lines. Perhaps they are stones. And now it's getting wider."

But it was not really getting wider, it was getting nearer. She realized this because of the way in which the shadow of the ship came rushing up towards her. And the road – she felt sure it was a road now – began to go in zig-zags. Obviously it was climbing up a steep hill. And when she held her head sideways and looked back, what she saw was very like what you see when you look down a winding road from the top of a hill. She could even see the shafts of sunlight falling through the deep water on to the wooded valley – and, in the extreme distance, everything melting away into a dim greenness. But some places – the sunny ones, she thought – were ultramarine blue.

She could not, however, spend much time looking back; what was coming into view in the forward direction was too exciting. The road had apparently now reached the top of the hill and ran straight forward. Little specks were moving to and fro on it. And now something most wonderful, fortunately in full sunlight – or as full as it can be when it falls through fathoms of water – flashed into sight. It was knobbly and jagged and of a pearly, or perhaps an ivory, colour. She was so nearly straight above it that at first she could hardly make out what it was. But everything became plain when she noticed its shadow. The sunlight was falling across Lucy's shoulders, so the shadow of the thing lay stretched out on the sand behind it. And by its shape she saw clearly that it was a shadow of towers and pinnacles, minarets and domes.

"Why! – it's a city or a huge castle," said Lucy to herself.

"But I wonder why they've built it on top of a high mountain?"

Long afterwards when she was back in England and talked all these adventures over with Edmund, they thought of a reason and I am pretty sure it is the true one. In the sea, the deeper you go, the darker and colder it gets, and it is down there, in the dark and cold, that dangerous things live – the squid and the Sea Serpent and the Kraken. The valleys are the wild, unfriendly places. The sea-people feel about their valleys as we do about mountains, and feel about their mountains as we feel about valleys. It is on the heights (or, as we would say, "in the shallows") that there is warmth and peace. The reckless hunters and brave knights of the sea go down into the depths on quests and adventures, but return home to the heights for rest and peace, courtesy and council, the sports, the dances and the songs.

They had passed the city and the sea-bed was still rising. It was only a few hundred feet below the ship now. The road had disappeared. They were sailing above an open park-like country, dotted with little groves of brightly-coloured vegetation. And then – Lucy nearly squealed aloud with excitement – she had seen People.

There were between fifteen and twenty of them, and all mounted on sea-horses – not the tiny little sea-horses which you may have seen in museums but horses rather bigger than themselves. They must be noble and lordly people, Lucy thought, for she could catch the gleam of gold on some of their foreheads and streamers of emerald- or orange-coloured stuff fluttered from their shoulders in the current. Then:

"Oh, bother these fish!" said Lucy, for a whole shoal of small fat fish, swimming quite close to the surface, had come between her and the Sea People. But though this spoiled her view it led to the most interesting thing of all.

Suddenly a fierce little fish of a kind she had never seen before came darting up from below, snapped, grabbed, and sank rapidly with one of the fat fish in its mouth. And all the Sea People were sitting on their horses staring up at what had happened. They seemed to be talking and laughing. And before the hunting fish had got back to them with its prey, another of the same kind came up from the Sea People. And Lucy was almost certain that one big Sea Man who sat on his sea-horse in the middle of the party had sent it or released it; as if he had been holdng it back till then in his hand or on his wrist.

"Why, I do declare," said Lucy, "it's a hunting party. Or more like a hawking party. Yes, that's it. They ride out with these little fierce fish on their wrists just as we used to ride out with falcons on our wrists when we were Kings and Queens at Cair Paravel long ago. And then they fly them – or I suppose I should say *swim* them – at the others. How –"

She stopped suddenly because the scene was changing. The Sea People had noticed the *Dawn Treader*. The shoal of fish had scattered in every direction: the People themselves were coming up to find out the meaning of this big, black thing which had come between them and the sun. And now they were so close to the surface that if they had been in air, instead of water, Lucy could have spoken to them. There were men and women both. All wore coronets of some kind and many had chains of pearls. They wore no other clothes. Their bodies were the colour of old ivory, their hair dark purple. The King in the centre (no one could mistake him for anything but the King) looked proudly and fiercely into Lucy's face and shook a spear in his hand. His knights did the same. The faces of the ladies were filled with astonishment. Lucy felt sure they had never seen a ship or a human before – and how should they, in seas beyond the world's end where no ship ever came?

"What are you staring at, Lu?" said a voice close beside her.

Lucy had been so absorbed in what she was seeing that she started at the sound, and when she turned she found that her arm had gone "dead" from leaning so long on the

rail in one position. Drinian and Edmund were beside her.

"Look," she said.

They both looked, but almost at once Drinian said in a low voice:

"Turn round at once, your Majesties – that's right, with our backs to the sea. And don't look as if we were talking about anything important."

"Why, what's the matter?" said Lucy as she obeyed.

"It'll never do for the sailors to see *all that*," said Drinian. "We'll have men falling in love with a sea-woman, or falling in love with the under-sea country itself, and jumping overboard. I've heard of that kind of thing happening before in strange seas. It's always unlucky to see *these* people."

"But we used to know them," said Lucy. "In the old days at Cair Paravel when my brother Peter was High King. They came to the surface and sang at our coronation."

"I think that must have been a different kind, Lu," said Edmund. "They could live in the air as well as under water. I rather think these can't. By the look of them they'd have surfaced and started attacking us long ago if they could. They seem very fierce."

"At any rate," said Drinian, but at that moment two sounds were heard. One was a plop. The other was a voice from the fighting top shouting, "Man overboard!" Then everyone was busy. Some of the sailors hurried aloft to take in the sail: others hurried below to get to the oars; and Rhince, who was on duty on the poop, began to put the helm hard over so as to come round and back to the man who had gone overboard. But by now everyone knew that it wasn't strictly a man. It was Reepicheep.

"Drat that mouse!" said Drinian. "It's more trouble than all the rest of the ship's company put together. If there is any scrape to be got into, in it will get! It ought to be put in irons — keel-hauled — marooned — have its whiskers cut off. Can anyone see the little blighter?"

All this didn't mean that Drinian really disliked Reepicheep. On the contrary he liked him very much and was therefore frightened about him, and being frightened put him in a bad temper — just as your mother is much angrier with you for running out into the road in front of a car than a stranger would be. No one, of course, was afraid of Reepicheep's drowning, for he was an excellent swimmer; but the three who knew what was going on below the water were afraid of those long, cruel spears in the hands of the Sea People.

In a few minutes the *Dawn Treader* had come round and everyone could see the black blob in the water which was Reepicheep. He was chattering with the greatest excitement but as his mouth kept on getting filled with water nobody could understand what he was saying.

"He'll blurt the whole thing out if we don't shut him up," cried Drinian. To prevent this he rushed to the side and lowered a rope himself, shouting to the sailors, "All right, all right. Back to your places. I hope I can heave a *mouse* up without help." And as Reepicheep began climbing up the rope – not very nimbly because his wet fur made him heavy – Drinian leaned over and whispered to him,

"Don't tell. Not a word."

But when the dripping Mouse had reached the deck it turned out not to be at all interested in the Sea People.

"Sweet!" he cheeped. "Sweet, sweet!"

"What are you talking about?" asked Drinian crossly. "And you needn't shake yourself all over *me*, either."

"I tell you the water's sweet," said the Mouse. "Sweet, fresh. It isn't salt."

For a moment no one quite took in the importance of this. But then Reepicheep once more repeated the old prophecy:

> "Where the waves grow sweet,
> Doubt not, Reepicheep,
> There is the utter East."

Then at last everyone understood.

"Let me have a bucket, Rynelf," said Drinian.

It was handed him and he lowered it and up it came again. The water shone in it like glass.

"Perhaps your Majesty would like to taste it first," said Drinian to Caspian.

The King took the bucket in both hands, raised it to his lips, sipped, then drank deeply and raised his head. His face was changed. Not only his eyes but everything about him seemed to be brighter.

"Yes," he said, "it is sweet. That's real water, that. I'm not sure that it isn't going to kill me. But it is the death I would have chosen – if I'd known about it till now."

"What do you mean?" asked Edmund.

"It – it's like light more than anything else," said Caspian.

"That is what it is," said Reepicheep. "Drinkable light. We must be very near the end of the world now."

There was a moment's silence and then Lucy knelt down on the deck and drank from the bucket.

"It's the loveliest thing I have ever tasted," she said with a kind of gasp. "But oh – it's strong. We shan't need to *eat* anything now."

And one by one everybody on board drank. And for a long time they were all silent. They felt almost too well and strong to bear it; and presently they began to notice another result. As I have said before, there had been too much light ever since they left the island of Ramandu – the sun too large (though not too hot), the sea too bright, the air too shining. Now, the light grew no less – if anything, it increased – but they could bear it. They could look straight up at the sun without blinking. They could see more light than they had ever seen before. And the deck and the sail and their own faces and bodies became brighter and brighter and every rope shone. And next morning, when the sun rose, now five or six times its old size, they stared hard into it and could see the very feathers of the birds that came flying from it.

Hardly a word was spoken on board all that day, till about dinner-time (no one wanted any dinner, the water was enough for them) Drinian said:

"I can't understand this. There is not a breath of wind. The sail hangs dead. The sea is as flat as a pond. And yet we drive on as fast as if there were a gale behind us."

"I've been thinking that, too," said Caspian. "We must be caught in some strong current."

"H'm," said Edmund. "That's not so nice if the World really has an edge and we're getting near it."

"You mean," said Caspian, "that we might be just – well, poured over it?"

"Yes, yes," cried Reepicheep, clapping his paws together. "That's how I've always imagined it – the World like a great round table and the waters of all the oceans endlessly pouring over the edge. The ship will tip up – stand on her head – for one moment we shall see over the edge – and then, down, down, the rush, the speed –"

"And what do you think will be waiting for us at the bottom, eh?" said Drinian.

"Aslan's country perhaps," said the Mouse, its eyes shining. "Or perhaps there isn't any bottom. Perhaps it goes down for ever and ever. But whatever it is, won't it be worth anything just to have looked for one moment beyond the edge of the world."

"But look here," said Eustace, "this is all rot. The world's round – I mean, round like a ball, not like a table."

"*Our* world is," said Edmund. "But is this?"

"Do you mean to say," asked Caspian, "that you three come from a round world (round like a ball) and you've never told me! It's really too bad of you. Because we have fairy-tales in which there are round worlds and I always loved them. I never believed there were any real ones. But I've always wished there were and I've always longed to live in one. Oh, I'd give anything – I wonder why you can get into our world and we never get into yours? If only I had the chance! It must be exciting to live on a thing like a ball. Have you ever been to the parts where people walk about upside-down?"

Edmund shook his head. "And it isn't like that," he added. "There's nothing particularly exciting about a round world when you're there."

CHAPTER SIXTEEN

THE VERY END OF THE WORLD

REEPICHEEP was the only person on board besides Drinian and the two Pevensies who had noticed the Sea People. He had dived in at once when he saw the Sea King shaking his spear, for he regarded this as a sort of threat or challenge and wanted to have the matter out there and then. The excitement of discovering that the water was now fresh had distracted his attention, and before he remembered the Sea People again Lucy and Drinian had taken him aside and warned him not to mention what he had seen.

As things turned out they need hardly have bothered, for by this time the *Dawn Treader* was gliding over a part of the sea which seemed to be uninhabited. No one except Lucy saw anything more of the People, and even she had only one short glimpse. All morning on the following day they sailed in fairly shallow water and the bottom was weedy. Just before midday Lucy saw a large shoal of fishes grazing on the weed. They were all eating steadily and all moving in the same direction. "Just like a flock of sheep," thought Lucy. Suddenly she saw a little Sea Girl of about her own age in the middle of them – a quiet, lonely-looking girl with a sort of crook in her hand. Lucy felt sure that this girl must be a shepherdess – or perhaps a fish-herdess – and that the shoal was really a flock at pasture. Both the fishes and the girl were quite close to the surface. And just as the girl, gliding in the shallow water, and Lucy, leaning over the bulwark, came opposite to one another, the girl looked up and stared straight into Lucy's face. Neither could speak to the other and in a moment the Sea Girl dropped astern. But Lucy will never forget her face. It did not look frightened or angry like those of the other Sea People. Lucy had liked that girl and she felt certain the girl had liked her. In that one moment they had somehow become friends. There does not seem to be much chance of their meeting again in that world or any other. But if ever they do they will rush together with their hands held out.

After that for many days, without wind in her shrouds or foam at her bows, across a waveless sea, the *Dawn Treader* glided smoothly east. Every day and every hour the light became more brilliant and still they could bear it. No one ate or slept and no one wanted to, but they drew buckets of dazzling water from the sea, stronger than wine and somehow wetter, more liquid, than ordinary water, and pledged one another silently in deep draughts of it. And one or two of the sailors who had been oldish men when the voyage began now grew younger every day. Everyone on board was filled with joy and excitement, but not an excitement that made one talk. The further they sailed the less they spoke, and then almost in a whisper. The stillness of that last sea laid hold on them.

"My Lord," said Caspian to Drinian one day, "what do you see ahead?"

"Sire," said Drinian, "I see whiteness. All along the horizon from north to south, as far as my eyes can reach."

"That is what I see too," said Caspian, "and I cannot imagine what it is."

"If we were in higher latitudes, your Majesty," said Drinian, "I would say it was ice. But it can't be that; not here. All the same, we'd better get men to the oars and hold the ship back against the current. Whatever the stuff is, we don't want to crash into it at this speed!"

They did as Drinian said, and so continued to go slower and slower. The whiteness did not get any less mysterious as they approached it. If it was land it must be a very strange land, for it seemed just as smooth as the water and on the same level with it. When they got very close to it Drinian put the helm hard over and turned the *Dawn Treader* south so that she was broadside on to the current and rowed a little way southward along the edge of the whiteness. In so doing they accidentally made the important discovery that the current was only about forty feet wide and the rest of the sea as still as a pond. This was good news for the crew, who had already begun to think that the return journey to Ramandu's land, rowing against stream all the way, would be pretty poor sport. (It also explained why the shepherd girl had dropped so quickly astern. She was not in the current. If she had been she would have been moving east at the same speed as the ship.)

And still no one could make out what the white stuff was. Then the boat was lowered and it put off to investigate. Those who remained on the *Dawn Treader* could see that the boat pushed right in amidst the whiteness. Then they could hear the voices of the party in the boat (clear across the still water) talking in a shrill and surprised way. Then there was a pause while Rynelf in the bows of the boat took a sounding; and when, after that, the boat came rowing back there seemed to be plenty of the white stuff inside her. Everyone crowded to the side to hear the news.

"Lilies, your Majesty!" shouted Rynelf, standing up in the bows.

"*What* did you say?" asked Caspian.

"Blooming lilies, your Majesty," said Rynelf. "Same as in a pool or in a garden at home."

"Look!" said Lucy, who was in the stern of the boat. She held up her wet arms full of white petals and broad flat leaves.

"What's the depth, Rynelf?" asked Drinian.

"That's the funny thing, Captain," said Rynelf. "It's still deep. Three and a half fathoms clear."

"They can't be real lilies – not what we call lilies," said Eustace.

Probably they were not, but they were very like them. And when, after some consultation, the *Dawn Treader* turned back into the current and began to glide eastward through the Lily Lake or the Silver Sea (they tried both these names but it was the Silver Sea that stuck and is now on Caspian's map) the strangest part of their travels began. Very soon the open sea which they were leaving was only a thin rim of blue on the western horizon. Whiteness, shot with faintest colour of gold, spread round them on every side, except just astern where their passage had thrust the lilies apart and left an open lane of water that shone like dark green glass. To look at, this last sea was very like the Arctic; and if their eyes had not by now grown as strong as eagles' the sun on all that whiteness – especially at early morning when the sun was hugest – would have been unbearable. And every evening the same whiteness made the daylight last longer. There seemed no end to the lilies. Day after day from all those miles and leagues of flowers there rose a smell which Lucy found it very hard to describe; sweet – yes, but not at all sleepy or overpowering, a fresh, wild, lonely smell that seemed to get into your brain and make you feel that you could go up mountains at a run or wrestle with an elephant. She and Caspian said to one another, "I feel that I can't stand much more of this, yet I don't want it to stop."

They took soundings very often but it was only several days later that the water became shallower. After that it went on getting shallower. There came a day when they had to row out of the current and feel their way forward at a snail's pace, rowing. And soon it was clear that the *Dawn Treader* could sail no further east. Indeed it was only by very clever handling that they saved her from grounding.

"Lower the boat," cried Caspian, "and then call the men aft. I must speak to them."

"What's he going to do?" whispered Eustace to Edmund. "There's a queer look in his eyes."

"I think we probably all look the same," said Edmund.

They joined Caspian on the poop and soon all the men were crowded together at the foot of the ladder to hear the King's speech.

"Friends," said Caspian, "we have now fulfilled the quest on which you embarked. The seven lords are all accounted for and as Sir Reepicheep has sworn never to return, when you reach Ramandu's Land you will doubtless find the Lords Revilian and Argoz and Mavramorn awake. To you, my Lord Drinian, I entrust this ship, bidding you sail to Narnia with all the speed you may, and above all not to land on the Island of Deathwater. And instruct my regent, the Dwarf Trumpkin, to give to all these, my shipmates, the rewards I promised them. They have been earned well. And if I come not again it is my will that the Regent, and Master Cornelius, and Trufflehunter the Badger, and the Lord Drinian choose a King of Narnia with the consent –"

"But, Sire," interrupted Drinian, "are you abdicating?"

"I am going with Reepicheep to see the World's End," said Caspian.

A low murmur of dismay ran through the sailors.

"We will take the boat," said Caspian. "You will have no need of it in these gentle seas and you must build a new one in Ramandu's island. And now –"

"Caspian," said Edmund suddenly and sternly, "you can't do this."

"Most certainly," said Reepicheep, "his Majesty cannot."

"No indeed," said Drinian.

"Can't?" said Caspian sharply, looking for a moment not unlike his uncle Miraz.

"Begging your Majesty's pardon," said Rynelf from the deck below, "but if one of us did the same it would be called deserting."

"You presume too much on your long service, Rynelf," said Caspian.

"No, Sire! He's perfectly right," said Drinian.

"By the Mane of Aslan," said Caspian, "I had thought you were all my subjects here, not my schoolmasters."

"I'm not," said Edmund, "and I say you can *not* do this."

"Can't again," said Caspian. "What do you mean?"

"If it please your Majesty, we mean *shall not*," said Reepicheep with a very low bow. "You are the King of Narnia. You break faith with all your subjects, and especially with Trumpkin, if you do not return. You shall not please yourself with adventures as if you were a private person. And if your Majesty will not hear reason it will be the truest loyalty of every man on board to follow me in disarming and binding you till you come to your senses."

"Quite right," said Edmund. "Like they did with Ulysses when he wanted to go near the Sirens."

Caspian's hand had gone to his sword hilt, when Lucy said, "And you've almost promised Ramandu's daughter to go back."

Caspian paused. "Well, yes. There is that," he said. He stood irresolute for a moment and then shouted out to the ship in general.

"Well, have your way. The quest is ended. We all return. Get the boat up again."

"Sire," said Reepicheep, "we do not *all* return. I, as I explained before –"

"Silence!" thundered Caspian. "I've been lessoned but I'll not be baited. Will no one silence that Mouse?"

"Your Majesty promised," said Reepicheep, "to be good lord to the Talking Beasts of Narnia."

"Talking beasts, yes," said Caspian. "I said nothing about beasts that never stop talking." And he flung down the ladder in a temper and went into the cabin, slamming the door.

But when the others rejoined him a little later they found him changed; he was white and there were tears in his eyes.

"It's no good," he said. "I might as well have behaved decently for all the good I did with my temper and swagger. Aslan has spoken to me. No – I don't mean he was actually here. He wouldn't fit into the cabin, for one thing. But that gold lion's head on the wall came to life and spoke to me. It was terrible – his eyes. Not that he was at all rough with me – only a bit stern at first. But it was terrible all the same. And he said – he said – oh, I can't bear it. The worst thing he could have said. You're to go on – Reep and Edmund, and Lucy, and Eustace; and I'm to go back. Alone. And at once. And what *is* the good of anything?"

"Caspian, dear," said Lucy. "You knew we'd have to go back to our own world sooner or later."

"Yes," said Caspian with a sob, "but this is sooner."

"You'll feel better when you get back to Ramandu's Island," said Lucy.

He cheered up a little later on, but it was a grievous parting on both sides and I will not dwell on it. About two o'clock in the afternoon, well victualled and watered (though they thought they would need neither food nor drink) and with Reepicheep's coracle on board, the boat pulled away from the *Dawn Treader* to row through the endless carpet of lilies. The *Dawn Treader* flew all her flags and hung out her shields to honour their departure. Tall and big and homelike she looked from their low position with the lilies all round them. And before she was out of sight they saw her turn and begin rowing slowly westward. Yet though Lucy shed a few tears, she could not feel it as much as you might have expected. The light, the silence, the tingling smell of the Silver Sea, even (in some odd way) the loneliness itself, were too exciting.

There was no need to row, for the current drifted them steadily to the east. None of them slept or ate. All that night and all next day they glided eastward, and when the third day dawned – with a brightness you or I could not bear even if we had dark glasses on – they saw a wonder ahead. It was as if a wall stood up between them and the sky, a greenish-grey, trembling, shimmering wall. Then up came the sun, and at its first rising they saw it through the wall and it turned into wonderful rainbow colours. Then they knew that the wall was really a long, tall wave – a wave endlessly fixed in one place as you may often see at the edge of a waterfall. It seemed to be about thirty feet

high, and the current was gliding them swiftly towards it. You might have supposed they would have thought of their danger. They didn't. I don't think anyone could have in their position. For now they saw something not only behind the wave but behind the sun. They could not have seen even the sun if their eyes had not been strengthened by the water of the Last Sea. But now they could look at the rising sun and see it clearly and see things beyond it. What they saw – eastward, beyond the sun – was a range of mountains. It was so high that either they never saw the top of it or they forgot it. None of them remembers seeing any sky in that direction. And the mountains must really have been outside the world. For any mountains even a quarter of a twentieth of that height ought to have had ice and snow on them. But these were warm and green and full of forests and waterfalls however high you looked. And suddenly there came a breeze from the east, tossing the top of the wave into foamy shapes and ruffling the smooth water all round them. It lasted only a second or so but what it brought them in that second none of those three children will ever forget. It brought both a smell and a sound, a musical sound. Edmund and Eustace would never talk about it afterwards. Lucy could only say, "It would break your heart." "Why," said I, "was it so sad?" "Sad!! No," said Lucy.

No one in that boat doubted that they were seeing beyond the End of the World into Aslan's country.

At that moment, with a crunch, the boat ran aground. The water was too shallow now for it. "This," said Reepicheep, "is where I go on alone."

They did not even try to stop him, for everything now felt as if it had been fated or had happened before. They helped him to lower his little coracle. Then he took off his sword ("I shall need it no more," he said) and flung it far away across the lilied sea. Where it fell it stood upright with the hilt above the surface. Then he bade them good-bye, trying to be sad for their sakes; but he was quivering with happiness. Lucy, for the first and last time, did what she had always wanted to do, taking him in her arms and caressing him. Then hastily he got into his coracle and took his paddle, and the current caught it and away he went, very black against the lilies. But no lilies grew on the wave; it was a smooth green slope. The coracle went more and more quickly, and beautifully it rushed up the wave's side. For one split second they saw its shape and Reepicheep's on the very top. Then it vanished, and since that moment no one can truly claim to have seen Reepicheep the Mouse. But my belief is that he came safe to Aslan's country and is alive there to this day.

As the sun rose the sight of those mountains outside the world faded away. The wave remained but there was only blue sky behind it.

The children got out of the boat and waded – not towards the wave but southward with the wall of water on their left. They could not have told you why they did this; it was their fate. And though they had felt – and been – very grown-up on the *Dawn Treader*, they now felt just the opposite and held hands as they waded through the lilies. They never felt tired. The water was warm and all the time it got shallower. At last they were on dry sand, and then on grass – a huge plain of very fine short grass, almost level with the Silver Sea and spreading in every direction without so much as a molehill.

And of course, as it always does in a perfectly flat place without trees, it looked as if the sky came down to meet the grass in front of them. But as they went on they got the strangest impression that here at last the sky did really come down and join the earth – a blue wall, very bright, but real and solid: more like glass than anything else. And soon they were quite sure of it. It was very near now.

But between them and the foot of the sky there was something so white on the green grass that even with their eagles' eyes they could hardly look at it. They came on and saw that it was a Lamb.

"Come and have breakfast," said the Lamb in its sweet milky voice.

Then they noticed for the first time that there was a fire lit on the grass and fish roasting on it. They sat down and ate the fish, hungry now for the first time for many days. And it was the most delicious food they had ever tasted.

"Please, Lamb," said Lucy, "is this the way to Aslan's country?"

"Not for you," said the Lamb. "For you the door into Aslan's country is from your own world."

"What!" said Edmund. "Is there a way into Aslan's country from our world too?"

"There is a way into my country from all the worlds," said the Lamb; but as he spoke his snowy white flushed into tawny gold and his size changed and he was Aslan himself, towering above them and scattering light from his mane.

"Oh, Aslan," said Lucy. "Will you tell us how to get into your country from our world?"

"I shall be telling you all the time," said Aslan. "But I will not tell you how long or short the way will be; only that it lies across a river. But do not fear that, for I am the great Bridge Builder. And now come; I will open the door in the sky and send you to your own land."

"Please, Aslan," said Lucy. "Before we go, will you tell us when we can come back to Narnia again? Please. And oh, do, do, do make it soon."

"Dearest," said Aslan very gently, "you and your brother will never come back to Narnia."

"Oh, *Aslan*!!" said Edmund and Lucy both together in despairing voices.

"You are too old, children," said Aslan, "and you must begin to come close to your own world now."

"It isn't Narnia, you know," sobbed Lucy. "It's *you*. We shan't meet *you* there. And how can we live, never meeting you?"

"But you shall meet me, dear one," said Aslan.

"Are – are you there too, Sir?" said Edmund.

"I am," said Aslan. "But there I have another name. You must learn to know me by that name. This was the very reason why you were brought to Narnia, that by knowing me here for a little, you may know me better there."

"And is Eustace never to come back here either?" said Lucy.

"Child," said Aslan, "do you really need to know that? Come, I am opening the door in the sky." Then all in one moment there was a rending of the blue wall (like a curtain being torn) and a terrible white light from beyond the sky, and the feel of Aslan's mane and a Lion's kiss on their foreheads and then – the back bedroom in Aunt Alberta's home in Cambridge.

Only two more things need to be told. One is that Caspian and his men all came safely back to Ramandu's Island. And the three lords woke from their sleep. Caspian married

Ramandu's daughter and they all reached Narnia in the end, and she became a great queen and the mother and grandmother of great kings. The other is that back in our own world everyone soon started saying how Eustace had improved, and how "You'd never know him for the same boy": everyone except Aunt Alberta, who said he had become very commonplace and tiresome and it must have been the influence of those Pevensie children.